A First Course in

BUSINESS ANALYSIS

A First Course in

BUSINESS ANALYSIS

V. J. Seddon, B. A., M. Sc.
Dean of the Faculty of Business,
Leeds Polytechnic

J. H. Butel, B. Sc. (Econ.), M. Sc.(Econ.)
Senior Lecturer in Economics and Business Studies,
Preston Polytechnic

Cassell

Cassell Educational Ltd: Artillery House, Artillery Row,
London SW1P 1RT

British Library Cataloguing in Publication Data

Seddon, V.
  A first course in business analysis.
  1. Business
  I. Title   II. Butel, J.
  338.7   HF 5500
ISBN 0–304–31567–2

Printed in Great Britain by Mackays of Chatham Ltd.

Last digit is print number: 9 8 7 6 5 4 3 2

To Sophie and 'Mojo'

Contents

Preface

In planning and writing this book we have been conscious of the need to combine a variety of quantitative methods into a set of basic tools for business analysis. It is intended, as the title indicates, to be a text for students commencing business studies at the BEC Higher level or on one of the many management courses now available. It does not deal solely with statistics for social scientists, nor mathematics for accountants: it combines elements of both with a problem-solving approach to realistic management applications. As a result, certain chapters may be unexpectedly elementary and others unusually advanced for a starting text. This is because we assume no prior mathematical knowledge beyond that usually achieved in Middle School or the fourth form or the eighth grade, but at the same time we intend the book to be useful in everyday management. By a gentle progression, without special regard to academic rigour, we have tried to extend simple concepts in arithmetic and geometry into a way of thinking about business problems and their solutions.

The central themes in business are covered explicitly within a framework of one of them, i.e. numeracy. Money, as a source, is the basis for most of the decisions taken by management and the search for its efficient use comprises much of the purpose of this book. People require special consideration and we introduce a variety of methods widely used in making decisions which involve labour and the pressure of human psychology.

The communication of information in business is crucial and we hope to encourage the skill in the form of recommendations, reports and the simplification of complex data.

The chapters fall into groups. The first three are intended to provide a foundation of simple applications, perhaps to help a tutor ensure that each student in a group has a roughly equivalent background. Chapters 4 to 8 introduce specific applications without which no aspiring manager would be equipped to take part in modern business. The final four chapters form an introduction to the management sciences and may be viewed as the culmination of a study course.

Each chapter commences with a statement of its objectives and the reader should use these as goals to be achieved in learning. Also, each chapter contains a basic business problem which will be solved in the course of the explanation of the methods. The reader should be able to follow the solution to this problem before proceeding to the assignments at the end of each chapter.

Certain chapters make reference to computer solutions but this book is not a computing text. If a simple computer program is useful in easing the tedium of calculation, then it is given using the BASIC language.

We acknowledge the co-operation of three 'generations' of BEC Higher National students at Preston Polytechnic. Their willingness to accept as tuition notes our experimental earlier drafts has proved invaluable and many improvements have resulted from their comments. Acknowledgements are due also to the following: Mrs A.M. Dickinson, Miss A.C. Ormsby and Mrs M.A. Harrison for their skill in typing and organizing our manuscripts; Preston Polytechnic for permission to reproduce a variety of items from the BEC Higher Assessment Programme and also certain tables of figures published by the Computer Services

Unit; Brian Booth, Dean of Business and Management, whose idea this book originally was; Lynne Haynes for her indispensable assistance in making final amendments. No doubt there remain inelegancies of exposition and perhaps a few uncorrected errors, for which we apologize.

V.J. Seddon
J.H. Butel

Preston, 1981

1—Numbers Are Useful In Business

1.1 INTRODUCTION AND OBJECTIVES

1.1.1 The Subject of the Chapter

In every situation and in all fields of human activity, whenever answers are required to complicated questions, the application of mathematical knowledge has proved advantageous. In the past, many activities have been analysed verbally, without recourse to numerical treatment, but the solutions so produced have either been approximate or else not quite totally believable. From weather-forecasting to economic history to the study of battle-strategy, arguments are becoming increasingly based on quantitative information and the application of scientific methods. Business science is no exception to this trend: so many basic management operations are now backed by mathematical analysis that every student of business activity must at least be aware of what questions can best be answered numerically and the forms those answers may take. However, there are a number of problems to be faced when the business environment is treated as a measurable entity governed by mathematical laws.

Generally, the business analyst is concerned with the relationships existing (or assumed to exist, which is often a completely different thing) between the *causes* of changes and the *results* of those changes having occurred. This involves him in setting up a theory which binds together the various elements in the argument and then making predictions about what will happen next. Clearly the basic theory may be wrong and this will be apparent if predictions are consistently in error. However, a situation may arise in which a theory is correct but the observations of the causes and results are so inaccurate that they can neither support nor disprove the theory. For example, self-service shops face a special problem as regards the service they provide: should they have a large number of checkouts (appropriately staffed) to facilitate a rapid turnover of customers, or should they economize on checkouts and risk large queues forming? In the first case, the cost of equipment and staff is high but customer satisfaction will be greater than if queues form. In the second case, the apparent cost is lower but customers may actively avoid that shop because it involves them in lengthy waits. The business analyst is called upon to estimate the loss of sales owing to overcrowding in the shop. In effect, he is asked to answer the question 'How many would-be customers decide not to enter the shop because of the queues, and how much on average would they have spent?' No matter how sophisticated his theory explaining the deterrent effect of queues, the fundamental problem is one of acquiring realistic data. Quite simply, it is not available, nor is there any reliable way of obtaining it.

The fact that a manager needs to ask questions involving numbers means that he must be able to understand answers presented to him in numerical form. It is the development of such an understanding that comprises the purpose of this book and the first chapter sets out the essential features of a mathematical approach to business management. The reader who felt confident in his mathematical ability at school will find this chapter merely a revision of ideas he met there. For others who found mathematics a difficult subject at school and who perhaps gave it up at the first opportunity, this chapter will lead them into certain basic methods with the intention that they should develop skills in arithmetic, using a calculator, reading tables, drawing graphs and thinking about money. Afterwards in later chapters, these simple concepts and methods will be extended into increasingly realistic applications.

1.1.2   Objectives

1.   To appreciate the role of numerical information in business decision-making.
2.   To be able to interpret a wide range of business data and to transform them into verbal or written form.
3.   To be able to make calculations involving realistic business data, using an electronic calculator and applying formulae.
4.   To revise and extend simple concepts of the mathematics of money and time.

1.2   WHERE DO NUMBERS FIT INTO BUSINESS?

There is a feeling that years of experience are always better than any investigation and recommendation based on mathematical methods. Sometimes this feeling is justified in the sense that every business has its quirks which the experienced manager knows about but which are often impossible to build into a scientific scheme of the firm's operations; in other words, the manager knows something which the mathematical analyst does not. Nonetheless, a more realistic manager will understand that the analyst's answers are *an aid to reducing the degree of risk* inherent in every decision-making process.

There is another aspect of this problem of veracity which centres on the use of *statistics*. In the past, management science has given the impression that an event with a 95 per cent likelihood of happening is more or less a fact. In reality, there is no such thing as a *statistical fact* of this type and the layman is wise to be wary of actions based on such information. However, provided the nature of statistical information is understood by the business manager, he will take it and use it to help him make up his mind about the situation in question. Examples of this particular problem are seen every day in any Organization and Methods Section when the investigation covers clerical work, particularly the proliferation of paperwork.

If an O and M expert states that he is 90 per cent confident that between one-third and one-quarter of all paperwork in an office is unnecessary, most listeners will ask themselves 'If he's not absolutely sure, why should I take any notice? It's only his opinion'. A more astute listener will realize that the 10 per cent uncertainty is related to the degree of precision in the estimate of wasted work. A greater spread in the estimate would allow greater confidence because more leeway is allowed for being wrong. One can be absolutely certain that the unnecessary paperwork is somewhere in the range 0 per cent to 100 per cent. In statistical work, the cost of acquiring near-absolute certainty is lack of precision and it is important to balance the need for high confidence against the precision of the final information. Chapter 4 explores this relationship in more detail.

Whenever an estimate is made, an important factor is '*Who estimated it*?' Behind the *who* lies a series of similar questions: 'Why did he estimate it in the first place?' 'Does he derive any benefit from its being big or small?' 'What is his record of estimates in the past?' And so on. It may seem unduly suspicious to treat a well-meaning man's figures in this way but it is often essential to be as sure of the sources of information as of the accuracy of the arithmetic which will be performed upon the data. As an example of this problem, consider a manager attempting to ensure that a particular project will be accomplished with the minimum disruption to other work-in-progress. He will ask the Management Services Section how many men they estimate will be required and for how long; then, no doubt, he must approach the trade union (or professional association) representative. This person's estimate of the same requirements is almost certain to be different because he has a different set of goals and different criteria for measuring the effort involved. Which estimate is *right*? The answer is that they are both *right* because really they are providing answers to two different questions. Upon whose estimate will the manager base his decision? Clearly it depends upon his experience of these two sources of information as reliable producers of data and upon his assessment of their tendency to be biased. If he knows of times in the past when the Work Study experts underestimated the requirements of a project, then he will ascribe more weight to the other information. Likewise, if the labour representative seems overconcerned with keeping the greatest number of his members in work, regardless of the real effort required, then his estimate will be discounted in favour of the other.

In business, sources of information are many. The Finance Department of any company will produce an endless stream of numbers relating to prices, quantities, sales, profits, interest rates and so on. The Personnel Department will produce a similar flood, this time about absences, holidays, qualifications, wage-rates, pensions and tax. Every employee is caught in the data flow either as a unit to be counted and 'processed' or as a producer whose output must be accounted for in detail. These are the sources of information within a company. Outside, there are government departments and industrial agencies each measuring, counting or analysing the day-to-day activity of the business community. These are the sources of official statistics, often published by the Central Statistical Office and HMSO. Without these data on prices, production, housing, sickness, education, wealth, trade or banking, business analysis would be impossible. Examples of such information will occur time and again in this book and, as we have said, knowledge of the source is often as valuable as knowledge of the contents.

1.3 WORKING WITH NUMBERS

1.3.1 A Calculator Makes Life Easy

A great many people, when faced with a numerical problem, feel that numbers have always been their 'weak point'. Yet mathematics is simply the application of the same set of thinking patterns as those involved in counting, or measuring or weighing. Fortunately, the drudgery of arithmetic has ended with the introduction of the electronic calculator and every student of business should possess one. This book assumes that the reader does and that it performs all the basic arithmetic operations and also the square-root function. No other special buttons are necessary but there are occasions when a memory (or store) and a power button to calculate X^y are useful.

The reader should practise with a calculator using the manufacturer's instruction leaflet, attempting the examples given in it. There is some variation in the operating procedures of different calculators and it is not possible to cover all models in this book. However, certain principles are common to all and the reader should soon become confident in three aspects of arithmetic.

1. *Simple arithmetic*, such as strings of numbers added together and subtracted. For example:

$$1250.75 + 982.90 + 641.72 + 595.21 + 320.94 = 3791.52$$

On almost all calculators this sort of sum is pressed on the buttons in the same order as one might speak it. The result is produced on the screen immediately after the 'equals' sign is pressed. Similarly, multiplication and division may be carried out quickly and accurately by performing the same kind of sequential button pressing. For example:

$$2.645 \times 13.460 \times 21.105 \times 36.421 \times 4.591 \times 1.095 = 137571.7844$$

Note that the product is accurate to a very high degree, that is, to many places of decimals. Even so, this answer from a 10-place calculator is not complete, since it should contain eighteen digits to the right of the decimal point. The calculator is said to have *truncated* the product by simply dropping those right-hand numbers which will not fit onto the screen. However, the answer is perfectly adequate for any practical purpose and no business analyst would be concerned about the truncation. Even so, the slight loss of accuracy must be borne in mind particularly if comparisons are to be made between two products, both of which are subject to truncation.

The reader should also check that the following sequential division is correct:

$$4927.42 \div 2.401 \div 11.6244 \div 3.0 = 58.848530$$

2. *Mixed arithmetic*, which means combinations of addition, subtraction, multiplication and division. For example:

$$\frac{14.26 + 21.19}{27.25 - 11.42} - \frac{146.14 - 39.21}{261.50 + 3.9276}$$

This is an instance where a memory is useful on a calculator, so that the right-hand part may be calculated first and stored. The left-hand part may then be calculated and the difference obtained directly in the memory. However, even without a store, the calculator simplifies the process.

First, obtain the numerators and denominators (upper and lower parts) throughout the problem to yield:

$$\frac{35.45}{15.83} - \frac{106.93}{265.4276}$$

Now these two elements may be simplified in turn by performing divisions to obtain $2.2394 - 0.4029$ after rounding to four places. The answer obtained by a final subtraction, is 1.8365. Calculations like this one occur very commonly in later sections of this book and readers should be sure of their ability to perform them. Again, the truncation error must be borne in mind.

3. *Square-roots*. This additional function is a worthwhile refinement and operates simply. Whatever number is on the screen will be acted upon by the pressing of the square-root button. For example:

$$\sqrt{42.67 \times 161.91 \times 27.204}$$

This may be calculated without writing down any intermediate results. Simply perform the sequence of multiplication to yield the product 187944.26. The square-root can now be found by pressing the square-root button to yield 433.53. The reader should practise the use of the square-root button; in particular, it should be noted that truncation also occurs in this operation so that the reverse calculation often produces a sizeable error. In the example above $\sqrt{187944.26} = 433.53$ to two places of decimals. By the rules, $(433.53)^2 = 433.53 \times 433.53$ should be 187944.26. However, because of truncation this does not happen and the error is sufficient to warrant caution in further operations upon square-rooted numbers.

Another important application for a calculator is the evaluation of formulae. A formula is the symbolic representation of the connection between a variety of related values. For example, temperature may be measured in Fahrenheit or in Celsius (sometimes called Centigrade). Most people know from watching television weather-forecasts, that $50°F$ is about $10°C$. Similarly, $61°F$ is about $16°C$. There must be some way of converting from one to the other, since they both measure the same condition and merely use different scales. The *formula* for conversion to Fahrenheit from Celsius can be obtained quite easily:

$$f = 32 + 1.8c$$

This says, 'Give me a temperature in $°C$ and I'll tell you it in $°F$'. Let us now try the conversion for a few commonly known temperatures. If:

$$c = 10°C \quad \text{then } f = 32 + (1.8 \times 10) \quad = 50°F, \text{ a cool day;}$$
$$c = 16°C \quad \text{then } f = 32 + (1.8 \times 16) \quad = 60.8°F, \text{ a typical day;}$$
$$c = 22°C \quad \text{then } f = 32 + (1.8 \times 22) \quad = 71.6°F, \text{ a hot day;}$$
$$c = 0°C \quad \text{then } f = 32 + (1.8 \times 0) \quad = 32°F, \text{ water freezes;}$$
$$c = 100°C \text{ then } f = 32 + (1.8 \times 100) = 212°F, \text{ water boils.}$$

Of course, the formula can be rearranged to obtain $°C$ from $°F$, as follows:

$$f = 32 + 1.8c$$

$$f - 32 = 1.8c$$

$$\frac{f - 32}{1.8} = c$$

This would normally be written with the 'finding' value on the left:

$$c = \frac{f - 32}{1.8}$$

The reader should now ensure that this reverse conversion works for commonly known temperatures. A calculator is very useful.

As an example of a business application of a formula, consider the case of a storekeeper at a large factory. He will maintain stocks of raw materials or input-components but must judge carefully between holding too few (and running out) or too many (high cash value lying idle). There are various formulae for deciding the ideal quantity to order and one is as follows:

$$\text{Order quantity } Q = \sqrt{\frac{2RC}{PM}}$$

where R = total annual requirement of material;
C = cost of making out an order;
P = current interest rate for loaned funds;
M = value of each unit of material.

Let us say that a factory uses 10 000 litres per year of a chemical at a cost of £2.50 per litre. The administration cost of placing an order is estimated to be £8 in time, telephone calls, postage and transport within the factory after delivery. Interest rates for lending are currently $9\frac{1}{2}$ per cent. By use of the formula, we obtain the ideal order quantity to be as follows:

$$Q = \sqrt{\frac{2 \times 10\,000 \times £8}{9\frac{1}{2}\% \times £2.50}}$$

$$= \sqrt{\frac{2 \times 10\,000 \times 8}{0.095 \times 2.50}}$$

$$= \sqrt{673\,684.21}$$

$$= \underline{820 \text{ litres per order (approximately)}}$$

This would mean that about 12 orders each year would be required to obtain the required 10 000 litres; that is, approximately an order every month. Now consider the effect upon the order quantity of a changing rate of annual usage of the chemical. For each of the following quantities let us calculate the ideal order quantity and frequency.

Annual Usage	Ideal Order Quantity	Number of Orders Per Year
20 000	1160	17.2
18 000	1100	16.3
16 000	1038	15.4
14 000	971	14.4
12 000	899	13.3
10 000	820	12.2
8 000		
6 000		
4 000		
2 000		
1 000		

The reader should complete the table: a calculator is essential. As a matter of realism, we should note that most orders for industrial materials will be sent in multiplies of 100 litres or even 250 litres. As a consequence the ideal order quantity may not be a practical quantity. The reader could gain expertise in the evaluation of formulae by fixing on an annual quantity and investigating the effects of a variable interest rate. For example, at a rate of only four per cent per year, the 10 000 litres would be ordered ideally in batches of 1265 litres. Now the reader should use 5 per cent, $7\frac{1}{2}$ per cent, 10 per cent, 11 per cent, $12\frac{1}{2}$ per cent, 14 per cent.

1.3.2   Measuring and Describing Numerical Relationships

As we have seen, it is an important aspect of any business analysis to be able to explain how *causes* and *effects* are linked. For example, the total cost of producing rubber tyres for cars and trucks will increase as the volume of output increases. It is inconceivable that one million tyres should cost as much to produce as two million tyres of the same specification. Hence

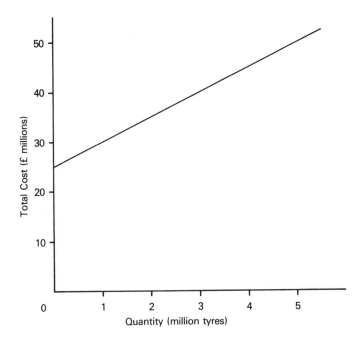

Figure 1.1   *Total cost of producing tyres*

we can say that increasing population (the cause) will raise total costs (the effect). Words like this are necessarily vague since they describe an imprecise relationship. There are other ways of describing such a cause–effect connection which permit greater precision of meaning; one way is to draw a graph. By definition, a graph is a diagram describing the relationship between variable quantities. Figure 1.1 is just such a diagram for the rubber-tyre example.

This graph tells us much more about the relationship than any simple sentence can. First, it says that the firm faces certain costs totalling £25 millions, even if annual production is zero. These costs are called overheads or fixed costs since they do not vary with output and they include rent, rates, water charges, directors' fees, interest on loans, building maintenance and so on. These fixed costs must be recovered from the sale of tyres just as certainly as the actual production costs of raw materials, labour, power and distribution, each of which *will* vary with production. If one million tyres are produced in a year, then each tyre must contribute £25 towards the overheads as well as cover its actual cost of production. Similarly, an annual output of two million tyres must recover the overheads at an average rate of £12.50 per tyre.

Second, the graph tells us that every production increase of one million tyres raises the total cost by £5 million. This is a constant cost-effect over the production range shown in Figure 1.1 and is interpreted to mean that the average tyre must cost £5 in the direct costs of materials, labour and so on. Every tyre that is produced and sold must contribute £5 towards the total cost to cover these direct costs. Thus, if one million tyres are produced, the total cost will be £30 million and each tyre must be sold at £30. If two million tyres are produced, they must be sold at £17.50 each to recover the £35 million total cost. At higher production rates, the cost of *each tyre* will gradually fall as the overheads are more and more thinly spread over the number of tyres.

Figure 1.1, then, describes the relationship between output and cost, and also permits the measurement of that relationship in everyday cash terms. In words, the graph can be described as follows: Overheads amount to £25 million per year and each tyre costs £5 in direct inputs. This sentence gives us the starting point of the graph and its slope. Given these two items of information for any line on a graph, that line can be drawn. The starting point is often referred to as the *intercept*, since it corresponds to a point on the vertical scale. The slope is often called the *gradient* of the line. The two scales which give the values along the line are each called an axis and are often called the vertical and horizontal axes. There is an assignment at the end of this chapter for the reader to practise constructing graphs. The important feature of any graph is that it shows, almost at a glance, the nature of the relationship. This requires that the graph be correctly labelled on its axes and be of an overall pleasing size: not so small that details are lost, nor so big that the line loses its visual impact.

The tyre-cost example we have considered has been translated into two representations, visual and verbal (diagram and words). Of course, we may also adapt the idea of a formula and instead write down the cost in terms of symbols. We already know that the fixed costs total £25 million per year and each tyre costs £5 in direct inputs. Therefore we could write:

$$\text{Total cost} = \text{fixed costs} + \text{direct costs}$$

$$= \text{£25 million} + (\text{£5} \times \text{number of tyres})$$

$$\underline{C = 25\,000\,000 + 5Q}$$

Where C = total annual cost;
       Q = annual quantity of tyres produced.

This symbolic statement looks like a formula and in one respect it is exactly that. It says, 'tell me a quantity and I'll tell you the annual cost'. But it is more than that: it is an algebraic (symbolic) statement of the relationship itself and would be called a *cost function* by the specialist. This use of the term 'function' has a particular purpose in mathematics, and means that the algebraic statement describes a theory. In this case, the theory concerns the production of tyres and the money spent in doing so. The function need not be a fact because the theory may be inadequate. Note that this concept is meaningless in the context of the Celsius–Fahrenheit conversion formula: there is no theory involved in it, only a re-definition of temperature scale.

If the theory of costs in tyre manufacture is changed, then the cost function will alter. Let us say that the *cost of each tyre* rises as the number of tyres increases. There is economic justification for such an assumption since increased output means increased maintenance on machinery, increased stocks of materials, increased road haulage and perhaps increased over-time payments to labour. Such a change in theory means that the graph of the cost function will change from a straight line (£5 per tyre) to a curve (changing cost per tyre) as shown in Figure 1.2.

If the function has changed, then the algebraic statement must also change. The graph below is for the function:

$$C = 25\,000\,000 + 3Q + 0.000001Q^2$$

This is clearly different from the straight line in Figure 1.1 since it includes a squared term. That is, the quantity of tyres adds to cost at more than a proportional rate and we must calculate Q^2 in the evaluation of cost. Whenever the right-hand side of a function's statement includes squared values (or higher powers), the graph will be a curve and not a straight line. The reader should check the values given by Figure 1.2 by calculating C for quantities of tyres of one million, two million, three million and other values. An assignment will give practice in manipulating non-linear functions.

Another aspect of functions that the business analyst finds useful is their ability to describe quite complicated theories which defy words or simple graphs. As an example of

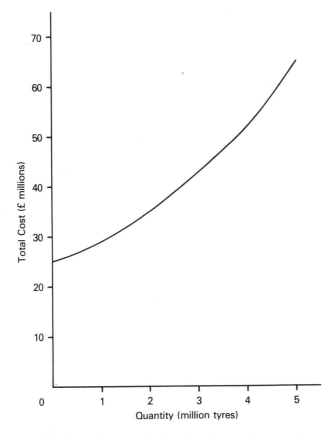

Figure 1.2 *Total cost of tyre production when direct cost per tyre is not constant*

this, let us say that the fixed costs of tyre manufacture are subject to inflation as the years go by, so that the original £25 million rises by £5 million per year. Thus the algebraic statement of the function would be written:

$$C = 25\,000\,000 + 5\,000\,000t + 3Q + 0.000001Q^2$$

Where $t =$ time in years.

This function cannot be drawn upon a simple graph, since it would need three axes (for C, t and Q). However, an approximate three-dimensional graph is shown in Figure 1.3 and the inflation effect can be seen clearly by a general rise in costs as time goes by. Such a graph is difficult to draw and does not convey an immediate impression of the underlying theory.

To describe Figure 1.3 in words would be almost impossible. If that is so, how *does* the analyst describe the function? The answer lies in the technique of *tabulation*, i.e. a table of values is used to convey the 'shape' of the function. Table 1.1 contains the cost data for a variety of tyre outputs over a number of years. To be able to construct and interpret such a table is an important skill for any business analyst. In this case, the interpretation is quite easy since, as we consider successive years, we can detect a general increase in costs superimposed on the basic function.

As we increase the complexity of the theory of costs to include further unknowns in the algebraic statement, more complex tabulations must be constructed to show the

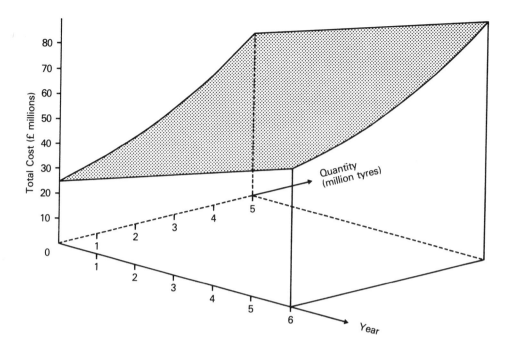

Figure 1.3   *Total cost of tyre production with overheads rising annually by £5 million*

Table 1.1   *The total costs of tyre manufacture as a function of quantity and time (total cost in £ per year)*

Year	Quantity of tyres per year			
	1 million	*2 million*	*3 million*	*4 million*
0	29 000 000	35 000 000	43 000 000	53 000 000
1	34 000 000	40 000 000	48 000 000	58 000 000
2	39 000 000	45 000 000	53 000 000	63 000 000
3	44 000 000	50 000 000	58 000 000	68 000 000
4	49 000 000	55 000 000	63 000 000	73 000 000
5	54 000 000	60 000 000	68 000 000	78 000 000

relationship. Eventually, the table is so complicated that it is not a simplification at all and probably ought not to be used for explanation. There are limitations on all non-mathematical representations of a function.

1.3.3   Numbers–The Only Way To Check On Money

Of all the quantities to be measured in business, money above all requires numbers since it needs counting and arithmetic to operate it in the way intended. It is inconceivable that track be kept of money-values without their representation being numerical. One important aspect of the use of money is that the passage of time is crucial to a discussion of value. The question: What is £5 worth? has meaning only when we define the £5. Is it borrowed money, or loaned money, or a promised amount? Five pounds today is 'worth' a different amount than five pounds next year or last year because time and money are interrelated.

Let us consider the question of borrowing money, to be repaid at a stated future date. The lender temporarily loses control of his money and so suffers loss of satisfaction in two respects. First, he loses what is called the *utility of possession*: in other words, the satisfaction of having the money in his possession. Second, he loses the benefit he might have obtained from spending the money on goods or services. To compensate for these it seems reasonable that the borrower should make a payment for obtaining possession of the money. Such a payment is called *interest*. Exactly how much interest is paid by a borrower will depend upon three things: how much money is borrowed, for how long and at what rate of interest. As each of these rises the total interest payment must rise also. The basic form of interest is called *simple interest* and it has this name because the debt increases in equal amounts over the years of the loan. The amount borrowed by a debtor is usually called the *principal* and we may analyse simple interest in the following way:

$$\text{Total amount to be repaid at any moment} = \text{principal} + \text{interest}$$

$$= \text{principal} + (\text{principal} \times \text{rate of interest} \times \text{no. of years})$$

$$= P + (P \times r \times n), \text{ using symbols}$$

$$\underline{\text{Amount} = P(1 + rn)}, \text{ when we simplify it}$$

Presumably, in a simple case, both the principal and the rate of interest are fixed for the life of the loan. In that case, only the amount and the number of years are variable, which means we should be able to draw a graph relating these two.

Let us take an example of a loan of £5000 at an interest rate of 10 per cent per year. Thus the symbolic statement can be derived as follows:

$$\text{Amount} = P(1 + rn)$$

$$= 5000\,(1 + 0.10n)$$

$$\underline{\text{Amount} = 5000 + 500n}$$

From this statement we may make a number of simple observations. First, if the loan were repaid immediately, then there would be no interest to pay. In this event, $n = 0$ and the amount repaid would be merely the £5000 loan. Second, for every year that passes, the amount increases by £500 interest. When $n = 1$, the amount = £5500. When $n = 2$, the amount = £6000 and so on. The graph of the debt is shown in Figure 1.4.

One of the advantages of drawing such a graph lies in its representation of time as a continuously changing number. The symbol n may take values like 0.5, 2.25, 3.125 and so so on just as easily as whole numbers, provided we remember that fractions of a year may be rounded up by banks to the nearest month or week. The reader should check from the graph, and from the function, that the debt doubles to £10 000 after ten years, equals £8000 after six years and £7750 after five years and six months.

Real-life banks and finance companies find simple interest inadequate for modern commercial lending. They argue as follows: after one year's life of the loan, the lender owes the principal plus that year's interest. Therefore in the second year he ought to pay interest on the total outstanding amount including the earlier interest. By this means, the lender is receiving and the borrower paying interest upon interest as each year goes by. This approach is called *compound interest*. We may obtain the symbolic statement as follows:

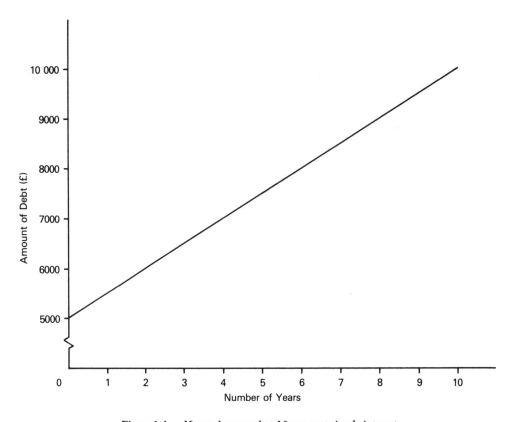

Figure 1.4   *Money borrowed at 10 per cent simple interest*

$$\text{Amount due at the end of year 1} = \text{principal} + \text{interest on principal}$$

$$= P + rP$$

$$= P(1 + r)$$

$$\text{Amount due at the end of year 2} = \text{amount from year 1} + \text{interest on amount from year 1}$$

$$= P(1 + r) + rP(1 + r)$$

$$= P(1 + r)(1 + r)$$

$$= P(1 + r)^2$$

By similar arguments, we can see that after three years the power near the brackets will be 3. After four years, it will be 4. Clearly after n years it will be n.

$$\underline{\text{Amount due at the end of } n \text{ years}} = P(1 + r)^n$$

Calculation of the right-hand side is less easy than with simple interest. If the reader has a 'power' button on his calculator there will be no problem: without the special button it may still be possible to calculate the power by repeated pressings of the multiplication and equals buttons. The maker's instructions will give details. Alternatively, we may use Table 1.2 which gives the amount to which £1 grows for various rates of interest and periods

Table 1.2 *The future value of £1 at compound interest*

Years	Rate of interest per year							
	6%	8%	10%	12%	14%	16%	18%	20%
1	1.060	1.080	1.100	1.120	1.140	1.160	1.180	1.200
2	1.124	1.166	1.210	1.254	1.300	1.346	1.392	1.440
3	1.191	1.260	1.331	1.405	1.482	1.561	1.643	1.728
4	1.262	1.360	1.464	1.574	1.689	1.811	1.939	2.074
5	1.338	1.469	1.611	1.762	1.925	2.100	2.288	2.488
6	1.419	1.587	1.772	1.973	2.195	2.436	2.700	2.986
7	1.504	1.714	1.949	2.211	2.502	2.826	3.185	3.583
8	1.594	1.851	2.144	2.476	2.853	3.278	3.759	4.300
9	1.689	1.999	2.358	2.773	3.252	3.803	4.435	5.160
10	1.791	2.159	2.594	3.106	3.707	4.411	5.234	6.192
15	2.397	3.172	4.177	5.474	7.138	9.265	11.974	15.407
20	3.207	4.661	6.727	9.646	13.743	19.461	27.393	38.338
25	4.292	6.848	10.835	17.000	26.462	40.874	62.669	95.396

of time. If the debt is £100, then the tabulated factor should be multiplied by 100, and so on for other debts.

For example, £5000 borrowed for seven years at a compounded 12 per cent rate of interest will amount to £11 055, as follows:

$$\text{Amount} = P(1 + r)^n$$

$$= P \times (\text{factor in table})$$

$$= 5000 \times 2.211 = \underline{£11\,055}$$

There is an assessment exercise at the end of the chapter which will explore further the use of Table 1.2. Note, however, what the table tells us about compound interest. As an extreme, £1 borrowed for 25 years at 20 per cent would amount to £95.40 approximately. This is much more than the simple interest amount, as may be shown for £100 over 25 years at 20 per cent.

Simple interest	*Compound interest*
$A = P(1 + rn)$	$A = P(1 + r)^n$
$\quad = 100\,(1 + 0.20 \times 25)$	$\quad = (1 + 0.20)^{25}$
$\quad = 100\,(1 + 5)$	$\quad = 100 \times (\text{factor in table})$
$\quad = 100 \times 6$	$\quad = 100 \times 95.396$
$\quad = \underline{£600}$	$\quad = \underline{£9539.60}$

This massive difference is often referred to as the *power of compound interest* and shows the effect of charging interest upon interest. Banks, building societies and finance companies all use compound interest. Figure 1.5 shows the linearity of simple interest and the curve of compound interest.

As an extension of the notion of interest, let us analyse now another important aspect of time and money. Consider, by way of introduction, the question: Which would you rather have, *£100 now or £100 in one year's time?* Most people would opt for the immediate cash rather than the promise. Why is that so? Because waiting for money robs it of some of

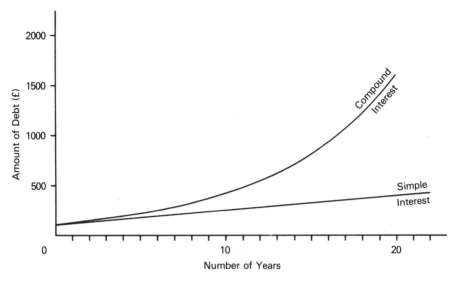

Figure 1.5   *Simple and compound amounts of £100 at 15 per cent per year*

its value: the eventual recipient suffers a loss of opportunity since he cannot spend it when he sees fit. This raises a second question: Which would you rather have, *£100 now or £120 in one year's time*? Here there seems to be a compensation for waiting and many people would prefer to wait for that larger amount. Of course, in the real world it is precisely this function which is served by interest: it compensates the lender for having to wait to use his money. If the current rate of interest is 12 per cent, then £100 now is worth £112 after one year. In other words, £100 is the *present value* of £112 in a year's time if the interest rate is 12 per cent per year. By the same argument, the present value of £112 in two years' time will be less than £100 since there must be compensation for a longer wait. We can find the present value by using the interest formula as follows:

$$
\begin{array}{ccc}
\text{Amount} & & \text{compound} \\
\text{in two} & = & \text{present amount} \times \text{interest} \\
\text{years} & & \text{factor}
\end{array}
$$

therefore:

$$
\frac{\text{Present}}{\text{amount}} = \frac{\text{amount in two years}}{\text{compound interest factor}}
$$

therefore:

$$
P = \frac{A}{(1 + r)^n}
$$

From Table 1.2 we obtain the factor for two years which at 12 per cent is 1.254. Therefore, the present value of the £112 is found:

$$
P = \frac{£112}{1.254} = £89.31
$$

Thus *£89.31 today is equivalent to £112 in two years' time* if the interest rate is 12 per cent. It is said to be the *discounted* value.

This concept of present value is crucial to all manner of business analysis and will be extended to realistic applications later in the book. For the time being, consider important implications of the theory. First, waiting for a long time for a sum of money can reduce its present value very considerably, since the power of compound interest works 'in reverse' against the person who waits. For example, waiting 25 years for £5000 reduces its present value to £294.11 if the interest rate is 12 per cent. At an interest rate of 15 per cent, its present value falls to £151.89. At 20 per cent, it falls to £52.41. It is not uncommon for insurance policies, due many years in the future, to be cashed early and we can see why such a decision may result in only a small sum being received. The reader should practise performing the calculation using, say, £1000 with time-periods of 10 and 15 years and with interest rates of 8, 12 and 16 per cent.

Second, present values may be added. For example, if £100 is to be received at the end of each of the next five years, the present value of the total cash flow is the sum of the individual present values. Assume an interest rate of 12 per cent again.

$$
\begin{aligned}
\text{Present value} &= \begin{matrix} £100 \\ \text{discounted} \\ \text{one year} \end{matrix} + \begin{matrix} £100 \\ \text{discounted} \\ \text{two years} \end{matrix} + \quad \dots \dots \quad + \begin{matrix} £100 \\ \text{discounted} \\ \text{five years} \end{matrix} \\[2mm]
&= \frac{100}{(1.12)} + \frac{100}{(1.12)^2} + \frac{100}{(1.12)^3} + \frac{100}{(1.12)^4} + \frac{100}{(1.12)^5} \\[2mm]
&= \frac{100}{1.120} + \frac{100}{1.254} + \frac{100}{1.405} + \frac{100}{1.574} + \frac{100}{1.762} \\[2mm]
&= 89.29 + 79.72 + 71.18 + 63.55 + 56.75
\end{aligned}
$$

Present value = £360.49

Clearly, the discounting process has reduced the £500 total cash flow to a present value of only about £360. Of course, total cash flow need not occur in five equal instalments and the reader should experiment with different divisions of the £500. For instance, what is the present value of five sums to be received in the following patterns,

1. £200, £100, £100, £50, £50.
2. £50, £50, £100, £100, £200.
3. £50, £100, £200, £100, £50.

The present value of each will be different from the others, since the amounts and waiting times are different in each case.

We shall return to present value at a later stage in the book to help evaluate expensive investment projects. For the time being, we have established the importance of numbers and arithmetic in dealing with money: without them no analysis would be possible.

ASSIGNMENTS

A1.1   The business analyst in a large firm of property agents has investigated the market for newly-built houses of a certain size. The average price of such houses is £24 000 and it is estimated that it will rise by £2000 per year in the foreseeable future. He therefore derives the simple function:

$$\text{Average price (£)} = 24\,000 + 2000t$$

Where t = years into future.

(a)   Calculate the average price for these houses 5, 6 and 10 years into the future.
(b)   Draw the graph of average price and time for the next 10 years.

A1.2   After a few years the analyst realized that his price-theory was too simple and deduced that another important influence was the rate of inflation. As the overall cost of living rose, households' abilities to repay mortgages were reduced and the house market suffered a decline. He has now estimated the function to be:

$$\text{Average price (£)} = 24\,000 + 2000t - 8R^2$$

Where R = percentage annual rise in cost of living.

(a)   Calculate the average price for these houses three years into the future when inflation is 10 per cent, 12 per cent and 20 per cent per year.
(b)   Calculate values to complete the following table:

Rate of inflation (%)

Years ahead	0	5	10	12	14	16	18	20
0	24 000							
1	26 000							
2	28 000							
3	30 000							
4	32 000							
5	34 000							
6	36 000							
7	38 000							
8	40 000							
9	42 000							
10	44 000							

(c)   A particular household bought a typical house for £24 000. They have decided to sell the house when the price has risen by at least £11 000. How long would you expect them to wait if there is zero inflation? How long would you expect them to wait if there is 20 per cent inflation?

A1.3   A company intends to increase the capacity of its factory at a cost of £1 million. This sum will be borrowed at a compound interest rate of 14 per cent per year, for five years.
(a)   What total sum must be repaid at the end of the fifth year?
     The sales of goods from the enlarged factory are estimated to be £500 000 in each of the five years.
(b)   Do you believe the proposed factory enlargement to be a worthwhile venture in simple accounting terms? (Note: there is more than one argument to be considered in this answer.)
     As an alternative to enlarging the factory, the company could spend £1 million acquiring subsidiaries to help increase output and reduce competition. The net sales of goods from this development are estimated to be as follows:

Year	1	2	3	4	5
Sales (£)	900 000	800 000	400 000	200 000	nil

(c)   Is this venture worth while in simple accounting terms?
(d)   Calculate the present values of the sales from both ventures and discuss which seems preferable and why.
(e)   On balance, which venture would you advise should be adopted?

2–Describing Business Situations

2.1 INTRODUCTION AND OBJECTIVES

2.1.1 The Subject of the Chapter

The topics discussed in this chapter are generally subsumed under the heading of 'statistics'. The term 'statistics' may refer to a collection of data, such as the population statistics of the United Kingdom. Indeed, the term derives from 'state' since it was governments who first recognized the need for information on area, population, wealth, and so on. The term is also used to describe a subject of study, which includes:

1. Collection;
2. Organization;
3. Analysis; and
4. Interpretation;

of numerical data. This fourfold process constitutes what is more properly known as 'statistical method'.

This chapter will follow this pattern, dealing first with the collection of data from various sources and second with the organization and presentation of such data. Third, a number of basic and widely used techniques aimed at measuring averages and the spread of data values will be considered. Finally, the usefulness of such calculated values will be shown.

2.1.2 Objectives

1. To be aware of the various sources and types of data and to appreciate their varying degrees of reliability.
2. To be able to prepare a report using numerical data and, where appropriate, employ visual forms of presentation.
3. To be able to calculate the most commonly employed measures of average and dispersion, for both ungrouped and grouped data.

2.2   BASIC PROBLEM DATA

As a result of government attempts to rationalize the allocation of long-haul airline routes between British airlines, Air Dodo have been given a choice between two routes, A and B. Route A is London to Caracas and Route B is London to Mexico City. The data contained in Tables 2.1 and 2.2 refer to the number of passengers carried on the two routes in 1981 by the current British operator, Pterodactyl Airways.

Table 2.1   *Passengers carried by Pterodactyl Airways on Route A in 1981*

Number of passengers	Number of days
0–49	5
50–99	10
100–149	30
150–199	75
200–249	140
250–299	87
300–349	18

Table 2.2   *Passengers carried by Pterodactyl Airways on Route B in 1981*

Number of passengers	Number of days
0–49	15
50–99	25
100–149	40
150–199	50
200–249	75
250–299	95
300–349	65

It is not expected that a change in operator will have any marked effect on the distribution of passenger traffic which in total is likely to be of similar magnitude to that of 1981.

This chapter will, by means of the appropriate techniques, provide a basis for rational choice between the alternative routes. The techniques will be illustrated largely by reference to the data for Route A contained in Table 2.1, although the corresponding values for Route B will be quoted for comparison where appropriate.

2.3   STATING STATISTICS

2.3.1   State Statistics

A major source of information is the Government and more particularly the Central Statistical Office (CSO), which is responsible for an extensive range of official statistics.

Official United Kingdom statistics are published by Her Majesty's Stationery Office (HMSO). Some are broadly based, such as the *Annual Abstract of Statistics* which includes data on population, output, consumption, investment, finance and foreign trade. Others are narrower and more specific, such as *Trade and Industry* (published weekly), which contains details of both wholesale and retail trade, and the *Department of Employment Gazette* relating to labour and the labour market.

By no means all data used in business are from government sources. Chambers of Commerce, banks, New Town Development Corporations, trade unions, private and public corporations, are just a few of the sources of non-government statistics.

The airline, in deciding between the two routes, may wish to avail itself of data from a variety of sources. Information on population, tourism and business trends would be useful as would past and current operator's accounts. Indeed, the problem data are of this last type.

2.3.2   First-hand or Second-hand Data?

First-hand data are known as *primary* or *crude data*. Such data, subject to reservations about accuracy, tend not to arouse emotions. An example would be census information showing the United Kingdom's population to be 56 million. However, second-hand or *secondary data* are derived (sometimes even manipulated) data, and as such require careful scrutiny and interpretation, and not least, recognition that they are in fact secondary. To illustrate this consider the statement that 'one-third of British workers receive an inadequate wage'. This immediately begs the question of what is defined as an inadequate wage. If a different definition is employed a different fraction of the labour force will be identified. It is here in the realm of secondary statistics that the subject has gained a bad name for deviousness or the equally damaging view that 'statistics can prove anything'.

In the context of the problem data, a list of the number of passengers carried on each day during the year would constitute primary data for the airline concerned but when obtained by the prospective carrier in the form shown in section 2.2 they represent secondary data.

2.3.3   Distinctions

The item being measured is termed the *variable* because it can assume various values. A *discrete variable* can take on only certain values (for example, shoe sizes) whereas a *continuous variable* can, within its lower and upper limits assume any value (for example, actual foot length). Given any two values of a continuous variable, it is always possible (subject to the degree of measurement accuracy) to find another value that lies between them. In the problem data the variable being measured is the number of passengers and this is clearly discrete. If the variable of interest were the age of the passenger, the data could be either discrete (age next birthday in years) or continuous (age in years, months, days, hours, etc.).

Another distinction is that between *population* and *sample*. The term 'population' refers to *all* values of a variable whether it be human or otherwise. A sample is a subset of the population. A set of data may function as both a population and a sample, depending on the purpose of the exercise. Thus the problem data represent the population of Pterodactyl Airways' passengers travelling on the London to Caracas route in 1981. On the other hand, the same data are merely a sample (although not random) of all passengers carried by Pterodactyl Airways on this route since it began in 1978.

The question of the purpose of the exercise leads to another important distinction, that between *descriptive statistics* and *inferential statistics*. The former are concerned, as the term suggests, with describing salient characteristics of the data. The latter go further, often involving calculated guesses on the basis of whatever data are available. The techniques discussed in this chapter are usually classified as descriptive measures, although they can form the basis for the drawing of inferences, as will be seen later.

Finally, we make the distinction between *ungrouped data* and *grouped data*. The former consists of original values separately listed whereas the latter does not display individual values but simply the number of items having a value which lies between two (class) limits. Thus the numbers 3, 7, 8, 10, 19, 15 are ungrouped. One possible grouping of the numbers would be:

Class	Number in that class
0–4	1
5–9	2
10–14	1
15–19	2

Although use of grouped data results in a loss of detail, it can make for more manageable calculations (witness the age-groupings in population statistics). Often however, as in the problem data, there is no choice but to use grouped data if that is all that is available.

2.3.4   Frequencies

Consider the following jumble of numbers which are observed values of a variable X: 2, 4, 4, 1, 3, 5, 2, 4, 5, 1, 6. If we wish to introduce some semblance of order into the data we could rewrite them as:

$$1, 1$$
$$2, 2$$
$$3,$$
$$4, 4, 4$$
$$5, 5$$
$$6$$

We see that the values 3 and 6 each occur once, that is, have a frequency (f) of 1; values of X of 1, 2 and 5 each have a frequency of 2; $X = 4$ three times and therefore has a frequency of 3. This may be conveniently written as a frequency distribution as in Table 2.3.

The example shown in Table 2.3 related to ungrouped data, that is, each value of X (1, 2, etc.) was included individually. Often, however, we deal (by necessity or design) with grouped data where two or more values of a variable are included together in a *class* and their respective frequencies summed to give a class frequency. The problem data are of this latter type.

To illustrate this let us consider the numerical data above. Suppose that we wish to use three classes, namely, 1–2, 3–4 and 5–6. We can draw up a *frequency distribution* for this grouped data as shown in Table 2.4.

The lowest and the highest values in a class are termed the *class boundaries* or *class limits* and the spread of values between boundaries defines the *class interval*. This interval is the same for all three classes in the above example, but this is not always the case.

Table 2.3 *A frequency distribution for ungrouped data*

Value of the variable (X)	Frequency (f)
1	2
2	2
3	1
4	3
5	2
6	1

Table 2.4 *A frequency distribution for grouped data*

Value of the variable (X)	Frequency (f)
1–2	4
3–4	4
5–6	3

There was no problem in deciding to which class particular values of the variable should be assigned; $X = 2$ goes in the first class (1–2), $X = 3$ in the second class (3–4) and so on. But what is wrong with the following?

Class

0–2

2–4

4–6

Suppose we have a value such as 2. Do we place it in the first or second class? Clearly the class boundaries are ambiguous and this should be avoided. One means of avoiding this is to use the following:

Class

0 but less than 2

2 but less than 4

4 but less than 6

Note that rounding off decimals may alter the class to which a value is assigned. Sometimes the final class is open ended. Thus in the above example, we might have had a final class of '6 or greater' as a catch-all for any remaining values of the variable. This is often encountered, for example, in population data where the final class may be 'aged 65 or over' because relatively few frequencies are encountered in these age groups and thus it would not be considered worth while or useful to have separate classes for 65 to 75 yrs, 75 to 85 yrs, and so on.

Table 2.5   *Distribution of Air Dodo passenger traffic in 1980 and 1981*

	1980		1981	
Europe	9	million	10	million
USA and Canada	5	million	7.5	million
Asia	2	million	3	million
Africa	2	million	2.5	million
Latin America	1.6	million	1.5	million
Australasia	0.4	million	0.5	million
TOTAL	20	million	25	million

2.3.5   Visualizing Data

Tables are a very useful means of organizing, presenting and summarizing data but they lack the obvious visual impact of charts and graphs. Thus, choosing the appropriate visual aid is an important aspect of data presentation. In this section we shall review some of the more commonly employed forms of visual presentation, using the data in Table 2.5 and the information relating to Route A.

Pictograms involve the use of stylized figures to represent the variable in question, the number of figures included indicating the quantities or magnitudes. Thus the number of passengers carried by Pterodactyl Airways and Air Dodo, on all routes, in 1981 (12 million and 25 million respectively) can be shown as in Figure 2.1.

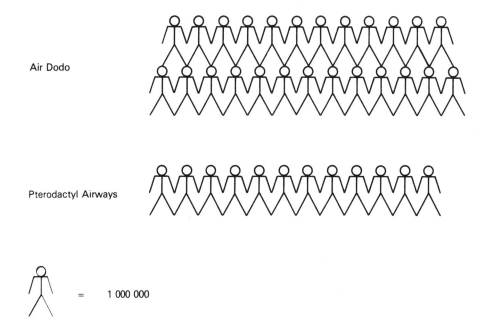

Figure 2.1   *A pictogram showing the number of passengers carried by Pterodactyl Airways and Air Dodo in 1981*

A *pie-chart* is a circle divided into segments, the areas of which are proportional to the corresponding data values. Where not only the relative sizes of the components but also the overall magnitude of the 'cake' or 'pie' is changing, the size of the circle needs to be altered accordingly. In view of the problems associated with it, this form is best suited to cases where the data are in percentage form, as illustrated in Figure 2.2.

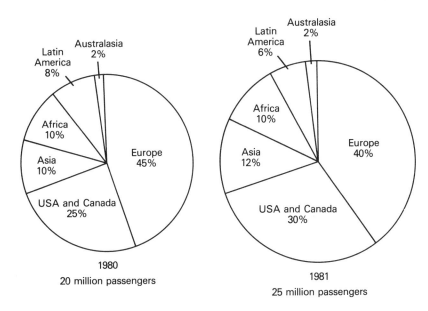

Figure 2.2   *A pie-chart showing the distribution of Air Dodo passenger traffic in 1980 and 1981*

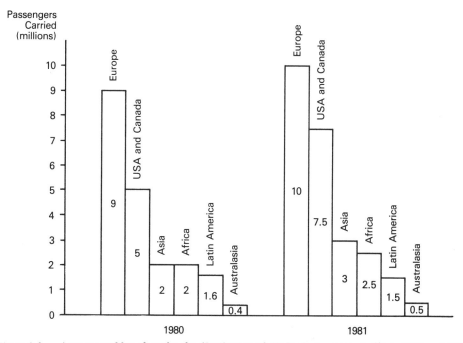

Figure 2.3   *A compound bar-chart for the distribution of Air Dodo passenger traffic in 1980 and 1981*

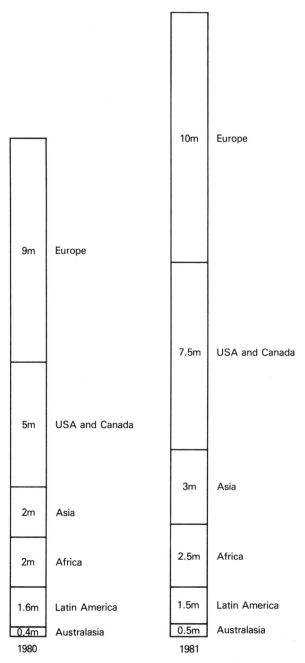

Figure 2.4   *A component bar-chart showing the distribution of Air Dodo passenger traffic in 1980 and 1981*

In a *bar-chart*, lines or blocks of different heights (or lengths if presented horizontally) represent the appropriate magnitudes. Not only can they be visually striking but it is possible to illustrate magnitudes of more than one variable at a time (*compound bar-chart*) or to illustrate the components of a variable (*component bar-chart*) either by absolute values or by a percentage of the total. These are illustrated in Figures 2.3 and 2.4 respectively.

A *histogram*, although superficially similar to the vertical bar chart, is a more complex chart widely used for grouped data. It is important to note that it is the *areas* of the blocks and not their heights which are proportional to the frequencies in each class. This last point is particularly important when dealing with unequal class intervals. The histogram, then, is a bar-chart of a frequency distribution and there should be no gaps between the blocks, even for discrete data. A histogram for the problem data (Route A) is shown in Figure 2.5.

A *frequency polygon* consists of a series of straight lines linking the centres of the tops of the blocks of a histogram. Note that in Figure 2.6 lines are continued beyond the two

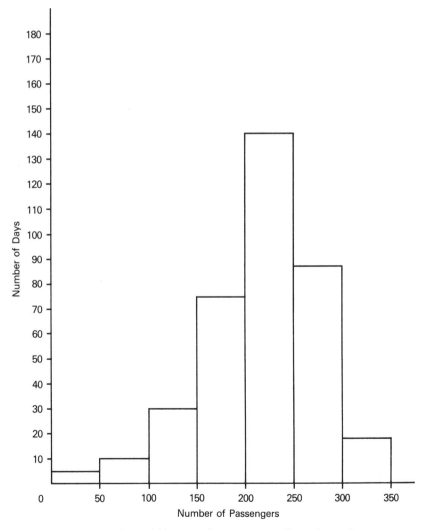

Figure 2.5   *A histogram for passenger traffic on Route A*

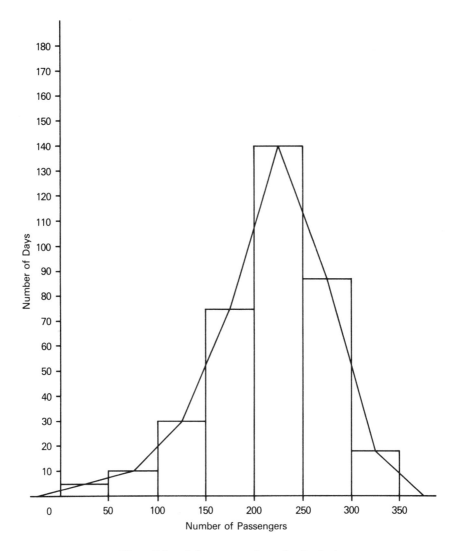

Figure 2.6   *A frequency polygon for Route A*

ends of the histogram on which it is based because the area under the polygon must equal the area under the histogram. In practice frequency polygons are less popular than histograms.

Just as the frequency polygon can be obtained from a histogram so, by smoothing the straight line, can the *frequency curve* be obtained from the frequency polygon. This can give a more general view of the variable, as Figure 2.7 illustrates, although strictly its use should be limited to continuous variables.

If instead of plotting frequencies separately for each class interval, we use accumulative frequencies class by class, the result is a *cumulative frequency polygon*. Before this can be drawn, it is necessary to calculate the appropriate cumulative frequencies as shown for the problem data in Table 2.6. When these cumulative frequencies are plotted against the upper class-limits the cumulative frequency polygon shown in Figure 2.8 is obtained.

It is often unrealistic to assume that frequencies accumulate in the form of a straight

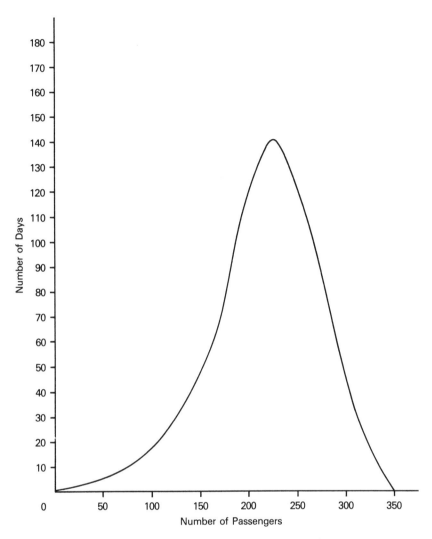

Figure 2.7 *A frequency curve for Route A*

Table 2.6 *A cumulative frequency table for Route A*

Number of passengers (X)	Number of days (f)	Cumulative frequency (Σf)
0–49	5	5
50–99	10	15
100–149	30	45
150–199	75	120
200–249	140	260
250–299	87	347
300–349	18	365

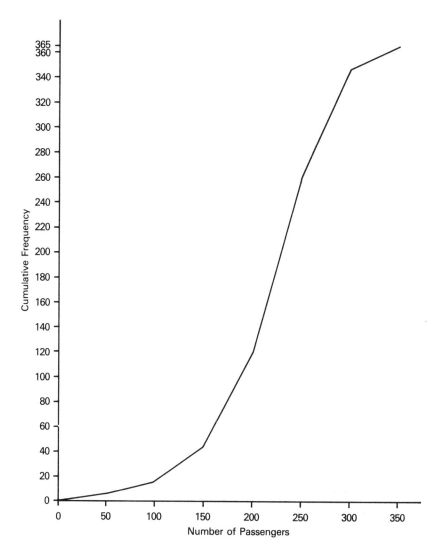

Figure 2.8   *A cumulative frequency polygon for Route A*

line, and so a *cumulative frequency curve*, more commonly called an *ogive*, is usually preferred. The ogive for the problem data is shown in Figure 2.9.

From Table 2.6 and Figure 2.9 we can see that on 120 days during 1981 less than
200 passengers were carried on Route A. From Figure 2.9 we may estimate that 185 or
fewer passengers were carried on 90 days in 1981. This technique becomes even more
useful if the vertical scale is converted to cumulative percentage. The final (topmost) value
of the ogive then becomes 100 (per cent) rather than the sum of all frequencies (365 days
in the problem data). Table 2.7 and Figure 2.10 illustrate the *percentage ogive* for the
problem data.

From Table 2.7 and Figure 2.10 we see that approximately 33 per cent of daily
flights on Route A carried less than 200 passengers.

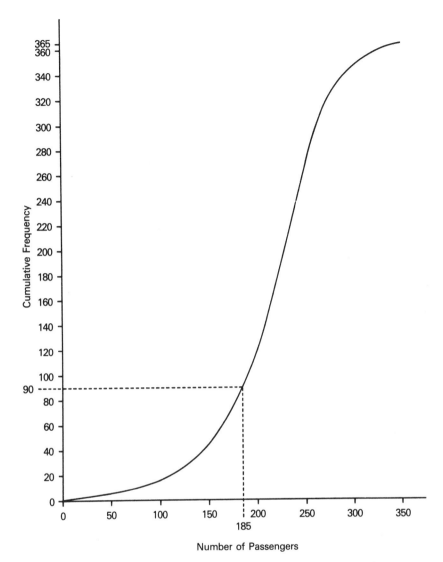

Figure 2.9   *A cumulative frequency curve (ogive) for Route A*

Table 2.7   *A cumulative percentage table for Route A*

Number of passengers (X)	Number of days (f)	Percentage of days (%)	Cumulative percentage (Σ%)
0–49	5	1.4	1.4
50–99	10	2.7	4.1
100–149	30	8.2	12.3
150–199	75	20.6[a]	32.9
200–249	140	38.4	71.3
250–299	87	23.8	95.1
300–349	18	4.9	100.0

[a] Rounded up to compensate for rounding errors and to ensure Σ% = 100

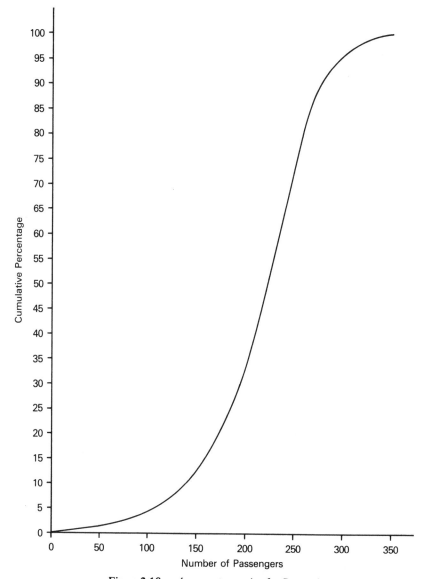

Figure 2.10   *A percentage ogive for Route A*

2.4   AVERAGES

2.4.1   The Arithmetic Mean

It is a basic human desire to categorize people, places, events and items so that general statements can be made about them. As a result, we speak of the typical Italian, or typical
Northern industrial town, or typical Cup Final. What is sought is a representative of what

may be a widely differing population or set of circumstances. Averages are attempts to find the representative: the difficulty with such an attempt arises from the reliability which may be placed on an average and from the fact that the average need not exist. The average amount spent by customers in a certain shop may be £3.65 but not a single customer need spend that actual amount.

Ask anyone for the average of the following numbers: 3, 5, 5, 7, 10 and the answer is likely to be '6'. This is simply obtained by adding the values and dividing by their number, five. This gives 30/5 = 6. This is but one of a number of types of average. It is know formally as the *arithmetic mean* (*AM*) or simply, the mean. If we call the variable being measured X, and the number of items n, the formal calculation is written as follows:

$$AM = \frac{\Sigma X}{n} = \frac{3+5+5+7+10}{5} = \frac{30}{5} = 6$$

The Σ sign indicates 'the sum of', in this case of the X values. It is a common symbol in quantitative work and will occur frequently in later chapters.

However, in business it is much more likely that the data will be grouped, as are the problem data. Basically the procedure is the same, with two modifications. First, in grouped data, by its very nature, actual values are unknown. For example, in the problem data we know that on five days the number of passengers carried was *somewhere* between 0 and 49 inclusive but the exact numbers are unknown. Under the circumstances the best we can do is assume that the numbers of passengers for the five days are evenly spaced within the 0–49 class. Given this assumption we can then proceed to use the *midpoint* (X') of the class, which is 24.5 as representative of the class as a whole.

The second modification involves us in the use of *frequencies*. Whereas in the example above the values were simply added, in the case of grouped data this would become tedious. This would involve us in a calculation beginning 24.5 + 24.5 + 24.5 + 24.5 + 24.5 and so on through the classes. Instead, we employ a shortcut. We simply multiply the midpoint of each class (X') by the relevant frequency (f). Thus for the class 0–49 the calculation is 24.5 x 5 = 122.5. In formal terms this is $X'f$ or fX'. The whole calculation then becomes:

$$AM = \frac{\Sigma fX'}{n} \quad \text{or} \quad \frac{\Sigma fX'}{\Sigma f}$$

Notice that in the denominator, n may be replaced by the equivalent Σf (sum of frequencies). Also, the *AM* for a population is often indicated by μ and the *AM* for a sample by $\bar{X}$. The full calculation is set out in Table 2.8.

Table 2.8   *Calculating the AM for Route A*

Number of passengers (X)	Class midpoint (X')	Number of days (f)	(fX')
0–49	24.5	5	122.5
50–99	74.5	10	745.0
100–149	124.5	30	3 735.0
150–199	174.5	75	13 087.5
200–249	224.5	140	31 430.0
250–299	274.5	87	23 881.5
300–349	324.5	18	5 841.0
		$\Sigma f = 365$	$\Sigma fX' = 78\,842.5$

$$AM_A = \frac{\Sigma fX'}{\Sigma f} = \frac{78\,842.5}{365} = 216 \text{ passengers}$$

From Table 2.8 we see that the *AM* for Route A is 216 passengers. By a similar cal-culation the *AM* of Route B is found to be 219 passengers. Therefore, on the basis of this information, the airline would be well advised to choose Route B. The *AM* is useful and easily understood, but can gloss over certain important characteristics of data. For example, an *AM* of 216 could also have been obtained from data with a frequency distribution markedly different from that for Route A. It is therefore often useful to calculate other measures of *central tendency* or *location*.

2.4.2   The Median

One such measure of location is the *median* (M_d). This is defined as the middle item when the data are arranged in ascending (or descending) order. For example, consider the following sample data arranged in ascending order: 3, 5, 5, 7, 10. The middle item is underlined. Thus the median is 5 ($M_d = 5$). In general, for an odd number of data, the median is identified as the $(n + 1)/2$th item. Thus for five numbers (as above) the median is the $(5 + 1)/2 =$ the third item. For an even number of values, say, 6, use of the expression $(n + 1)/2$ identifies the $7/2 = 3.5$th item. Of course, no such item exists, so what we do is take the average of the third and the fourth item. Thus if our data values were: 3, 5, 5, 7, 10, 12, the median would be $(5 + 7)/2 = 6$. In such cases the median value may not be an actually observed value.

The problem is compounded in the case of grouped data where we do not know any specific values to start with! We start by identifying the *median class*, that is, the class interval containing the middle term. This is done by calculating cumulative frequencies. Thus in the problem data, the median is the $n/2$th item (use of $(n + 1)/2$ would give a false impression of precision), that is, $365/2 =$ the 182.5th item. This item clearly lies in the 200–249 class, as can be seen from Table 2.9.

Table 2.9   *Identification of the median class for Route A*

Number of passengers (X)	Number of days (f)	Cumulative frequency (Σf)
0–49	5	5
50–99	10	15
100–149	30	45
150–199	75	120
200–249	140	260
250–299	87	347
300–349	18	365

This fixes a lower and upper limit to its value: 200 and 249 respectively. The next step is to place the median *within* its class. The first item in the median class is the 121st item, the second is the 122nd item and so on. The 182.5th item is thus the $(n/2 - 120)$th item into the median class, that is, the 62.5th item along in the median class. Is this a long way into the median class? Well, since there are 140 items in total in the median class, it represents 62.5/140 of the class interval, or roughly halfway along. But what does this mean in terms of passengers? The class interval is 50 passengers and so $(62.5/140) \times 50 = 22.32$ or to the nearest passenger, 22, measures how far above the lower limit (in terms of numbers of passengers) the median lies. Thus the median number of passengers is $200 + 22 = 222$. In formal terms all this may be expressed as:

$$M_d = L_{M_d} + \left(\frac{\frac{n}{2} - \text{cum } fp}{f_{M_d}} \right) \times CI$$

Where
- M_d = median value;
- L_{M_d} = lower limit of median class;
- $n/2$ = middle item in the data;
- cum fp = cumulative frequency up to and including the class immediately preceding the median class;
- f_{M_d} = frequency in the median class;
- CI = class interval of the median class.

Substituting in the appropriate values we obtain:

$$M_d = 200 + \left(\frac{\frac{365}{2} - 120}{140} \right) \times 50$$

$$M_d = 200 + \left(\frac{182.5 - 120}{140} \right) \times 50$$

$$M_d = 200 + (0.446) \times 50$$

$$M_d = 200 + 22.3 = 222.3$$

$$M_d = 222, \text{ to the nearest passenger}$$

An alternative, though less precise, method of estimating the median for grouped data involves the use of the appropriate ogive. A horizontal line is drawn halfway along the vertical (cumulative frequency or cumulative percentage) axis. The value on the horizontal axis (value of the variable) corresponding to the point of intersection of the horizontal line and the cumulative frequency curve is the estimated value of the median. This is shown in Figure 2.11.

Let us review the main points. The first requirement is to identify the median class, that is, the class in which the middle item is to be found. The next step is to specify where in that class the median lies. It is assumed that the values are distributed evenly within the median class as if in fact they were set out in ascending order. It is then a question of how far into (what fraction of the way along) the median class the median item lies. Clearly, having identified the median class, the smallest possible value for the median is the lower limit of that class (L_{M_d}) and to this is added a measure of how much further into the class we must look for the median (62.5/140ths in the example), multiplied by the extent or width of the class interval (50 in the example).

Remember that calculation of the median for grouped data is subject to the same qualifications as that of the *AM*, and hence the value obtained, by whatever means, must be considered approximate.

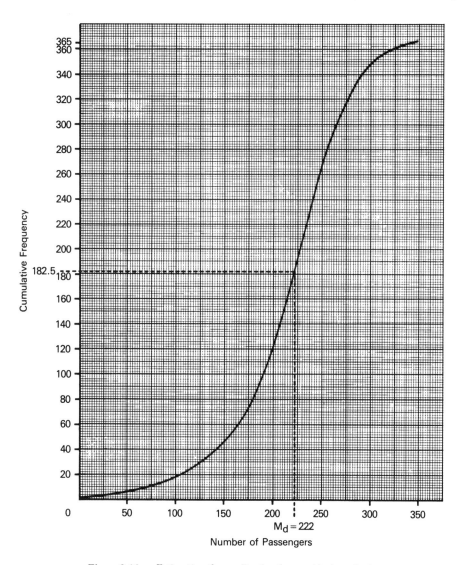

Figure 2.11   *Estimating the median by the graphical method*

2.4.3   The Mode

The *mode* (M_o) is simply the value which occurs most frequently in a set of data, or, in other words, has the highest frequency. Consider the following ungrouped data: 3, 5, 5, 7, 10, 12. Here the value 5 occurs most frequently (twice) and is thus the mode. Where there is only one mode the distribution is termed unimodal, but it is possible for there to be no mode (all items having the same frequency) or for there to be more than one mode (the highest frequency being shared by more than one value).

Subject to the usual reservations about grouped data it is possible to estimate the mode by two methods. First, the *graphical method* requires the construction of the histogram

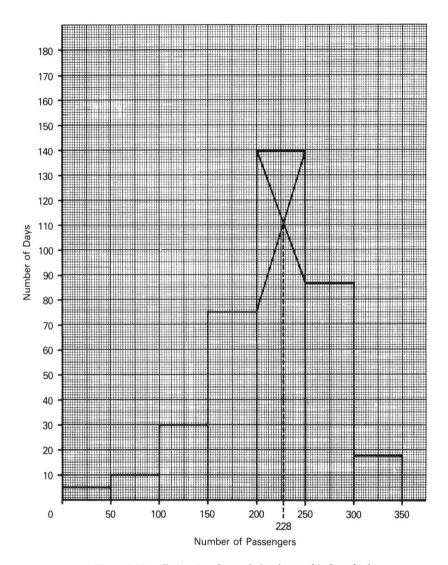

Figure 2.12 *Estimating the mode by the graphical method*

for the data as shown in Figure 2.5 and reconstructed in Figure 2.12. The mode is then found at the intersection of the two lines, the value (228 passengers) being read off on the horizontal axis.

The alternative method involves use of the following formula:

$$M_o = L_{M_o} + \left(\frac{d_1}{d_1 + d_2}\right) \times CI$$

Where L_{M_o} = lower limit of the modal class;
d_1 = difference in frequencies between the modal class and the preceding class;
d_2 = difference in frequencies between the modal class and the following class;
CI = class interval of the modal class.

Substituting the data values into this we obtain:

$$M_o = 200 + \left(\frac{65}{65 + 53} \right) \times 50$$

$$M_o = 200 + \left(\frac{65}{118} \right) \times 50$$

$$M_o = 200 + 27.54$$

$$M_o = 228, \text{ to the nearest passenger}$$

Again, it will be seen that the first step is to identify the modal class (the class with the highest frequency) and then to ascertain where within these bounds the mode is expected to lie. The lower limit of the modal class therefore is the minimum value that the mode can have when estimated in this way.

If the frequencies in the two adjoining classes are equal, then $d_1 = d_2$ and the mode is reckoned to lie halfway along the modal class. A moment's thought, however, should make it clear that the actual mode could in fact lie in the class with the lowest frequency, or indeed any other class. In our example, for instance, it is possible that the 140 values in the modal class are in fact widely spread, whereas the five values in the 0–49 class are all the same value. The point is that since the data are grouped we just do not know the actual values and hence our estimate of the mode should be viewed as simply an educated guess.

2.4.4   Other Related Measures of Location

Just as the median divides the data into halves, so *quartiles* divide the data into quarters. In fact, the median is the central quartile (Q_2) while the *lower quartile* (dividing the data below the median into half again) is termed Q_1 and the *upper quartile* (dividing the upper half of the distribution into half again) is termed Q_3.

For the following ungrouped data: 3, 5, 5, 7, 10, the lower quartile (Q_1) is the $(n + 1)/4$th item, that is, $6/4 = 1\frac{1}{2}$th item. This is midway between the first (3) and the second (5) item and so an average is taken $(3 + 5)/2$ to give a Q_1 value of 4. If a fraction other than half occurs, the nearer data value may be chosen. Thus if Q had been identified as the $1\frac{1}{3}$rd item, 3 (the first item) would have been chosen as the Q_1 value. The upper quartile (Q_3) is expressed as $3(n + 1)/4$ which identifies the $18/4 = 4\frac{1}{2}$th item. This is $(7 + 10)/2 = 8.5$.

For grouped data, Q_1 and Q_3 are identified by the use of the following formulae:

$$Q_1 = L_{Q_1} + \left(\frac{\frac{n}{4} - \text{cum} fp_{Q_1}}{fQ_1} \right) \times CI_1$$

$$Q_3 = L_{Q_3} + \left(\frac{\frac{3n}{4} - \text{cum} fp_{Q_3}}{fQ_3} \right) \times CI_3$$

Where L_{Q_1} and L_{Q_3} = lower limits of the respective quartile classes (i.e. that containing the $n/4$ and $3n/4$ items respectively);

cum fp_{Q_1} and cum fp_{Q_3} = cumulative frequencies up to and including the class prior to the respective quartile classes;

f_{Q_1} and f_{Q_3} = frequencies in the respective quartile classes;
CI_1 and CI_3 = class intervals in the respective quartile classes.

The quartile classes are identified in Table 2.10.

Table 2.10 *Identification of the quartile classes for Route A*

	Number of passengers (X)	Number of days (f)	Cumulative frequency (Σf)
	0–49	5	5
	50–99	10	15
	100–149	30	45
Q_1 class:	150–199	75	120
	200–249	140	260
Q_3 class:	250–299	87	347
	300–349	18	365

Substituting in appropriate values from the problem data we obtain:

$$Q_1 = 150 + \left(\frac{\frac{365}{4} - 45}{75} \right) \times 50$$

$$Q_1 = 150 + \left(\frac{46.25}{75} \right) \times 50$$

$$Q_1 = 150 + 30.8$$

$$Q_1 = 181, \text{ to the nearest passenger}$$

and for the upper quartile (Q_3):

$$Q_3 = 250 + \left(\frac{\frac{1095}{4} - 260}{87} \right) \times 50$$

$$Q_3 = 250 + \left(\frac{13.75}{87} \right) \times 50$$

$$Q_3 = 250 + 7.9$$

$$Q_3 = 258, \text{ to the nearest passenger}$$

Alternatively, the graphical method may be used. This involves reading off the values a quarter and three-quarters of the way along the ogive, as shown in Figure 2.13.

Deciles (D) divide data into tenths. The formula for the quartiles can be used with the amendment that instead of $n/4$ or $3n/4$, the first decile (D_1) will use $n/10$, the second decile (D_2) $2n/10$ and so on. The other items of the formula will correspond accordingly. *Percentiles* (P) divide the data into hundredths and, again with suitable amendments, the formula for the quartiles can be used. Alternatively, the graphical method may be employed.

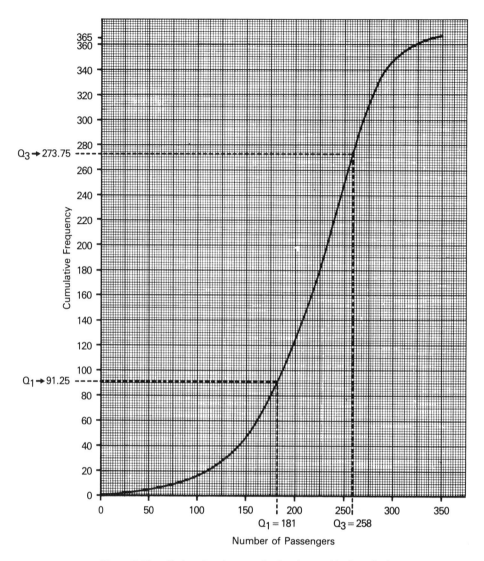

Figure 2.13   *Estimating the quartiles by the graphical method*

2.4.5   The Geometric Mean

The geometric mean (GM) is appropriate when dealing with ratios and percentages such as population and economic growth rates. It is obtained as the Nth root of the product of N values of a variable thus:

$$GM = \sqrt[N]{X_1 \times X_2 \times \ldots X_N}$$

To illustrate this, let us consider the following values of X: 3, 5, 5, 7, 10;

$$GM = \sqrt[5]{3 \times 5 \times 5 \times 7 \times 10} = 5.5$$

Note that the *GM* for the same data gives a lower value than the *AM*. Computationally, it is often convenient to work in logarithms, in which case the expression becomes:

$$\log GM = \frac{\Sigma \log X}{N}$$

the antilog then gives the value of the *GM* as follows:

$$\log GM = \frac{\log 3 + \log 5 + \log 5 + \log 7 + \log 10}{5}$$

$$= \frac{0.4771 + 0.6990 + 0.6990 + 0.8451 + 1.0000}{5} \quad \text{from ordinary log-tables}$$

$$= \frac{3.7202}{5}$$

$$= 0.7440$$

From antilog tables we obtain the result *GM* = 5.5 as above.

If your calculator has a 'power button', the result may be obtained by finding the fifth root; that is, the one-fifth power using the decimal equivalent 0.2. The manufacturer's handbook will give detailed instructions.

In order to measure, say, the average rate of growth in passenger air traffic between two time-periods the following expression can be used:

$$r = \sqrt[N]{\frac{P_N}{P_0}} - 1$$

Where r = rate of increase;
      P_N = value at end of N periods;
      N = number of time-periods;
      P_0 = value at beginning of periods.

By way of example, imagine the number of passengers carried increases from 1 million to 1.5 million over ten years. What has been the average rate of growth per year? If the *AM* were used we would obtain an annual rate of growth of five per cent since the increase has been 50 per cent over 10 years. However, this gives a patently false impression of the nature of growth since it does not grow by the same absolute amount each year but is in fact similar to compound, as opposed to simple, interest. Use of the *GM* would give:

$$r = \sqrt[10]{\frac{1\,500\,000}{1\,000\,000}} - 1$$

$$r = 1.04 - 1 = 0.04 \text{ or } 4\% \text{ per year (approximately)}$$

Incorrect use of the *AM* instead of the *GM* results in an overstatement of the average annual rate of growth.

2.5   DISPERSION

2.5.1   The Spread

In section 2.4 we saw how various measures of central tendency could be employed to describe a set of data and indeed to distinguish between different sets of data. However, it is possible for two different sets of data to share the same average values, as is illustrated below. There is a need therefore for the identification of a further characteristic of the data to enable the distinction to be made.

The second characteristic is the *spread* or *dispersion* of the values of the variable in the data. Here some of the more important measures of dispersion, each employing a different criterion, will be examined. The following ungrouped data will be used:

Set (a)   10, 11, 15, 15, 17, 20.
Set (b)   6, 10, 15, 15, 18, 24.

The *AM* for both (a) and (b) is 14.67 and they have the same median value, 15, and the same modal value, also 15. However, even a cursory glance indicates that the data are not as uniform as their averages suggest; data (b) contain a greater spread of values.

2.5.2   The Range

The *range* is the simplest measure of dispersion and is found by subtracting the smallest value in the data from the largest. Thus for Set (a):

$$\text{range}_a = 20 - 10 = 10$$

and for Set (b):

$$\text{range}_b = 24 - 6 = 18$$

Thus the spread or dispersion of values as indicated by the range is greater for Set (b) than for Set (a).

For grouped data, such as the airline problem data, the procedure is to take the lower limit of the first class and the upper limit of the last class as the most extreme values. Thus, from Tables 2.1 and 2.2 we obtain:

$$\text{range}_A = 349 - 0 = 349 \text{ passengers for Route A}$$
$$\text{range}_B = 349 - 0 = 349 \text{ passengers for Route B}$$

Clearly in such cases the range is determined by the class intervals chosen for the data and the *actual* smallest and largest values cannot be identified.

While simple to calculate, the range does have the drawback that it totally ignores all but the two extreme values. Thus the range for the two sets of data below is the same $(33 - 3 = 30)$:

Set (c)   3, 8, 13, 18, 23, 28, 33.
Set (d)   3, 17, 18, 19, 20, 21, 33.

Clearly, we would prefer a measure which, in some way, takes into account *all* values.

2.5.3   The Mean Deviation

The mean deviation *MD* is the average difference between each value and the arithmetic mean, $(X - \bar{X})$. This involves finding the difference between each of the values and the arithmetic mean to give a set of $(X - \bar{X})$, summing each of those *ignoring the sign* (otherwise they would sum to zero) and dividing the total by the number of items (n). Note that here dispersion is measured as *dispersion of values about the AM*. In formal terms for ungrouped data this gives:

$$MD = \frac{\Sigma |X - AM|}{n}$$

Where the $| \quad |$ sign (the modulus) indicates that we ignore negative signs, so that all values are taken as positive.

The procedure is shown for Set (a) in Table 2.11, where MD_a is found to be 2.78. A similar calculation for Set (b) reveals an *MD* of 4.44. The larger value for MD_b clearly reflects the greater spread of values in Set (b).

Table 2.11   *Calculation of the mean deviation for ungrouped data in Set (a)*

X	AM ($\bar{X}$)	X − AM	|X − AM|
10	14.67	− 4.67	4.67
11	14.67	− 3.67	3.67
15	14.67	+ 0.33	0.33
15	14.67	+ 0.33	0.33
17	14.67	+ 2.33	2.33
20	14.67	+ 5.33	5.33
			$\Sigma |X - AM| = 16.66$

$$MD_a = \frac{\Sigma |X - AM|}{N} = \frac{16.66}{6} = 2.78$$

For grouped data the procedure is basically the same as for ungrouped data. The two differences are, first, as the actual values of X are unknown the midpoint value of each class is used, and second, it is necessary to take into account the frequencies in each class. This gives:

$$MD = \frac{\Sigma f |x|}{n}$$

Where f = frequency in the class;
x = deviation of the midpoint of the class from the *AM* (i.e. $X' - AM$);
n = Σf.

Table 2.12 illustrates the calculation of the *MD* for Route A. It is found that MD_A is 45 passengers.

Table 2.12   *Calculation of the mean deviation for grouped data (Route A)*

Number of passengers (X)	Class midpoint (X')	AM ($\bar{X}$)	X' − AM (X' − $\bar{X}$)	|X' − AM| (|X' − $\bar{X}$|) (|x|)	Number of days (f)	f|X' − $\bar{X}$| f|x|
0–49	24.5	216	− 191.5	191.5	5	957.5
50–99	74.5	216	− 141.5	141.5	10	1 415.0
100–149	124.5	216	− 91.5	91.5	30	2 745.0
150–199	174.5	216	− 41.5	41.5	75	3 112.5
200–249	224.5	216	+ 8.5	8.5	140	1 190.0
250–299	274.5	216	+ 58.5	58.5	87	5 089.5
300–349	324.5	216	+ 108.5	108.5	18	1 953.0
					$\Sigma f = 365$	$\Sigma f\|x\| = 16\,462.5$

$$MD_A = \frac{\Sigma f|x|}{\Sigma f} = \frac{16\,462.5}{365} = 45.1 \text{ passengers for Route A}$$

2.5.4   Variances

In calculating the *MD* the problem of signs was overcome by ignoring them. An alternative solution is to square the deviations. The *variance* is simply the average of the squared deviations from the *AM*. For ungrouped data this is shown as:

$$\text{Var} = \frac{\Sigma(X - AM)^2}{n} = \frac{\Sigma(x)^2}{n}$$

The calculation of the variance for the data in Set (a) is shown in Table 2.13. The resultant value is $\text{Var}_a = 11.6$.

A similar calculation for the data in Set (b) gives $\text{Var}_b = 32.6$. Again the dispersion of values (measured as the average of the squared deviations from the arithmetic mean) is shown to be greater in the case of Set (b).

The variance is a widely used measure but suffers from one particular drawback,

Table 2.13   *Calculation of the variance for ungrouped data in Set (a)*

X	AM ($\bar{X}$)	X − AM (x)	(X − AM)^2 (x^2)
10	14.67	− 4.67	21.81
11	14.67	− 3.67	13.47
15	14.67	+ 0.33	0.11
15	14.67	+ 0.33	0.11
17	14.67	+ 2.33	5.43
20	14.67	+ 5.33	28.41
			$\Sigma x^2 = 69.34$

$$\text{Var}_a = \frac{\Sigma(X - AM)^2}{n} = \frac{69.34}{6} = 11.6$$

namely, that the value calculated is in *original units squared*. Thus if the data in Set (b) were in pounds the variance would read as 32.6 £^{2}. All is not lost, however, because we can convert back into the original units by taking the square-root of the variance. This measure is termed the standard deviation and will be discussed in section 2.5.5.

For grouped data the formula for variance is:

$$\text{Var} = \frac{\Sigma f(X' - AM)^2}{n} = \frac{\Sigma f x^2}{n}$$

Again this involves taking midpoints (X') of classes and weighting these by the frequencies, otherwise the procedure is the same as for ungrouped data. The calculation of the variance for problem data (Route A) is shown in Table 2.14.

Table 2.14 *Calculation of the variance for grouped data (Route A)*

Number of passengers (X)	Class midpoint (X')	AM ($\bar{X}$)	(X' − AM) (x)	(X' − AM)² (x)²	Number of days (f)	f(X' − AM)² (f(x)²)
0–49	24.5	216	− 191.5	36 672.25	5	183 361.25
50–99	74.5	216	− 141.5	20 022.25	10	200 222.50
100–149	124.5	216	− 91.5	8 372.25	30	251 167.50
150–199	174.5	216	− 41.5	1 722.25	75	129 168.75
200–249	224.5	216	+ 8.5	72.25	140	10 115.00
250–299	274.5	216	+ 58.5	3 422.25	87	297 735.75
300–349	324.5	216	+ 108.5	11 772.25	18	211.900.50
					$\Sigma f = 365$	$\Sigma f(X' - AM)^2 = 1\,283\,671.25$

$$\text{Var}_A = \frac{\Sigma f(X' - AM)}{\Sigma f} = \frac{1\,283\,671.25}{365} = 3516.9$$

$$\text{Var}_A = 3517 \text{ passengers}^2$$

2.5.5 Standard Deviation

The most widely used measure of dispersion, *standard deviation (SD, σ or s)*, is obtained simply from the variance by taking the square-root. Thus, for ungrouped data:

$$SD = \sqrt{\frac{\Sigma(X - AM)^2}{n}} = \sqrt{\frac{\Sigma(x)^2}{n}}$$

Thus for Set (a) SD_a is 3.4. And similarly, for Set (b) SD_b is 5.7.

The difference in the standard deviation of Set (a) and the standard deviation of Set (b) again reflects the greater dispersion of values about the *AM* in the latter.

For grouped data:

$$SD = \sqrt{\frac{\Sigma f(X - AM)^2}{n}} = \sqrt{\frac{\Sigma f(x)^2}{N}}$$

The calculation for the problem data (Route A) using this expression is the same as in Table 2.14; the *SD* being obtained as the square-root of the variance, i.e.

$$SD_A = \sqrt{\text{Var}_A} = \sqrt{3517} = 59.3$$

Although the whole basis of the *SD* rests on deviations from the *AM*, it is not necessary to calculate each of these individually before computing the *SD*. Original (rather than deviation) values can be used if the following expression is employed:

$$SD = \sqrt{\frac{\Sigma f(X')^2 - n(\bar{X})^2}{n}}$$

where X' are the class midpoints. Note that in such expressions Σf is often used in place of n although they are, of course, exactly the same. The calculation of the standard deviation for problem data (Route A) using this expression is shown in Table 2.15.

Table 2.15   *An alternative calculation for standard deviation on Route A*

Number of passengers	Class midpoints		Number of days	
(X)	(X')	(X')²	(f)	f(X')²
0–49	24.5	600.25	5	3 001.25
50–99	74.5	5 550.25	10	55 502.50
100–149	124.5	15 500.25	30	465 007.50
150–199	174.5	30 450.25	75	2 283 768.70
200–249	224.5	50 400.25	140	7 056 035.00
250–299	274.5	75 350.25	87	6 555 471.70
300–349	324.5	105 300.25	18	1 895 404.50
			$\Sigma f = n = 365$	$\Sigma f(X')^2 = 18\,314\,190$

$$SD_A = \sqrt{\frac{\Sigma f(X')^2 - N(\bar{X})^2}{n}}$$

$$SD_A = \sqrt{\frac{18\,314\,190 - (365 \times 216^2)}{365}}$$

$$SD_A = \sqrt{\frac{18\,314\,190 - 17\,029\,440}{365}}$$

$$SD_A = 59.3 \text{ passengers}$$

The general formula for *SD* is given above but the reader will encounter the use of σ to indicate the standard deviation of a population and s for the standard deviation of a sample. One point which may be confusing is the use of N, n or $n-1$ as the divisor in *SD* formulae. First, N is often reserved for the population, while n refers to a sample. Second, when the population standard deviation (σ) is being calculated, N is the divisor. N (or n) is used to calculate a sample standard deviation if the result is to be considered solely with reference to that sample. $N-1$ (or $n-1$) is used to calculate a sample standard deviation (s) when the result is intended to be used to draw inferences about the population from which it has been taken. This 'correction' is referred to again in Chapter 4, where it is crucial. Readers with pre-programmed calculators should ascertain whether it computes standard deviation by using N (or n) or else $N-1$ (or $n-1$). Although in practice the error will be slight, business analysis sometimes uses relatively few observations and the difference could be important, as we shall see in the next chapter.

2.5.6   More Deviation

It will be seen that the *MD*, variance and standard deviation all measured dispersion by reference (in some way) to the deviations of values from the *AM*. An alternative base for measures of dispersion would be the relative values of the lower and upper quartiles. The *interquartile range* is simply the positive difference between the two values, that is the interquartile range is $Q_3 - Q_1$. For the problem data of Route A this gives an interquartile range of $258 - 181 = 77$ passengers.

   Quartile deviation (QD), sometimes known as the *semi-interquartile range*, is given by:

$$QD = \frac{Q_3 - Q_1}{2}$$

For the problem data of Route A the *QD* is 38.5. Thus, if one can identify the upper and lower quartiles from a set of data, calculation of *QD* is straightforward.

2.5.7   Relativity

All the above measures of dispersion dealt in *absolute* terms. Often, however, we require a *relative* measure of dispersion in each set of data. One such measure is the *coefficient of variation (CV)*. If the *SD* has been used to measure dispersion, the *CV* will measure the relative size of *SD* to *AM*. In other words, how dispersed are the data in relation to their overall magnitude? Thus:

$$CV = \frac{SD}{AM} \times 100$$

Thus for the ungrouped data in Set (a):

$$CV_a = \frac{3.4}{14.67} \times 100 = 23.2\%$$

and for Set (b):

$$CV_b = \frac{5.7}{14.67} \times 100 = 38.9\%$$

For the problem data in Route A, the coefficient of variation is given by:

$$CV_A = \frac{SD_A}{AM_A} \times 100$$

$$CV_A = \frac{59.3}{216} \times 100$$

$$CV_A = 27.45\%$$

   Another measure of relative dispersion is the coefficient of quartile variation *CVQ* which compares the interquartile range $(Q_3 - Q_1)$ with the sum of Q_1 and Q_3. Thus:

$$CVQ = \frac{Q_3 - Q_1}{Q_3 + Q_1} \times 100$$

For the problem data of Route A this gives:

$$CVQ_A = \frac{258 - 181}{439} \times 100$$

$$CVQ_A = 17.5\%$$

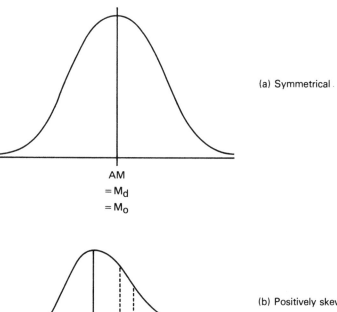

(a) Symmetrical

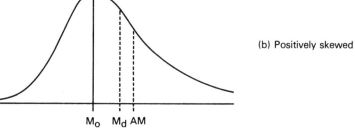

(b) Positively skewed

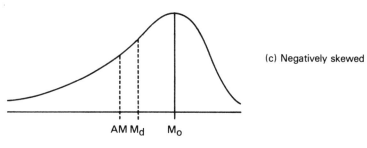

(c) Negatively skewed

Figure 2.14 *Skewness*

2.5.8 Skewness

Figure 2.14 illustrates three frequency distributions. The first, (a), being *symmetrical*, is characterized by having the *AM*, median and mode all equal. The distribution in (b) is termed *positively skewed* since the 'tail' spreads to the right. In this case, the median is to the right of the mode and the *AM* is even further to the right since it is 'dragged up' by some extremely large values on the right. The negatively skewed distribution (c) is the reverse of (b).

Skewness then is a measure of the relative positions of the three major forms of average; the arithmetic mean, the median and the mode. One commonly employed measure, *Pearson's coefficient of skewness* (S_k), can be calculated by means of either formula shown below:

$$S_k = \frac{3(AM - M_d)}{SD}$$

or

$$S_k = \frac{AM - M_o}{SD}$$

Note that if the distribution is symmetrical, $AM = M_d = M_o$, and thus $S_k = 0$. For the problem data for Route A, however:

$$S_k(A) = \frac{3(216 - 222)}{59.3} = -0.30$$

or

$$S_k(A) = \frac{216 - 228}{59.3} = -0.20$$

The difference in calculated values of S_k between the two formulae is in most cases likely to be slight. Both show that the Route A data are negatively skewed.

Table 2.16   *Summary table for both Routes A and B*

	Route A	Route B
AM	216	219
Median	222	235
Mode	228	270
Q_1	181	161
Q_3	258	286
Range	349	349
MD	45	69
Variance	3517	7025
SD	59	84
Interquartile range	77	125
QD	38.5	62.5
CV	27.5%	38%
CV_Q	17.5%	28%
Skewness $\left[\dfrac{3(AM - M_d)}{SD}\right]$	−0.30	−0.57

2.6   REPORT AND CONCLUSION

Now is the time to take stock of the various calculations made and to utilize them in the preparation of a report advising Air Dodo on the choice between Routes A and B. Table 2.16 summarizes the values obtained for each route.

First, Route B is superior in terms of all three types of average, most markedly in the case of the mode, which suggests that the most common number of passengers carried on Route B's daily flight is 270, compared with Route A's 228. However, the spread, or variability, of passenger load is much greater on Route B, as evidenced by, for example, a standard deviation of 84 passengers compared with 59 passengers on Route A. This may have implications for the type of aircraft to be assigned to the route.

Thus Air Dodo will have to weigh a higher average passenger load (suggesting higher revenue) against the greater variability (perhaps increasing costs) of Route B compared with Route A.

ASSIGNMENTS

A2.1 (a) For the problem data in the text calculate the corresponding values for Route B, and check your answers against those shown in Table 2.16. Where appropriate use both the formula and the graphical method. Draw up a detailed report and advise Air Dodo.

  (b) What other data would be most useful in preparing such a report?

A2.2 (a) Explain (and check) the calculations necessary to make the statement: 'On Route A 40 per cent of flights carried no more than 209 passengers'. Hint: this refers to the fourth decile (D_4).

  (b) Air Dodo operate two types of aircraft, the Starling, with a maximum capacity of 240 and a breakeven load of 185 passengers, and the Pelican, with a capacity of 349 and a breakeven load of 220 passengers.

  Advise Air Dodo on the better aircraft for each route. (Hint: look for the number of days on which passengers would be turned away if the Starling were chosen, and the number of days for which an operating profit, or loss, is made.)

A2.3 The following data are the amounts (to the nearest £) spent by a sample of 13 customers in a supermarket one Monday morning: 7, 3, 3, 4, 6, 2, 10, 1, 19, 12, 5, 16, 9 (in £s).

  (a) Calculate the *AM*, the median and the mode.
  (b) Calculate the *MD, SD* and *QD*.

  Group the data into a suitable frequency distribution and:

  (c) Calculate the *AM*, median and mode by the formula and graphical method.
  (d) Calculate the *MD, SD* and *QD*.
  (e) Compare your results under (a) with (c) and (b) with (d) and comment.
  (f) Comment on the usefulness or otherwise to the supermarket of your calculations.

A2.4 Rolls of wallpaper are sold as being 10 metres in length. However, the rolling machinery cannot produce the rolls exactly to that length and the following data are obtained from a random selection of output.

Actual length (metres)	Number of rolls
Below 9.60	11
9.60–9.80	17
9.80–10.00	41
10.00–10.20	70
10.20–10.40	38
10.40 and over	23

(a)   Construct the ogive for these data.

(b)   It has been decided that no roll shorter than 10 metres may be sold retail. State the proportion of rolls that cannot be sold.

(c)   The machine is set to produce rolls longer than 10 metres. What is the evidence for this?

(d)   Estimate the actual amount of paper on 200 retail rolls which is in excess of the stated 10 metres per roll.

A2.5   Consider the following data relating to a firm's workforce.

Weekly earnings £	Numbers of workers
Under 50	5
50 but under 60	13
60 but under 70	29
70 but under 80	39
80 but under 90	42
90 but under 100	37
100 but under 110	20
110 but under 120	9
120 but under 130	4
130 and over	2

(a)   What weekly wage might a prospective employee expect to receive?

(b)   Explain how you would justify the answer to (a) to a young employee who earns £62 per week.

3—Measuring Uncertainty In Business

3.1 INTRODUCTION AND OBJECTIVES

3.1.1 The Subject of the Chapter

It is a fact of life that businesses operate in an uncertain world. Decisions need to be made on the basis of certain assumptions that may, or may not, be borne out. The uncertainty begins with the decision to start up in business and is inherent in later decisions such as whether or not to expand production, develop a new product, enter a new market, and so on. It is easy to say with hindsight that a particular decision should or should not have been made, but decision-making cannot wait and calculated risks have to be taken.

In fact, a distinction is often made between absolute or total uncertainty and calculated uncertainty, the latter being termed 'risk'. In the case of risk, the likelihood or probability of a particular event may be estimated. While not infallible, probabilities can be a useful guide to decision-making, as football-pools punters who study form will testify!

In this chapter we shall examine the basic concept of probability and the means of calculating probabilities. Later, in Chapter 10, we shall examine its application to business strategy.

3.1.2 Objectives

1. To understand the nature and meaning of probability and of expectation.
2. To appreciate the usefulness of the concept of probability when applied to business situations.
3. To be able to calculate probabilities using the basic rules of probability arithmetic.

3.2 BASIC PROBLEM DATA

A student, whose brother works for a wholesale stationery supplier, operates a 'sideline' among his fellow students selling just three items: paper pads, pens and file-binders. In an analysis of one term's sales it is found that 90 paper pads, 180 pens and 30 file-binders were sold. In addition, classified according to country of origin, the sales are comprised as follows:

Paper pads : British makes only;
Pens   : 50% British, 50% Italian;
File-binders : 80% British, 20% French

Thus, in terms of the total number of items sold we have:

British: 90 + (50% of 180) + (80% of 30)
           = 204 items representing 68% of all items;
Italian: 0 + (50% of 180) + 0
           = 90 or 30% of all items;
French: 0 + 0 + (20% of 30)
           = 6 items, 2% of all items

In addition it is known that the profit per item, irrespective of country of origin, is as follows:

Paper pad : 20p
Pen   : 5p
File-binder : 50p

3.3   ARITHMETIC OF RISK

3.3.1   What is probability?

Probability may be approached by either the classical (*a priori*) or the empirical (experimental) route. In the former, we have sufficient knowledge before the event (*a priori*) to calculate probabilities. Thus, when rolling a fair die, since it has six sides, the probability of getting, say, a '6' is 1/6, since a '6' is one of just six possible results, each of which is equally likely. The empirical approach should arrive at the same result, but by repeated throwing of the die. If the result of each throw is recorded, when a large number of throws has been made, we should find that a '6' occurred one-sixth of the time, or at least approximately so. In this case, probability may be seen as relative frequency; relative, that is, to the total number of outcomes. Often, however, probabilities are calculated on a more subjective basis: a combination of past experience, advice and a hunch. In such cases, although our arithmetic may be correct, the results may be 'wrong'. In this chapter we shall calculate objective probabilities based on actual sales, although if these are taken as indicators of the future, they become subjective since we are assuming that they remain substantially unaltered. However approached, if all possible outcomes are considered, the sum of the probabilities must be 1. Thus probabilities (p) must be in the range $0 \leqslant p \leqslant 1$.

3.3.2   First Steps in Calculating Probability

It can be seen from the problem data that since 204 out of 300 items are British made, British goods constitute 68 per cent of all items. Now, if we were to select, *at random*, a sales ledger entry for one item that term, the probability that it refers to the sale of a British good is $204/300 = 0.68$. We may write this as:

$$p(\text{British}) = \frac{204}{300} = 0.68$$

Similarly, the probability that one entry taken *at random* would refer to the sale of, say, a pen, would be:

$$p(\text{pen}) = \frac{180}{300} = 0.60$$

In the two calculated probabilities we have considered just one characteristic (country of origin, or item type) at a time. Now we shall see how probabilities are calculated when both characteristics are considered.

3.3.3   The Italian Pad: Mutual Exclusiveness

In our audit of the term's sales, how likely are we to come across an Italian paper pad? The answer is clear, 'Not at all—it is impossible', since all paper pads are of British make. Formally, we say that the categories 'Italian' and 'paper pad' are *mutually exclusive*—an item which is one cannot be the other. On the other hand, a pen may also be Italian (indeed, half of all pens sold are) and so these are *non-exclusive* categories. The importance of this distinction in calculating probabilities will be seen in the following section.

3.3.4   The 'Or' Principle

Often we will ask questions like 'what is the probability of . . . or . . . ?' The appropriate calculation depends on the distinction made betwen non-exclusive and mutually-exclusive events. Consider our problem data. What is the probability that a randomly selected ledger entry refers either to a paper pad *or* to a French product? Note that either of these two characteristics (paper pad, French) constitutes 'success', and that they are mutually exclusive; a paper pad cannot be French, and a French item cannot be a paper pad.

This is conveniently shown in diagram form. Figure 3.1 is a square with the breakdown by item type measured on the vertical axis and by country of origin on the horizontal scale. The areas represent the proportions found in our problem data, which in terms of our audit represent the probability of selection. The total area, since it represents the sum of probabilities, must equal 1 as indeed it does because each side is of length 1, giving an area $1 \times 1 = 1$.

In order to find the probability of a paper pad or a French item, we simply *add* the appropriate probabilities. The paper pads occupy an area $0.3 \times 1 = 0.3$, and the French items the area $0.2 \times 0.1 = 0.02$. Adding them we obtain an area or probability of 0.32. More formally we have:

$$p(\text{paper pad or French}) = p(\text{paper pad}) + p(\text{French})$$

$$= \frac{90}{300} + \frac{6}{300}$$

$$= \frac{96}{300}$$

$$= 0.32$$

The probability is a little less than one-third.

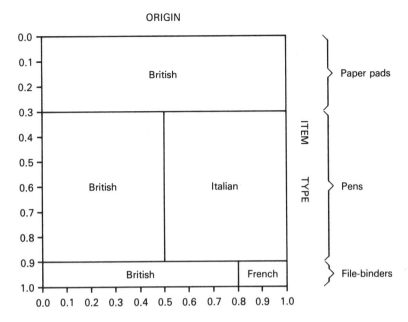

Figure 3.1 *A probability square for the problem data*

In general, for two mutually-exclusive events (*A* and *B*) we have:

$$p(A \text{ or } B) = p(A) + p(B)$$

We see that the appropriate probabilities are simply added together.

However, what if the two categories are not mutually exclusive? Consider the probability of an item being either a file-binder or British. Clearly they are not mutually exclusive since 80 per cent of the files are British made. It would be *wrong* to write:

$$p(\text{file or British}) = p(\text{file}) + p(\text{British})$$

$$= \frac{30}{300} + \frac{204}{300}$$

$$= \frac{234}{300}$$

$$= 0.78$$

Why? Well, note that the 30 files include the 24 that are British made, while the 204 British items also include these 24 British-made file-binders. We are, in fact, double-counting these British file-binders, which is represented by the overlapping area in Figure 3.2.

To overcome this we must subtract the number of British-made file-binders once. Thus we should write:

$$p(\text{file or British}) = p(\text{file}) + p(\text{British}) - p(\text{British file})$$

$$= \frac{30}{300} + \frac{204}{300} - \frac{24}{300}$$

$$= \frac{210}{300}$$

$$= 0.70$$

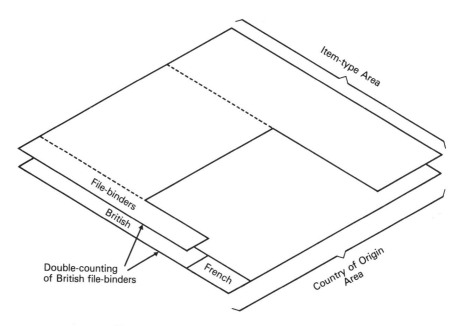

Figure 3.2   *Overlap represents double-counting*

In general for non-exclusive events we write:

$$p(A \text{ or } B) = p(A) + p(B) - p(A \text{ and } B)$$

The procedure outlined in this section is often termed 'the rule of addition'.

3.3.5   The French Connection: Dependence and Independence

Two events are *independent* when the occurrence or non-occurrence of one event has no effect on the probability of the other event. For example, whether a coin was minted in 1981 or not, does not affect the probability of obtaining a head in one toss. The two events, date minted and result when tossed, are completely independent. Events are dependent when the outcome of the first event dictates the probability of the second event occurring. In our problem data, for example, the two events, item type (paper pad, pen and file) and country of origin (British, French, Italian) are dependent. To appreciate this at the intuitive level note that the probability of an item being French, given that the item is a paper pad, is zero, since there are no French paper pads. On the other hand, if the item is a file-binder, the probability of the item being French is certainly not zero, since 1/5 of the file-binders are French. The formal rules for obtaining probabilities under conditions of dependence and independence follow in section 3.3.6.

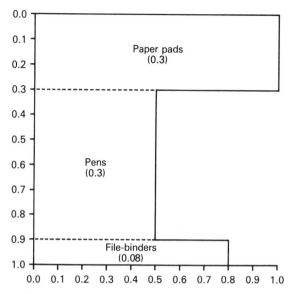

Figure 3.3   *British items only: conditional probability*

3.3.6   The 'And' Principle

Let us calculate the probability that an item selected at random will be British *and* a pen (that is, a British pen). We first calculate the probability associated with one event, say, its being British. This is 204/300 since 204 out of the total of 300 items are British. Then we *multiply* this by the probability that an item is a pen *given that it is British*. Since there are 204 British items and 90 of them are pens, this *conditional probability* (conditional, that is, upon the first event being British) is 90/204. This is illustrated in Figure 3.3.

The British area is $0.3 + 0.3 + 0.08 = 0.68$. Of this, 0.3 represents pens. Thus, given that we are concerned only with British items ($p = 0.68$) the probability of an item being a pen is $0.3/0.68 = 0.441$ or 90/204. The calculation in formal terms is:

$$p(\text{British and a pen}) = p(\text{British}) \times p(\text{a pen, given that it is British})$$

$$= \frac{204}{300} \times \frac{90}{204}$$

$$= \frac{90}{300}$$

$$= 0.30$$

In general we write:

$$p(A \text{ and } B) = p(A) \times p(B|A)$$

where $p(B|A)$ is the conditional probability of B given that A has occurred and may be obtained in the following way:

$$p(B|A) = \frac{p(A \text{ and } B)}{p(A)}$$

In our worked example this would give us:

$$\frac{p(\text{British and a pen})}{p(\text{British})} = \frac{90/300}{204/300}$$

$$= \frac{90}{204}$$

which is the conditional probability obtained from the probability square in Figure 3.3.

To consolidate this, let us calculate the probability of an item being French and a file-binder.

$$p(\text{French and a file}) = p(\text{French}) \times p(\text{file given that it is French})$$

$$= \frac{6}{300} \times \frac{6/300}{6/300}$$

$$= \frac{6}{300}$$

$$= 0.02$$

Note that the conditional probability in this case is 1 (that is $(6/300)/(6/300)$, since if an item is French it cannot be anything other than a file.

One final point, the resultant overall probability is unaffected by the order in which we take events, thus in general:

$$p(A \text{ and } B) = p(A) \times p(B|A)$$

and

$$p(B \text{ and } A) = p(B) \times p(A|B)$$

give an identical answer. The reader should check the two worked examples shown above.

To consider the case for independent events suppose in our selection of ledger entries we select an item at random, consider only its country of origin and then without removing it, close the ledger. We then open the ledger again and randomly select an item, but this time consider only whether it is a paper pad, pen or file. In this case the probability of the item being, say, a pen, is completely independent of the country of origin noted at the first stage. Thus we have:

$$p(\text{British and a pen}) = p(\text{British}) \times p(\text{pen})$$

$$= \frac{204}{300} \times \frac{180}{300}$$

$$= 0.408$$

In general, for independent events we write:

$$p(A \text{ and } B) = p(A) \times p(B)$$

The procedure outlined in this section is often termed the 'rule of multiplication'.

3.4   A SEQUENCE OF EVENTS

3.4.1   Sampling and Replacement

Our analysis so far has been essentially static, in the sense that it considered just one item taken at random from the ledger. Often, however, we are interested in a sequence of events. To illustrate this let us consider the probability that the first two items taken from the ledger will be pens. The probability of the first item being a pen is 180/300 since 180 out of a total of 300 items are pens. The probability that, having already obtained a pen, the second item will also be a pen is 179/299 because only 179 pens remain and there are now only 299 items in total. By sampling without replacement we obtain:

$$p(2 \text{ pens}) = \frac{180}{300} \times \frac{179}{299}$$

This is an extension of the concept of dependence discussed in section 3.3.6.

In this context, independence occurs if sampling takes place with replacement; for example, if having obtained a pen as the first item we do not remove it but simply close the ledger and then re-open it to select randomly an item a second time. In this case, the original item (a pen in our example) may well be selected again. Thus the probability remains unchanged. We obtain by sampling with replacement:

$$p(2 \text{ pens}) = \frac{180}{300} \times \frac{180}{300}$$

3.4.2   The Probability Tree

A convenient means of presenting sequential probabilities is by means of a probability tree where the branches represent possible sequences (Figure 3.4). Consider the possible sequences, by item type, for the drawing of two items from our ledger. Each selection involves three possible outcomes: paper pad, pen or file-binder.

Note that there are nine possible sequences, but are they equally likely? The answer clearly is no, because since pens constitute 60 per cent of all sales, it must be more likely that both items will be pens than, say, files. The next step is to insert the appropriate probabilities in the tree. These probabilities are arrived at by straightforward multiplication because each selection is an independent event. Figure 3.5 depicts the probabilities for sampling without replacement (dependence) and Figure 3.6 for sampling with replacement (independence). It can be seen that there is little difference between the two sets of probabilities, and for this reason dependence is often ignored. Furthermore, in either case, the probabilities must add up to 1 because each sequence is unique and mutually exclusive, covering every possible outcome.

The resultant probabilities should be intuitively reasonable. For instance, the most likely of all sequences is two pens ($p = 0.36$), not unreasonable, given that pens comprise 60 per cent of all items. Conversely, the least likely sequence must be two files ($p = 0.01$).

By adding the appropriate sequential probabilities we may answer basic questions like: What is the probability of both items being the same type? Assuming replacement, the answer is:

$$p(2 \text{ paper pads}) + p(2 \text{ pens}) + p(2 \text{ files})$$

$$= 0.09 + 0.36 + 0.01$$

$$= 0.46$$

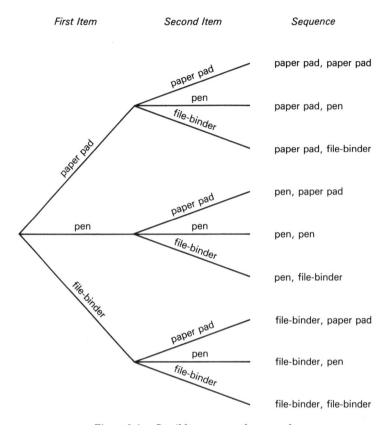

First Item *Second Item* *Sequence*

Figure 3.4 *Possible sequences for two sales*

3.4.3 A Shortcut

One useful shortcut may conveniently be mentioned here. Suppose we wish to calculate the probabilities that the two items chosen will be different, we could proceed as before by summing the following probabilities from Figure 3.6:

$$p(\text{paper pad and pen}) + p(\text{paper pad and file}) + p(\text{pen and file})$$

that is, $0.36 + 0.06 + 0.12 = 0.54$.

However, since the sum of all probabilities must be 1.0, and only two sets of sequences are possible, namely, both are the same, or they are different, we could obtain the probability that the two items will be different by subtracting from 1.0 the probability that they will be the same. We obtain:

$$p(\text{different}) = 1.0 - p(\text{same})$$

$$= 1.0 - 0.46$$

$$= 0.54$$

which is the result obtained above.

First Item   Second Item   Overall
Probability

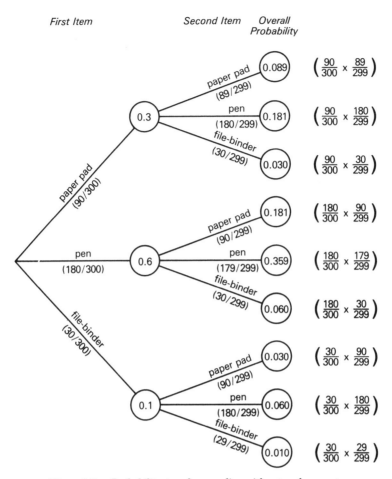

Figure 3.5   *Probability tree for sampling without replacement*

3.5   IS ORDER IMPORTANT?

From the probability tree in Figure 3.6 we see that the probability of both a pen and a file being chosen is the sum of the sequential probabilities:

$$p(\text{pen, file}) + p(\text{file, pen})$$

$$= 0.06 + 0.06$$

$$= 0.12$$

Suppose we were to ask 'What is the probability of the sequence, a file followed by a pen?' The answer is not 0.12 because the order of the events has been specified, and only p(file, pen) should be taken into account. The answer is 0.06.

    In technical terms we would say that there is one possible combination (a file and a pen) but two possible permutations (a file followed by a pen, and a pen followed by a file).

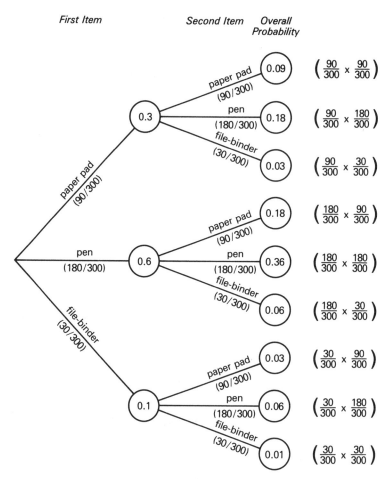

Figure 3.6   *Probability tree for sampling with replacement*

Unlike combinations, in permutations the order of events is important. For this reason, the 'Full Perm' used by football-pools companies is a misnomer, it in fact refers to a combination!

3.6   THE USEFULNESS OF PROBABILITY

In order to establish the basic rules of probability we have analysed just one term's sales. Since this is something which has already occurred and is well documented—the sales ledger says it all—it might appear a pointless exercise. What then is the point of it all?

First, although the information was available from the sales ledger as it stood, it was not 'working' for us. It was purely a list—a historical record. What we have done so far is to classify the data into a form suitable for other purposes.

Second, we may use our calculated probabilities in order to predict the future pattern of sales. For example, the aim of the one-term analysis may have been to ensure adequate future inventory levels. Clearly, much depends on how typical our chosen term is. For this reason, in practice, a much longer period would be analysed to provide probability values.

Of course, in business, probabilities are rarely of intrinsic interest; it is what they indicate about possible profit, sales, losses and the like, that make them interesting. It is to this that we now turn, carrying our calculated probabilities forward into the future (for this reason we can assume an infinite population and hence independence).

3.7   WHAT DO YOU EXPECT TO GAIN?

3.7.1   Expectation

Mathematical expectation refers to the long-run average value. Thus, if a fair coin is tossed 100 times, the expectation is 50 heads; that is the probability for each toss (0.5) multiplied by the number of trials (100) = 50 heads.

3.7.2   Introducing Money

Expected monetary value (whether profits, revenues or losses, etc.) is obtained by multiplying the probability of an event (or sequence of events) by the money value ('pay-off') which will result if it does occur. Let us illustrate by reference to our problem data, utilizing the probability tree in Figure 3.6.

We recall that the profit per item is as follows:

$$\begin{aligned} &\text{Paper pad} : 20\text{p} \\ &\text{Pen} \quad\quad : \ 5\text{p} \\ &\text{File} \quad\quad : 50\text{p} \end{aligned}$$

What is the expected profit on the first two items sold in a day? Figure 3.7 shows the nine possible sequences for two items, the relevant probabilities and the appropriate profit. The first pay-off of 40p results if both items are paper pads, since a profit of 20p is made on each. The remaining profits are calculated similarly.

The expected profit for two sales is 28p obtained as follows:

Events	*Probability*		*Profit*		*Expected contribution*
Paper pad, paper pad	0.09	×	40p	=	3.6p
Paper pad, pen	0.18	×	25p	=	4.5p
Paper pad, file-binder	0.03	×	70p	=	2.1p
Pen, paper pad	0.18	×	25p	=	4.5p
Pen, pen	0.36	×	10p	=	3.6p
Pen, file-binder	0.06	×	55p	=	3.3p
File-binder, paper pad	0.03	×	70p	=	2.1p
File-binder, pen	0.06	×	55p	=	3.3p
File-binder, file-binder	0.01	×	100p	=	1.0p
			Expected profit		28.0p

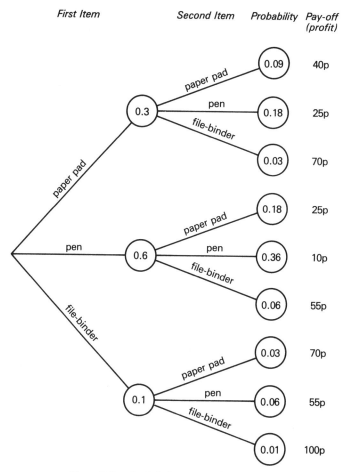

Figure 3.7 *Probability tree with pay-offs*

3.7.3   Expecting the Impossible

Notice that in our example an *actual* profit of 28p on two sales cannot occur (the nearest we get is 25p when a paper pad and a pen are sold), but this is not altogether surprising since the expected profit is simply a long-run average value (a weighted average).

3.7.4   Expectation as an Aid to Decision-making

To illustrate the use of expectation in decision-making, imagine that the student, in order to prepare for his forthcoming examinations, wishes to appoint a temporary replacement. A suitable applicant is offered a choice between two bonus schemes. The first is the payment of 5p per item sold, and the second is 50 per cent of the profit per item sold. Which should the applicant choose, if his aim is to maximize his pay?

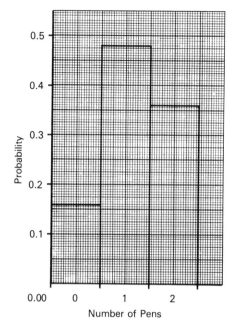

Figure 3.8 *Probability distribution for two sales*

If he selects Bonus Scheme 1 he is certain to receive 5p per item sold. For Scheme 2 he needs first to calculate the expected profit for one item sold.

Expected profit = sum of expected profit on each item for sale

$$= (0.3 \times 20p) + (0.6 \times 5p) + (0.1 \times 50p)$$
$$\text{for pads} \qquad \text{for pens} \qquad \text{for files}$$

$$= 14p$$

If he receives 50 per cent of this his share of expected profit amounts to 7p. Thus it would be wise for him to opt for Scheme 2.

3.7.5   Psychology Versus Probabilities

Finally, let us note that decisions are not always made in such a purely mechanical fashion. Suppose we were offered £100 or the chance of £300 depending upon the single toss of a (fair!) coin. Which would we choose? Although the expected value of the chance is 0.5 × £300 = £150, perhaps a great many people would opt for the certainty of £100. After all, somebody has to lose in the toss.

3.8   PICTURES OF PROBABILITY

3.8.1   Discrete Probability Distributions

If we take the results shown in Figure 3.6, we can construct a histogram indicating the probability associated with 0, 1 and 2 pens in two sales. This is shown in Figure 3.8.

This may be extended to any number of sales. The histogram for 10 sales is shown in Figure 3.9.

The probabilities for the ten sales case may be obtained by means of a probability tree in just the same way as our two sales example, although, clearly, it would be much more time-consuming.

These are examples of discrete probability distributions because the variable, the number of pens, can only take on specified values, such as 0, 1, 2, and so on. A value such as 1.2 cannot occur and thus the probability of such a value is 0.

3.8.2   An Infinity of Values

It can be seen from Figure 3.9 that the greatest probabilities are to be found in the middle, around the mean (expected) value. The histogram gives a distinct pattern of bunching around the mean with probabilities falling off markedly either side. This pattern is also found in continuous variables, but by its very nature we would not expect steps as in a histogram, but rather a smooth falling off either side of the mean as shown in Figure 3.10.

3.8.3   The Normal Distribution

In drawing the curve in Figure 3.10 it is assumed that the greatest probabilities occur around the mean and fall off smoothly in either direction from it. Also, it is symmetrical. As before, the total area under the curve, representing as it does the sum of all probabilities, must equal 1.0. Since the distribution is symmetrical, the area below the mean is 50 per cent ($p = 0.5$) and that above the mean is 50 per cent ($p = 0.5$). Notice how probabilities are reflected in the area under the curve. Thus the probability of a value Z or less is indicated by the area shaded in Figure 3.11.

It would obviously be useful if we knew the area (probability) associated with various values like Z. In fact, one widely used example of a continuous distribution, the normal distribution, does just that. The secret is to measure how far Z is from the mean in *units of standard deviation*. One very useful value and the corresponding areas (probabilities) are shown in Figure 3.12.

Thus 95 per cent of the area (probability $= 0.95$) is found between $Z = -1.96$ and $Z = +1.96$. Therefore 2.5 per cent ($p = 0.025$) lies below (to the left of) -1.96 and 2.5 per cent lies above (to the right of) $+1.96$.

This is all very convenient, but how common is the normal distribution? The answer is very. Many natural phenomena such as heights, weights and lengths follow this pattern, at least approximately.

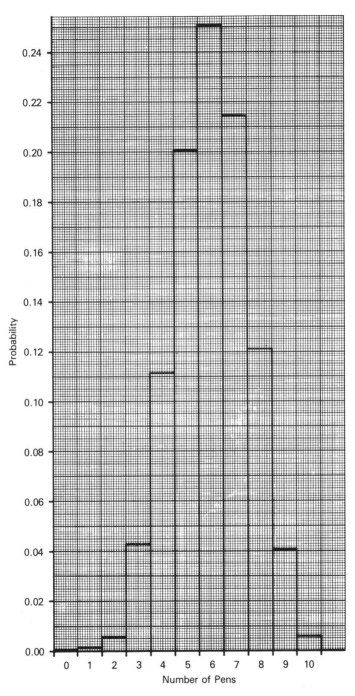

Figure 3.9 *Probability distribution for ten sales*

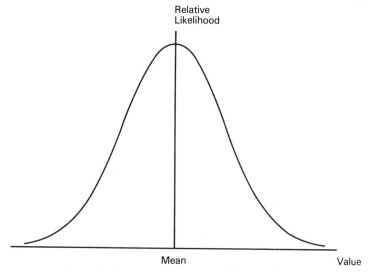

Figure 3.10   *A continuous probability distribution*

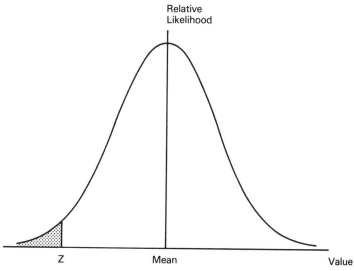

Figure 3.11   *The normal distribution*

3.8.4   The Normal Table

For this reason, the areas (probabilities) associated with various values of Z, not just ± 1.96, are tabulated. An example of such a table (it comes in various, but equivalent, forms) is given in Table 3.1. Before we apply the normal distribution to our problem data, let us see how the normal table is used.

First we need to know the Z value, which measures how far our value is from the mean, measured in standard deviations. Suppose it is $+ 0.78$. We then look up the Z column for $Z = 0.70$ and then across that row until we reach the 08 column. The figure in the table is 0.21770. What does this represent? Figure 3.13 illustrates.

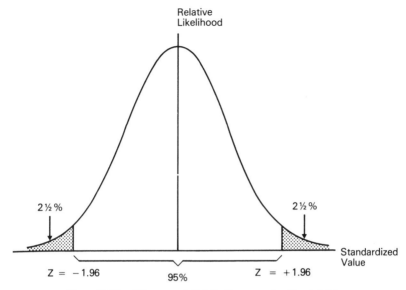

Figure 3.12   *The normal distribution areas for Z = ± 1.96*

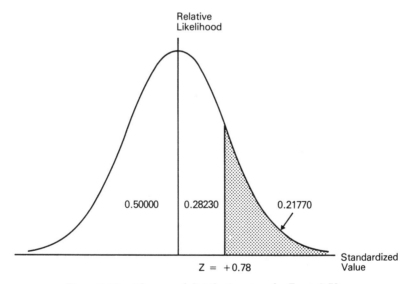

Figure 3.13   *The normal distribution areas for Z = + 0.78*

Thus 21.77 per cent of the area (representing a probability of 0.21770) lies to the right of $Z = +0.78$. The area to the left of $Z = 0.78$ is $1.00000 - 0.21770$ or 0.78230. Because of its symmetry, 0.5 lies to the left of the mean, and thus the area between $Z = +0.78$ and the mean is $0.7823 - 0.5000 = 0.2823$.

Table 3.1   *Areas under the normal curve.*

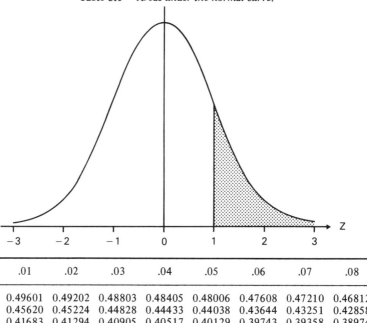

Z	.00	.01	.02	.03	.04	.05	.06	.07	.08	.09
0.0	0.50000	0.49601	0.49202	0.48803	0.48405	0.48006	0.47608	0.47210	0.46812	0.46414
0.1	0.46017	0.45620	0.45224	0.44828	0.44433	0.44038	0.43644	0.43251	0.42858	0.42465
0.2	0.42074	0.41683	0.41294	0.40905	0.40517	0.40129	0.39743	0.39358	0.38974	0.38591
0.3	0.38209	0.37828	0.37448	0.37070	0.36693	0.36317	0.35942	0.35569	0.35197	0.34827
0.4	0.34458	0.34090	0.33724	0.33360	0.32997	0.32636	0.32276	0.31918	0.31561	0.31207
0.5	0.30854	0.30503	0.30153	0.29806	0.29460	0.29116	0.28774	0.28434	0.28096	0.27760
0.6	0.27425	0.27093	0.26763	0.26435	0.26109	0.25785	0.25463	0.25143	0.24825	0.24510
0.7	0.24196	0.23885	0.23576	0.23270	0.22965	0.22663	0.22363	0.22065	0.21770	0.21476
0.8	0.21186	0.20897	0.20611	0.20327	0.20045	0.19766	0.19489	0.19215	0.18943	0.18673
0.9	0.18406	0.18141	0.17879	0.17619	0.17361	0.17106	0.16853	0.16602	0.16354	0.16109
1.0	0.15866	0.15625	0.15386	0.15151	0.14917	0.14686	0.14457	0.14231	0.14007	0.13786
1.1	0.13567	0.13350	0.13136	0.12924	0.12714	0.12507	0.12302	0.12100	0.11900	0.11702
1.2	0.11507	0.11314	0.11123	0.10935	0.10746	0.10565	0.10383	0.10204	0.10027	0.09853
1.3	0.09680	0.09510	0.09342	0.09176	0.09012	0.08851	0.08691	0.08534	0.08379	0.08226
1.4	0.08076	0.07927	0.07780	0.07636	0.07493	0.07353	0.07215	0.07078	0.06944	0.06811
1.5	0.06681	0.06552	0.06426	0.06301	0.06178	0.06057	0.05938	0.05821	0.05705	0.05592
1.6	0.05480	0.05370	0.05262	0.05155	0.05050	0.04947	0.04846	0.04746	0.04648	0.04551
1.7	0.04457	0.04363	0.04272	0.04182	0.04093	0.04006	0.03920	0.03836	0.03754	0.03673
1.8	0.03593	0.03515	0.03438	0.03362	0.03288	0.03216	0.03144	0.03074	0.03005	0.02938
1.9	0.02872	0.02807	0.02743	0.02680	0.02619	0.02559	0.02500	0.02442	0.02385	0.02330
2.0	0.02275	0.02222	0.02169	0.02118	0.02068	0.02018	0.01970	0.01923	0.01876	0.01831
2.1	0.01786	0.01743	0.01700	0.01659	0.01618	0.01578	0.01539	0.01500	0.01463	0.01426
2.2	0.01390	0.01355	0.01321	0.01287	0.01255	0.01222	0.01191	0.01160	0.01130	0.01101
2.3	0.01072	0.01044	0.01017	0.00990	0.00964	0.00939	0.00914	0.00889	0.00866	0.00842
2.4	0.00820	0.00798	0.00776	0.00755	0.00734	0.00714	0.00695	0.00676	0.00657	0.00639
2.5	0.00621	0.00604	0.00587	0.00570	0.00554	0.00539	0.00523	0.00508	0.00494	0.00480
2.6	0.00466	0.00453	0.00440	0.00427	0.00415	0.00402	0.00391	0.00379	0.00368	0.00357
2.7	0.00347	0.00336	0.00326	0.00317	0.00307	0.00298	0.00289	0.00280	0.00272	0.00264
2.8	0.00256	0.00248	0.00240	0.00233	0.00226	0.00219	0.00212	0.00205	0.00199	0.00193
2.9	0.00187	0.00181	0.00175	0.00169	0.00164	0.00159	0.00154	0.00149	0.00144	0.00139
3.0	0.00135	0.00131	0.00126	0.00122	0.00118	0.00114	0.00111	0.00107	0.00104	0.00100
3.1	0.00097	0.00094	0.00090	0.00087	0.00084	0.00082	0.00079	0.00076	0.00074	0.00071
3.2	0.00069	0.00066	0.00064	0.00062	0.00060	0.00058	0.00056	0.00054	0.00052	0.00050
3.3	0.00048	0.00047	0.00045	0.00043	0.00042	0.00040	0.00039	0.00038	0.00036	0.00035
3.4	0.00034	0.00032	0.00031	0.00030	0.00029	0.00028	0.00027	0.00026	0.00025	0.00024
3.5	0.00023	0.00022	0.00022	0.00021	0.00020	0.00019	0.00019	0.00018	0.00017	0.00017

Notes
The table shows the area to the right of any positive Z value, when Z is measured in standard deviations from the mean.
    The total area under the curve is 1.00000, divided symmetrically by the mean. Consequently, the area for negative Z is not given.

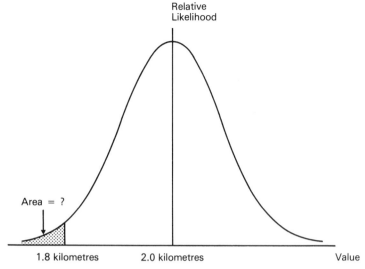

Figure 3.14 *The problem stated*

3.8.5 Applying the Normal Distribution

The British manufacturer of our pens has set the production process to ensure that, on average, the pens contain sufficient ink to write for two kilometres, with a standard deviation of 100 metres. It is known that the distribution is normal.

What is the probability that one pen chosen at random will last for less than 1.8 kilometres? Let us formulate the problem in a diagram. Figure 3.14 sets it out.

Remembering that area represents probability, we need to calculate the shaded area in Figure 3.14. As it stands we are unable to do so. What we need to do is to convert (standardize) the units of measurement. So instead of saying that we are interested in a value 0.2 kilometres or more below the mean, we wish to express this difference as so many standard deviations or more below the mean. This is effected by means of the following expression for Z:

$$Z = \frac{X - \mu}{\sigma}$$

Where: Z = standardized value;
      X = value of interest;
      μ = population mean;
      σ = population standard deviation.

Substituting in our values we obtain:

$$Z = \frac{1800 - 2000}{100} = \frac{-200}{100} = -2$$

Thus, if the actual difference, in original units, is 200 metres and the standard deviation (σ) is 100 metres, this represents a difference of two standard deviations.

Let us now consult Table 3.1. We see that the probability in the tail corresponding to $Z = -2.00$ is 0.02275. This is shown in Figure 3.15. Thus the probability of a pen not writing for at least 1.8 kilometres is 0.02275 or, to put it another way, 2.2275 per cent of all pens produced by this firm will run out before they have written for 1.8 kilometres.

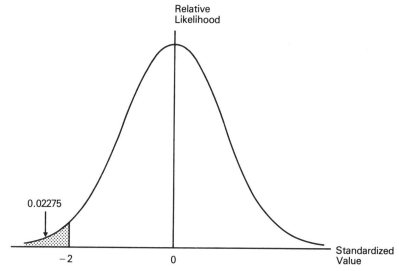

Figure 3.15   *The standardized normal distribution areas for the problem data*

Clearly, *any* normal distribution, regardless of its units of measurement, can be converted to standard form so that the table of areas can be used.

3.8.6   A Word of Caution

Because of the nature of a continuous variable we are unable to state the probability associated with any one particular value. Thus we calculated the probability of a pen writing for less than 1.8 kilometres. To establish the possibility of a pen writing for exactly 1.8 km would not be possible, although we could create a small area with 1.8 at the centre, say, 1.79 to 1.81, and calculate this.

Finally, it is important that the data being considered are in fact normally, or at least approximately normally, distributed if the tabulated areas are to be used as probabilities.

3.9   CONCLUSION

The calculation of probabilities is often an invaluable aid to decision-making. In this chapter we have dwelled on the basic rules of probabilities. In Chapter 10 we shall examine the application of probability and expected values to business strategy.

ASSIGNMENTS

A3.1 Entry into a large firm's management division is by examination. There are three levels or stages. All those passing Stage I will be offered a position in the company. Those who also pass Stage II will be offered a more senior position, while those who also pass Stage III will move into the most senior new-entrant positions. The starting salaries are commensurate with seniority of post, being £6000, £8500 and £10 000 respectively.

Only 15 per cent of applicants will pass Stage I. Of those 25 per cent will pass Stage II and of those 10 per cent will pass Stage III.

(a) Draw a probability tree for the problem.
(b) What is the probability that an applicant will be accepted by the company?
(c) What at the outset is the probability that an applicant will pass Stage III?
(d) Given that a candidate has passed Stage I, what is his/her chance of passing Stage III?
(e) What is the expected salary for:

  (i)   those successful at Stage I;
  (ii) those successful at Stage II;
  (iii) those successful at Stage III?

A3.2 The first stage of a new Anglo-French aircraft project involves inviting tenders for the engine and wings. The first item to be considered is the engine. The probability of a British one being chosen is estimated at 0.80. If this is chosen, there is a probability of 0.60 that the wings will also be made by a British firm. On the other hand, if a French engine is chosen ($p = 0.20$), there is a probability of 0.90 that the wings will also be French built. The British firms involved in tendering expect the engine order to create an additional 4000 jobs and the wings order an extra 2000 jobs.

(a) Draw the appropriate probability tree.
(b) What is the probability that the engine and wings will be built by different countries?
(c) What, initially, is the expected increase in British employment as a result of the first stage of the project?
(d) If a British engine is chosen, what is the overall expected increase in employment in the British aircraft industry?

A3.3 A firm assembles saucepans from three components, the bowl, the handle and the lid. From experience it is known that 1 in 25 bowls, 1 in 50 handles and 1 in 40 lids are faulty. However, automation means that it is not feasible to identify any faults until the saucepan is assembled. If all three components are perfect, the saucepan is sold at a profit of £4.50; if one component is faulty, it is classed as sub-standard and sold at a profit of £2.00. If two components are faulty, the saucepan is sold at cost price, while if all three components are faulty, it is scrapped at a loss of £1.50.

(a) Draw a probability tree for the data.
(b) How likely is a perfect saucepan?
(c) In a production run of 1000 saucepans what is the expected profit?
(d) If it were possible to eliminate faults entirely in just one of the components at no extra cost, which should be chosen? Explain your decision by calculating the change in expected profits for each of the three possibilities.
(e) What gain in profit would result from your decision in (d), per production run of 1000 saucepans?

A3.4 The output of 'kilo' bags of sugar is known to be normally distributed with a mean weight of 1.025 kilos and a standard deviation of 10 grams.

(a) What percentage of bags weigh between 1.015 kilos and 1.035 kilos?

(b)   If, under the Trade Descriptions Act, the firm is liable to be prosecuted if it sells a bag weighing less than 1 kilo, what percentage of bags render the firm liable to be prosecuted?

(c)   If the firm decides to take a gamble and increase the percentage of bags weighing less than 1 kilo to 2.5 per cent of output, at what mean weight should the packing machines be set? (Hint: use the Z expression, where the new μ is the only unknown.)

A3.5   A firm producing specialist steel casings for a local shipbuilder knows that its output is normally distributed with a mean diameter of 50 cm and a standard deviation of 0.4 cm. The shipbuilder's tolerance levels are 50 ± 0.75 cm.

   The casings cost £40 to make and those within the tolerance limits are sold to the shipbuilder for £85. Anything exceeding 50.75 cm in diameter is sold as scrap at a price of £8.00 per casing. Items less than 49.25 cm in diameter require reboring at an additional cost of £12.00 per item. All items rebored satisfy the tolerance limits.

(a)   What percentage of output is acceptable without reboring?

(b)   In a production run of 500 casings, for what level of costs (including reboring) should the firm budget?

(c)   What level of profit can the firm expect from a production run of 500?

(d)   In order to avoid a penalty clause in the contract of an order for 705 casings, the firm wishes to meet the order in one production run without any delay for reboring. What minimum size of production run should it aim for?

4—Obtaining and Using Business Data

4.1 INTRODUCTION AND OBJECTIVES

4.1.1 The Subject of the Chapter

Business decisions can be made only upon the basis of information: ignorance is the killer of good management. As a result, the business analyst must be able to obtain information, usually of a numerical nature, and then use it in advice to managers. Often information is obtained by counting items on shelves or reading ledgers or abstracting from files. These activities may be easy or impossible depending upon the care taken when the items were stored or written. Much more difficult to obtain is information tied up in people's brains in the form of attitudes or intentions.

Analysis of such intangible data requires a *survey* and this chapter considers the principles of survey methods and designs. One of the crucial decisions to be made is between a whole-population survey and a sample survey. It is obvious that the former will be expensive if it refers to the population of a country, but even if the population is defined only as the inhabitants of a housing estate, a mass survey could be time-consuming and costly. If 'population' refers to objects, such as light-bulbs, and the aim of the survey is to establish life expectancies, the investigation will involve destruction of the light-bulbs in the course of the experiments thus rendering a mass survey nonsensical. What is required in such cases is the *sample* approach, in which a group of people or items is selected to represent the whole population. This chapter will consider methods of selecting samples.

The second aspect of business information (considered first in this chapter) is that of making estimates and assessing people's preconceived ideas. This area is usually referred to as *sampling and estimation theory*. Sample findings cannot be assumed to be the same as whole-population findings and there are methods for making worthwhile statements about the latter using the former. They use the material of previous chapters and introduce the reader to ideas of applied probability, significance and the testing of hypotheses.

4.1.2 Objectives

1. To introduce the notion that sample results can be made to represent the whole population.
2. To calculate and analyse sample statistics in terms of the sampling distribution of the mean and proportions.

3. To calculate spot and interval estimates for a population mean and proportion with a variety of degrees of confidence.
4. To test simple hypotheses concerning the population mean and proportion.
5. To consider methods whereby samples may be selected to ensure representativeness of their parent population.
6. To consider the design of questionnaires, to criticize on the basis of good practice and psychological principles, and to construct acceptable samples.

4.2 BASIC PROBLEM DATA

Laundromatic Holdings Ltd is the owner of a chain of launderettes and dry-cleaning shops across the country. About a year ago, the Regional Manager (South West) placed a proposal before the directors suggesting that a shop be opened in a large housing development, recently completed. It is agreed that a shop could be opened if the typical weekly spending in the launderette and on dry-cleaning was in excess of £2 per household. The Regional Manager is given the responsibility for obtaining the necessary information.

Every twentieth address on the housing estate is visited by a member of the three-person survey team employed part-time by the Regional Manager. They visit on two successive Friday evenings between 7.30 and 9.00 pm with the following questions:

1. Do you *regularly* use a launderette or have clothes dry-cleaned?
    Yes/No.
2. How much did you spend in the last seven days in a launderette or on dry-cleaning?
    Up to £1/Up to £2/Up to £3/Up to £5/Over £5
3. Would you welcome and support a launderette/dry-cleaning shop situated on this estate?
    Yes/No/Don't know

The results from the survey are given below, and the Regional Manager believes that they vindicate his original recommendation:

Question 1

Yes:	38 addresses
No:	11 addresses
No-one at home:	15 addresses

Question 2

Weekly spending	*Up to £1*	*Up to £2*	*Up to £3*	*Up to £5*	*Over £5*
Number of replies	8	10	15	10	6

Mean spending: £2.78
Standard deviation: £1.76

Question 3

Yes:	40
No:	nil
Don't know:	9

The Regional Manager reports to the directors and concludes with four statements which he derives from the survey.

(a) Over 77 per cent of households surveyed use our type of shop regularly.
(b) The average weekly expenditure on our type of service is nearer £3 than £2.
(c) Over 80 per cent of households surveyed would support our new shop.
(d) There are 1280 addresses on the estate, and an average weekly spending of £2.78 means a weekly income to the shop of about £3500.

Laundromatic's problem now is to approve or reject the plan to open a new shop. Although the mean spending exceeds £2, the variation among households is so great that further analysis is desirable. Also, the methods used in the survey will be questioned by at least one director.

4.3 WHAT SAMPLES SHOW

4.3.1 Sample and Population

A population is defined as all the members or items with the properties or attributes under investigation. Of course, it may be a human population (of a town or certain age-range) or an inanimate one. Once a population is defined, a sample can be chosen: methods for doing so are considered later in the chapter. The basic idea is that the sample should be *representative* of the population. If nothing is known about the population, this can never be achieved with any degree of certainty. However, if a *random sample* is selected, it is very probable that this will represent the population. A random sample is defined as a sample drawn from a population in such a way that each individual in the population has the same chance of being selected. Thus it is improbable that a sample drawn in this way from a population with 50 per cent males and 50 per cent females will contain 80 per cent males and only 20 per cent females, though it is possible. It is more likely that the sample will contain about 50 per cent of both males and females. In the Laundromatic case, a random sample should ensure that the mean and the standard deviation for the entire population are closely estimated by the sample results.

As a general principle, it can be shown that the larger the sample, the more closely will its statistics approximate to those of the parent population. Analysts have agreed that, whenever possible, large samples should be selected and that 'large' means in excess of thirty separate items. Thus the Laundromatic sample can be defined as large, even though 15 houses were vacant, because there were 49 useful interviews. Since the sample mean of £2.78 is the only available information, and assuming it to be obtained from a random sample, we can state as follows:

Best estimate of
mean spending by = £2.78 per week (sample mean)
all households

As regards the population dispersion in household spending, the sample data are inadequate as an estimate. The sample standard deviation of £1.76 was calculated from 49 data points and must be an underestimate of the population standard deviation. It is reasonable to assume that no sample will contain the same *range* of data as exists in the population at large, because random samples are unlikely to pick up extreme values far from the mean. Since the sample mean and the population mean will be close in value for a large random sample, a reduced range in the sample must result in a reduced standard deviation. It can be shown that the best estimate of the population standard deviation is obtained by multiplying the sample standard deviation by a correction factor which will increase it, as follows:

$$\text{Best estimate of standard deviation of spending for all households} = \text{Sample standard deviation} \times \sqrt{\frac{\text{number in sample}}{\text{number in sample less one}}}$$

$$= s \times \sqrt{\frac{n}{n-1}}$$

This correction factor has the effect of increasing the sample value and corresponds to the calculation mentioned in section 2.5.5. For the Laundromatic sample, the correction factor is $\sqrt{49/48}$ which is 1.0104. Clearly, for larger samples, the correction factor has only a small effect upon the estimation of population standard deviation: a sample of 100 items would yield a correction factor of only 1.005 which is negligible for most practical business analyses. In the Laundromatic case, we would estimate the population standard deviation as follows:

$$\text{Best estimate of standard deviation of spending for all households} = £1.76 \times 1.0104 = £1.78$$

We shall use, and regard, this figure as the population standard deviation. The reader should note that such a sampling correction should *always* be applied, though it will have little effect in the case of a large sample.

There is one obvious problem with these estimates. If another one-twentieth sample were to be taken, there is no guarantee that its mean and dispersion would be the same as those the Regional Manager obtained. Samples must be variable because they will probably include and exclude different individuals or items each time they are chosen, whether it be with or without replacement. If samples are variable in their composition, then we must expect the 'best estimate' to change at each sample. How can it be 'best' when it is certain to change? Because the only available information must be 'best'. Consider a simple numerical example:

1. Let five plastic chips be hidden in a black bag, each with a number between 1 and 5 written on it.
2. We are required to estimate the average value on the chips by taking a sample of just three at once without looking into the bag.
3. The sample yields 5, 4, 1, which have a mean value of $3\frac{1}{3}$.

Since this is the only available information, we estimate the mean value for all the chips to be $3\frac{1}{3}$. In fact, the mean of 5, 4, 3, 2, 1 is 3 so that our estimate contains a *sampling error* of about 11 per cent. The different samples of three chips that can be selected from the population of five are just ten in number. Each sample will have its own mean and each mean is an estimate of the population mean. Consider all possible combinations:

Combination	Mean value
5 4 3	4
5 4 2	$3\frac{2}{3}$
5 4 1	$3\frac{1}{3}$
5 3 2	$3\frac{1}{3}$
5 3 1	3
5 2 1	$2\frac{2}{3}$
4 3 2	3
4 3 1	$2\frac{2}{3}$
4 2 1	$2\frac{1}{3}$
3 2 1	2

This shows that the sample mean could vary between 2 and 4 depending upon the combination chosen. The mean of the sample means is 3 as may be seen by constructing the frequency distribution and the symmetrical bar chart in Figure 4.1.

Sample mean	Frequency
2	1
$2\frac{1}{3}$	1
$2\frac{2}{3}$	2
3	2
$3\frac{1}{3}$	2
$3\frac{2}{3}$	1
4	1

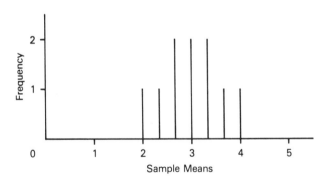

Figure 4.1 *Sampling distribution for samples of three chips from a population of five chips*

We may derive two general principles about samples from this information. First, that sample means are less dispersed than are individuals in the population: the means are bounded by 2 and 4 but the population has values between 1 and 5. Second, that the expected value of the sample mean equals the population mean. Figure 4.1 is known as the *sampling distribution of the mean* and it is clear that the mean of this distribution is equal to the population mean. Of course, only one sample will actually be taken so that Figure 4.1 can never be drawn in practice. Laundromatic have just the single sample mean of £2.78. They do not know whether this value is close to the 'true' mean or in one of the tails of the sampling distribution.

As a matter of interest, consider the five chips again, this time taking random samples of just two chips. The sampling distribution is listed below and shown in Figure 4.2. There are ten combinations.

Combinations of two chips	Mean value	Sample mean	Frequency
5 4	$4\frac{1}{2}$	$1\frac{1}{2}$	1
5 3	4	2	1
5 2	$3\frac{1}{2}$	$2\frac{1}{2}$	2
5 1	3	3	2
4 3	$3\frac{1}{2}$	$3\frac{1}{2}$	2
4 2	3	4	1
4 1	$2\frac{1}{2}$	$4\frac{1}{2}$	1
3 2	$2\frac{1}{2}$		
3 1	2		
2 1	$1\frac{1}{2}$		

Figure 4.2   *Sampling distribution for samples of two chips from a population of five chips*

Once again we see that the sample means are less dispersed than the original data and have a mean value of 3. But note that the dispersion is not so reduced as it was for samples of three chips. In fact, there is a general principle at work here. It is called a *central limit theorem* and may be stated briefly: *the dispersion of sample means will diminish as the number of items in the sample increases*. In a sense, the theorem is intuitive. Consider the sequence:

Question: If a sample is taken, will its mean equal the true mean?

Answer: No, because samples will vary somewhat among themselves and each sample mean is an estimate of the true mean.

Question: If the samples themselves are variable, how can I learn anything useful about a population?

Answer: The means of the samples will not be as dispersed as the parent population because each sample will include some items from each side of the mean and will average out extreme values.

Question: How effective are samples at doing this?

Answer: The greater the sample size, the better is each estimate of the true mean and the less dispersed will be the sample means.

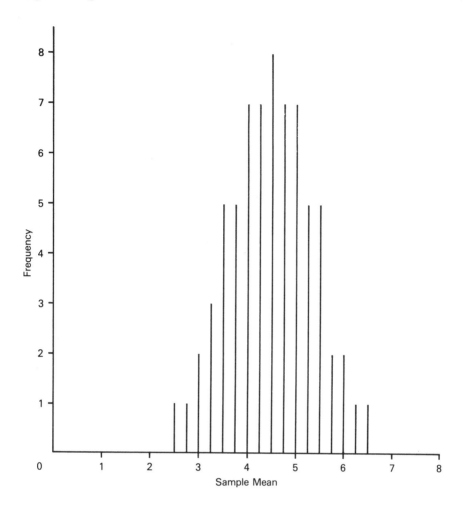

Figure 4.3 *Sampling distribution for samples of four chips from a population of eight chips*

In later sections, this theorem and its development will be given quantitative form and will be used as a basis for important decision techniques.

4.3.2 The Normal Distribution

The frequency charts in Figures 4.1 and 4.2 show that sampling has the effect of producing symmetrical unimodal distributions. We cannot progress with sampling from so small a population as just five ships but Figure 4.3 shows the frequencies of sample means for samples of four chips from a population of eight bearing the values 1 to 8 inclusive. Note that the most likely (the commonest) sample mean is 4.5 which is the population mean for the eight chips and that sample means are bounded by 2.5 and 6.5. It is not possible for a sample of four chips to have a mean outside this interval, so that the population dispersion has been greatly reduced in the sampling process.

If we were to continue this sample mean investigation for increasingly larger populations, we should find the frequency charts becoming even more bell shaped. In fact, for an
infinite population and samples of at least thirty items, the frequency chart will be indis-
tinguishable in shape from the normal distribution introduced in Chapter 3. This is the prediction of another *central limit theorem: for large samples chosen randomly from any
infinite population, the means of the samples will tend to be normally distributed with the
expected sample mean equal to the population mean and the standard deviation of the
sample means diminishing as the sample size increases.*

The notion of 'standard deviation of sample means' is sometimes confusing but it
merely refers to the degree of dispersion in sampling distributions such as Figures 4.1, 4.2
and 4.3. For large samples from infinite populations, this dispersion can be predicted. It can
be shown that the following relationship applies:

$$\text{Standard deviation of sample means} = \frac{\text{Standard deviation of population}}{\text{Square-root of number in sample}}$$

symbolically,
$$s_{\bar{X}} = \frac{\sigma}{\sqrt{n}}$$

As the sample size (n) increases in the denominator, the value of $s_{\bar{X}}$ diminishes as the
theorem states.

The standard deviation of sample means is often referred to as the *standard error of
the mean* and we shall adopt this term. Of course, to calculate the standard error of the
mean we need to know the population standard deviation but normally it is one of the main
purposes of the sampling procedure to estimate just that statistic. From section 4.3.1 we
now know that σ may be estimated from the sample standard deviation, using the correction
factor. Therefore, the dispersion in sample means may be calculated as follows:

$$\begin{array}{l}\text{Best estimate of standard}\\ \text{deviation of spending for} = \pounds 1.78\\ \text{all households}\end{array}$$

and so,
$$\text{Standard error of mean} = \frac{\pounds 1.78}{\sqrt{49}} = \pounds 0.25, \text{ to the nearest penny}$$

Consider the £2 per household limit placed upon the Regional Manager by the
directors. It is a cut-off value, so that a mean spending of £2 or less over all households
would preclude the shop's being opened. Let us assume that the true mean for the estate is
indeed £2 per household, then samples could be as variable as shown in Figure 4.4. A sample
of 49 households could yield a mean spending of £2.20 or £1.80 or £2.40 or £1.60 and so
on, but with diminishing likelihood the further it is from the mean. A sample is extremely
unlikely to yield a mean of £3 if the population mean really is £2. Note that Figure 4.4 is
marked off in standard errors.

If the central limit theorems and assumptions are valid, then we are now in a position
to test the Regional Manager's beliefs and help the board of directors decide on a course of
action.

4.3.3   Could the Regional Manager be Right?

There is no such thing as a statistical fact, only a weight of evidence in favour of a theory, or
else opposed to it. In the Regional Manager's case, he interprets the survey findings to show

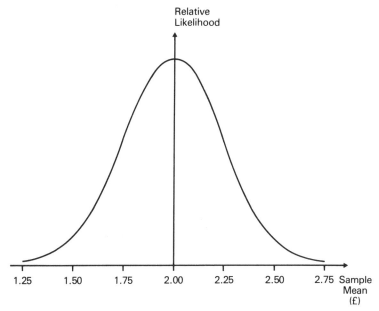

Figure 4.4 *Sampling distribution for the Laundromatic data*

mean spending on launderettes and dry-cleaning to be in excess of £2 per household. Unfortunately, he has reported the £2.78 sample mean as a spot-estimate of the true mean and used it as such.

From an analytical point of view, the findings should be properly assessed in relation to a *hypothesis* about mean spending. Let us say initially that the findings do not support the Regional Manager; that the £2 limit has not been overcome by sufficient counter-evidence. This is usually called the *null hypothesis* since it implies that no strong evidence exists, and is usually written as follows:

H_0: population mean spending $= $ £2, at most

The alternative to this statement is called the *alternative hypothesis* with the symbol H_1:

H_1: population mean $> $ £2

One of these must be correct and the other incorrect: if we reject one, we must assume the other to be correct on the available evidence. The question to be answered is: Is the discrepancy between the hypothetical value and the sample mean too great for the former to be probable? The answer depends on the particular logical argument which follows:

1. If H_0 is true, the sample mean will not be very different from the hypothetical mean.
2. If the sample mean is very different from the hypothetical mean, then either the sample is unrepresentative or else the hypothesis must be under doubt.
3. If the sample *is* representative, then a large discrepancy must lead to the rejection of the null hypothesis.

Rejection of the null hypothesis in the Laundromatic case means that the £2 limit is exceeded and the Regional Manager's recommendation is given added weight.

From Chapter 3, you will recall that the area under the normal distribution curve can be split into known proportions by reference to the standard deviation. Since the sampling distribution for the mean in the Laundromatic case is normal, by the central limit theorem,

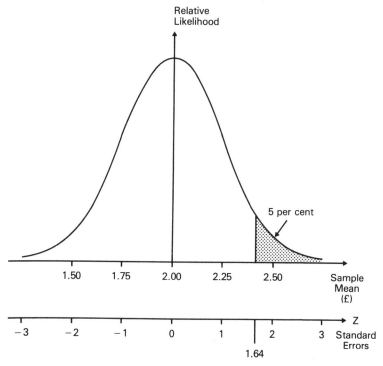

Figure 4.5   *The five per cent cut-off value for the Laundromatic data*

and since its dispersion can be estimated, we are able to make probability statements about sample results. Only five per cent of the area under the normal curve will lie in a tail beyond a value of 1.64 standard deviations measured on the horizontal axis, as shown in Figure 4.5. One standard error in the sampling distribution is £0.25 so that 1.64 standard errors is about £0.41. Therefore, it could be stated that only five per cent of samples (that is, one in twenty) will have a mean in excess of £2.41 *if the true mean is £2.00*. Similarly, the table of normal areas in Chapter 3 indicates that only one per cent of samples will have a mean in excess of £2.58 *if the true mean is £2.00*. Table 4.1 gives the Z values (number of standard errors) which cut off various areas in one tail of the normal distribution. The reader should check these values against the table in Chapter 3.

Table 4.1   *Areas in one tail of a normal distribution.*

Z standard errors	1.28	1.64	1.96	2.33	3.09
Per cent area in one tail	10	5	2.5	1	0.1

Each of the Z values in Table 4.1 can be regarded as a *critical value* for the purpose of testing the hypothesis that the true mean is £2.00. For example, there is a probability of 0.001 (0.1 per cent) that a sample could have a mean equal to or greater than £2.77 as follows:

For $Z = 3.09$, area in tail $= 0.001$;
$Z = 3.09$ indicates $3.09 \times £0.25$ above £2.00;
$Z = £3.09$ indicates $£2.00 + £0.77$, i.e. £2.77.

This shows how very unlikely such a result is and yet the Regional Manager's sample did exceed £2.77. Consequently, if the sample itself was truly representative, there must be considerable doubt cast upon the null hypothesis.

A practical approach to the test could be stated as follows:

Step 1: State the null and alternative hypotheses $H_0: \mu = £2.00$
$H_1: \mu > £2.00$

Step 2: Assume H_0 is true and calculate a 'test statistic' for the sample
$$Z = \frac{£2.78 - £2.00}{£0.25}$$
$Z = 3.12$ standard errors

Step 3: Compare this 'test statistic' with tail values for Z in Table 4.1
$Z > 1.96$, the 0.025 level
$Z > 2.33$, the 0.01 level
$Z > 3.09$, the 0.001 level

Step 4: If the result is in the low probability part of the tail, reject H_0 as unlikely
Since $Z > 3.09$, the probability of £2.78 occurring from a true mean of £2.00 is less than 0.001; therefore H_0 must be rejected

Step 5: If H_0 is rejected, the alternative must be assumed to be correct
H_1 is not rejected so we must assume that the true mean exceeds £2.00

A business analyst would state this conclusion as: The sample result is *statistically significant* at the 0.001 level and the null hypothesis is rejected. Use of the term 'significance' implies that the sample findings and the hypothetical value are significantly different, so different in fact that there is only a 0.001 probability (0.1 per cent chance) of its arising. Therefore, the hypothesis must be rejected by an overwhelming weight of evidence. The directors should accept instead the Regional Manager's recommendation, provided the sample is believed to be representative.

4.3.4 Confidence in an Estimate

The Laundromatic Regional Manager has a spot-estimate of £2.78 for the true mean spending but he ought not to present it as the true mean itself. It is a single value from the wide range of possible means of samples. What would be useful, and more honest, is a statement of the values between which the true mean could lie, with a probability attached to it. For example, such a statement could be: Population mean is contained by interval £2.37 to £3.19 with 90 per cent confidence (that is, probability 0.90). This gives a clear indication of the accuracy of the estimate and also an assessment of its probability of being incorrect. There is a 0.10 probability (a 10 per cent chance) of this interval's failing to include the true mean.

The approach to making such statements is simple. Using the notation introduced in Chapter 3, we may state that

$$p \left(\begin{array}{c} \text{Sample} \\ \text{mean} \end{array} \text{falls within} \begin{array}{c} \text{True} \\ \text{mean} \end{array} \pm 1.64 \begin{array}{c} \text{Standard} \\ \text{errors} \end{array} \right) = 0.90$$

This is because 1.64 standard errors either side of the mean cuts off five per cent of the normal area in each tail, as shown in Figure 4.6. The probability statement can be

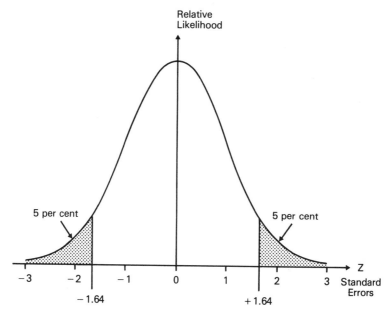

Figure 4.6   *The 90 per cent interval for a sampling distribution*

manipulated to yield the following result which is what we require:

$$p\left(\begin{array}{c}\text{True}\\\text{mean}\end{array}\text{included within}\begin{array}{c}\text{Sample}\\\text{mean}\end{array}\pm 1.64\begin{array}{c}\text{Standard}\\\text{errors}\end{array}\right) = 0.90$$

i.e.

$$p\left(\mu \text{ in interval } \bar{x} \pm 1.64\,\frac{\sigma}{\sqrt{n}}\right) = 0.90$$

For other probabilities (degrees of confidence) the 1.64 would be replaced. For example, 95 per cent confidence requires $2\frac{1}{2}$ per cent in each tail which, from Table 4.1, leads to a Z value of 1.96. Thus $p(\mu$ in interval $\bar{x} \pm 1.96(\sigma/\sqrt{n})) = 0.95$ and so on for other percentage points. Table 4.2 summarizes commonly applied Z values for various degrees of confidence.

Table 4.2   *Areas included in confidence intervals.*

Z value	1.64	1.96	2.33	2.58	3.29
Per cent area within ± Z	90	95	98	99	99.9

For the Laundromatic data, the Regional Manager could obtain an *interval estimate* of the true mean instead of merely reporting the spot-estimate of £2.78. The calculation is as follows if we assume that he wishes to be 90 per cent confident.

$$p\left(\mu \text{ in } £2.78 \pm 1.64 \frac{£1.78}{\sqrt{49}}\right) = 0.90$$
$$p(\mu \text{ in } £2.78 \pm 1.64 \times £0.25) = 0.90$$
$$p(\mu \text{ in } £2.78 \pm £0.41) = 0.90$$
$$p(\mu \text{ in } £2.37 \text{ to } £3.19) = 0.90$$

He can be 90 per cent confident that the true or population mean spending will be between £2.37 and £3.19, with a best estimate of £2.78. Perhaps he should report that he is 'pretty sure the mean spending exceeds £2.37'. If he wishes to be more confident, he must broaden the interval by using bigger Z values:

For confidence level	*Interval estimate*
90 per cent	£2.37 to £3.19
95 per cent	£2.29 to £3.27
99 per cent	£2.13½ to £3.42½
99.9 per cent	£1.96 to £3.60

Accuracy is lost as confidence is increased and vice versa, as Figure 4.7 shows. A business analyst must decide on the appropriate combination and it is conventional to state 90 and 95 per cent confidence intervals since higher levels are regarded as unnecessary. Note that a confidence level of 99.9 per cent means that the true mean spending could be below £2.00. In this instance, the search for excessive confidence could result in the proposed shop not being approved by the directors.

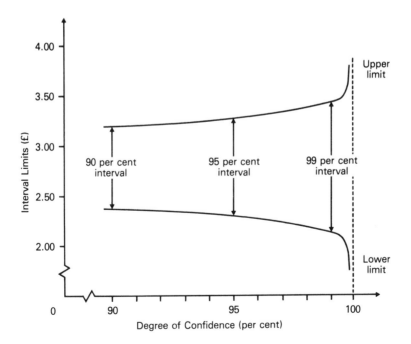

Figure 4.7 *Loss of precision in the search for greater confidence*

4.3.5   Percentage Support for the New Shop

In the same way that we have been able to make useful statements and apply statistical tests to the mean expenditure, it is also possible to analyse *proportions* in a population. Forty households out of a random selection of 49 said they would support Laundromatic's new shop; that is, 81.6 per cent or 0.816. The Regional Manager has reported this observation to the directors as if it were true also for the entire population, but we know that sample results ought not to be interpreted in such a manner. There are theorems governing sample proportions and the following results can be shown to be true for large samples in which the proportion is not less than about one-tenth nor greater than about nine-tenths:

$$\text{Best estimate of population proportion} = \text{Sample proportion} = 0.816$$

$$\text{Standard deviation of sample proportions (called } \textit{standard error} \textit{ of the proportion)} = \sqrt{\frac{\left(\text{Population proportion}\right) \times \left(1 - \text{Population proportion}\right)}{\text{Number in sample}}}$$

$$= \sqrt{\frac{\pi(1-\pi)}{n}} \quad \text{where } \pi \text{ is the population proportion}$$

$$= \sqrt{\frac{0.816 \times 0.184}{49}} \quad \text{since } \pi \text{ is estimated by the sample proportion}$$

$$= 0.055$$

We may use these results to obtain an interval estimate for the population proportion of households supporting the new shop. By recourse to the normal distribution, we may state the following for 95 per cent confidence:

$$p\left(\text{Population proportion included within Sample proportion} \pm 1.96 \text{ Standard errors}\right) = 0.95$$

$$p(\pi \text{ in the interval } 0.816 \pm 1.96 \times 0.055) = 0.95.$$

Thus we may be 95 per cent confident that π lies between 0.708 and 0.924. This shows how wide the interval must be to yield a high probability. The reader should use the Z values in Table 4.2 and verify the following results.

For confidence level	Interval estimate
90 per cent	0.725 to 0.906
95 per cent	0.708 to 0.924
99 per cent	0.674 to 0.958
99.9 per cent	0.635 to 0.997

Note again, as for the mean, that confidence and accuracy are inversely related. To gain 99.9 per cent confidence, the Regional Manager must be prepared to report a proportion 'somewhere between 63 per cent and about 100 per cent' of households expressing support for the new shop. Quite clearly, the directors would regard such a statement as rather vague and perhaps view it as a weakness in the survey. It could be overcome only by increasing the sample size and thereby reducing the standard error.

Knowledge of the sampling distribution of a proportion permits also the testing of hypotheses about its value. In the Laundromatic case there is no requirement that a large proportion of the housing estate should express support for the new shop but we can envisage such a proviso being made. Let us say that the directors require more than three-quarters of households to express support before they would consider going ahead with the plan. Does the sample evidence suggest that such a condition will be fulfilled? Using the approach adopted for the mean, the evidence may be judged as follows:

Step 1: State the null and alternative hypotheses

$H_0: \pi \leqslant 0.750$
$H_1: \pi > 0.750$

Step 2: Assume H_0 is true and calculate the test statistic

$$Z = \frac{0.816 - 0.750}{0.055}$$
$$Z = +1.200$$

Step 3: Compare the test statistic with the values in Table 4.1

$Z < 1.96$, the 0.025 level
$Z < 1.64$, the 0.050 level
$Z < 1.28$, the 0.100 level

Step 4: If the result is not in the extreme tail of the normal distribution, the sample value could occur under H_0: it cannot be rejected

Since $Z < 1.28$, the probability that a sample value of 0.816 could occur from a population proportion of 0.750 is not very small

Step 5: If H_0 cannot be rejected, then H_1 must be

We must assume that the true proportion does not exceed 0.750

A business analyst would state this conclusion as: The sample result is *not statistically significant* at the 0.10 level and the null hypothesis cannot be rejected. In this event, the directors of Laundromatic should reserve judgement on the new shop since there is not over-powering evidence in favour of customer support.

4.4   THE NATURE OF THE SAMPLE DATA

4.4.1   How Was the Sample Chosen?

The Laundromatic sample was chosen simply by selecting one-twentieth of the houses in street order. This is called a *systematic sample.* If carried out properly, it should be about as random as a *simple random sample*, in which every household is allocated a number and individuals are picked out from a device like a tombola drum. On the whole, systematic sampling would be appropriate for interviewing on doorsteps. But there are other approaches and these are listed briefly.

Multistage sampling

1. Make a random selection of streets; this is the first stage.
2. Make a random selection of houses in the selected streets; this is the second stage.

Stratified sampling

1. Divide all the houses on the estate into categories such as detached, semi-detached and linked since this probably will affect usage of launderettes.
2. Obtain a systematic sample from each 'stratum'; say one-twentieth of each type of house.

Quota sampling

1. Give each interviewer a quota such as five houses with a car in the driveway, two women at a bus-stop, six mothers outside a school and four retired people.
2. The validity of the sample will depend upon the ability of the interviewer to distinguish between the various groups in the population.

Cluster sampling

1. On a map of the estate, split the houses into forty, roughly equal, clusters.
2. Select at random two of the clusters.
3. Interview *every* house in both clusters.

The purposes of such sampling procedures is to ensure representativeness within the sample. In other words, the randomness of the sample must be arranged in order to avoid *bias* in the results; that is, to prevent specific results far removed from that which is typical in the population. Although systematic sampling would be acceptable in the Laundromatic case, there are other features in the survey that could cause adverse comment, as we shall see.

4.4.2   Timing a Survey

To interview people on their own doorsteps in the early evening presupposes that the typical household is available at that time. Such may not be the case for various reasons. First, the use of a launderette is probably more common among manual and semi-skilled workers than among professionals or the self-employed. Which of these various groups of people is most likely to be at home early on a Friday evening? Possibly the latter two because Friday evening is the start of the weekend for many weekly-paid households, and they are more likely to be out enjoying their leisure time. Consequently, the survey was carried out at precisely those times that an important element in the population was absent. Perhaps that accounts for the fifteen vacant houses encountered by the interviewers, and if so, the sample would be seriously biased away from true representativeness. Indeed, if the vacant houses were occupied by launderette-users, an important element within the data has been lost. For randomness, timing can be crucial and the interviewers should have been sent out at a variety of different times of the day.

4.4.3 Asking the Right Questions

The questions in the Regional Manager's survey are each open to criticism. Consider them in turn.

Question 1. Do you regularly use a launderette or have clothes dry-cleaned?

The word 'regularly' is not precise. If a household dry-cleans its curtains and suite covers once a year in April, then that is regular and the respondent could truthfully answer, 'Yes'. Conversely, a housewife may use the launderette frequently but not regularly; that is to say, not every week or fortnight but whenever necessary. Such a respondent could answer, 'No'. Also, the question is fundamentally vague: it uses the examples of clothes being cleaned but households may use the launderette or dry-cleaning only for items other than clothes, which are cleaned at home. For example, a shop-keeper may use the launderette to wash the dust-covers off the counters because they are too big to fit in a domestic washing machine. A better question could be, 'How many times have you visited the launderette or the dry-cleaners in the last month?' The responses would yield a secondary benefit in that the Regional Manager could estimate the mean frequency of use of the proposed facilities.

Question 2. How much did you spend in the last seven days in a launderette or on dry-cleaning?

As a first criticism, the 'or' should be replaced by 'and' because use of the launderette does not exclude any dry-cleaning. Secondly, why restrict the question to the last seven days? A housewife may take all her laundry to be washed once a fortnight at a cost of £2.00, and may also have some items dry-cleaned once a month at a cost of £3.00. If those activities occurred earlier than a week ago, she will answer, 'Nothing'. But she is spending £7 per month, i.e. £1.75 per week. A better question could be, 'When did you last visit the launderette or dry-cleaners and how much did you spend on either?' This is not very much more complicated than the original and would yield data on frequency of use as well as mean spending.

Question 3. Would you welcome and support a launderette/dry-cleaning shop situated on this estate?

It would take a hard-faced, even cruel, respondent to answer 'No' to this question. The wording does not encourage honesty but rather agreement with the interviewer's obvious interest. It is said to be a *leading question* since it leads to a particular response. We are all subject to such pressure when asked a question starting, 'Don't you agree with me that . . .?' To disagree seems to insult or even to break a potential short-term friendship, whereas to agree is to please the questioner even though the agreement is a lie. At least this question does not ask explicitly for agreement but is worded to imply that disagreement is unco-operative, unfriendly, even anti-social. It is not surprising that not a single respondent said, 'No' and nine 'Don't know' replies were probably from people trying to be honest but unable to bring themselves to say it. A better question would take out the personal commitment from the wording and transform it into opinion about the neighbourhood. For example, 'Do you think the people on the estate would find a local launderette useful and use it regularly?' This permits the respondent to answer truthfully without appearing unfriendly, such as 'Of course, I would, but I'm not so sure about the neighbours'. The interviewer would interpret this as a 'No'.

4.4.4 How to Ask Better Questions

There are basic rules that should be followed in the design of questionnaires whether they are to be distributed in a postal survey or used for interviews. They may be listed briefly.

1. Questions must be simple and unambiguous.
2. Avoid 'leading questions' at all costs.
3. Avoid over-personal questions if possible.
4. Keep the questionnaire as short, and to the point, as possible.
5. Always try to adopt a logical sequence of questions.
6. Use preprinted answers whenever possible.
7. With interviews consider the use of probe questions; that is, ask the question twice in different forms to test the truthfulness of the respondent.
8. It is usual to undertake a pilot study using the questionnaire with a small sample of respondents. Ambiguities and other such difficulties in the questionnaire are usually identified at this stage and can be amended. Also, a few open-ended questions included in the pilot study may indicate areas of information which are relevant, but which have not been covered by specific questions in the initial draft of the questionnaire.

4.4.5 The Directors Do Not Approve

The Laundromatic Regional Manager undertook the survey to prove a point; that his region should have another shop. The selection of the sample was reasonable and could be expected to yield adequately representative results. Analysis of the findings was less than adequate, since he presented only the spot-estimate for the mean without reference to any probability or confidence. Consequently, his conclusions about weekly takings must be viewed as speculative rather than definite. Finally, the questions asked in the survey itself are not valid in their intention or their wording. They are couched in terms designed to support his recommendations and the directors of the company should realize it. The questions are the main weakness in the exercise and no findings derived from them should be regarded as useful statistical data. If the exercise is to be carried out again, it will be of prime importance to start by phrasing the questions in accordance with the guidelines given above.

The directors of Laundromatic Holdings Ltd should not approve the opening of a new shop on the basis of currently available data. The Regional Manager should be reprimanded or at least advised or perhaps sent on a management training course!

ASSIGNMENTS

A4.1   At a certain college the library closes at 7.00 pm on Friday evenings and re-opens at 9.00 am the following Monday morning. The part-time students' representatives on the Business and Management Board of Studies ask that consideration be given to Saturday opening of the library to enable them and their fellows to obtain essential books out of working hours. The Library Committee reply that part-time students should obtain books in the evening, when the library is open until 9.00 pm Monday to Thursday. Saturday opening could be considered only if there was substantial support from full-time students.

The Students' Union undertake a survey of student opinion by interviewing selected groups as follows:

Monday 16 November at 12.00 noon:	10 first-year students.
Monday 16 November at 5.00 pm:	10 second-year students.
Wednesday 18 November at 9.00 am:	10 third-year students and 5 mature students in any year of their studies.
Thursday 19 November at 12.00 noon:	10 fourth-year students and 5 married women in any year of their studies.
Friday 20 November at 9.00 am:	5 more mature students and 5 more married women.

Each interviewed student is asked three questions:

1.   Do you believe that the library should open on Saturdays to help part-time students?
     Yes/No
2.   Would you support Saturday opening by using the library yourself?
     Yes/No
3.   How often would you use the library on a Saturday?
     Once a term/Twice a Term/Once a Month/More Often

The replies from the interviews are as follows:

Question 1:	Yes	60
	No	nil
Question 2:	Yes	52
	No	8
Question 3:	Once a Term	41
	Twice a Term	16
	Once a month	3
	More often	nil

(a)   Criticize this survey with reference to its sampling procedure, its questions and its findings. Hence explain why the Library Committee probably ought not to accept it as evidence of substantial support.
(b)   Redesign the survey taking into account your criticisms in (a) and any other features of the situation which you regard as important. For example, is student demand for weekend library facilities constant throughout the year?

A4.2   The bookshop at a certain college is managed by an ex-student who was also recently elected as a County Councillor. There has been adverse publicity in the local newspaper in which a group of students admitted that the £90 book allowance in the full-time student grant is not usually spent on books or stationery. Instead, it seems to be spent in the Union Bar. The bookshop manager understandably is incensed by the revelation and decides to survey student book-purchasing habits not only in his capacity as supplier but also as an elected representative of local rate-payers.

(a) Discuss the problems of population and sampling in this instance, and advise the manager of one acceptable method.

(b) Design a questionnaire of no more than four questions to assesss students' knowledge about their grants, their spending habits and their attitude towards books in general.

A4.3 The bookshop manager in A4.2 has followed the advice of a fellow bookseller and has used his own statistical knowledge to obtain the following results from a random sample:

Number of books bought in year	Up to 4	5–9	10 or more
Number of replies	42	37	2

Cost of most expensive book	Below £4	£4 to £7.99	£8 or more
Number of replies	16	44	21

How much do you think you should spend on books?	Below £25	£25 to £74	£75 to £89	£90 or more
Number of replies	10	48	18	5

(a) Calculate the mean and standard deviation for:

   (i) The number of books purchased.
   (ii) The cost of the most expensive book purchased.
   (iii) The expectations of the total spending on books.

(b) Establish 90 per cent and 95 per cent interval estimates for (i), (ii) and (iii) above.

(c) The bookshop manager has a suspicion that typical students buy only five books each year, limit themselves to editions costing under £7 and really believe that they should not be asked to spend more than £50 each year. Test these three beliefs at the 0.05 level of significance, clearly stating your conclusions.

(d) Would you agree that the manager is right to be disturbed about students' book-purchasing habits?

A4.4 Bags of sugar are sold as being one kilo in weight. However, the filling machine cannot yield an exact weight, but works to a standard deviation of 2.5 grams about its setting.

A random sample of 100 bags of sugar upon the shelves of a supermarket is weighed and found to contain a mean weight of 998 grams.

(a) Does this sample provide evidence that the filling machine is incorrectly set at a weight below one kilo? (Test at the 0.05 level of significance.)

(b) Each bag bears the legend 'Min-contents 995 grams'. What proportion, therefore, of packed bags would you expect to be withheld from sale because they are underweight?

A4.5 A building society's Chief Accountant believes that the value of the average mortgage is rising at ten per cent per year. In mid 1982 the mean mortgage offered by the society was £14 600. In May 1983 the Chief Accountant takes a random sample of 256 mortgages registered since January 1 and obtains the following results: 31 May 1983 sample mean mortgage £15 910; sample standard deviation £2450.

(a) Use this information to test the Chief Accountant's belief. Specify precisely the nature of your test and any assumptions you need to make. (Test at the 0.05 level.)

(b) Obtain an interval estimate for the society's mean mortgage which gives 90 per cent confidence.

(c) The Chief Accountant decides to formalize this annual review by setting a decision rule for 1984, of the form, 'If the mean value of 100 random mortgages is below £x, please inform me'. The value of x is to be such that it indicates a less than ten per cent increase over the year.

Deduce the value of x if the decision rule is to be correctly applied with a probability of 0.90

A4.6 The Senior Cashier of a large store has made a check of a random sample of working days and noted a daily discrepancy between the till-books and the cash placed in the vault. He obtained the following results:

Discrepancy *(£)*	*Frequency* *(Days)*
Excess 20 or more	10
10–20 excess	30
0–10 excess	60
0–10 short	20
10–20 short	10
Short 20 or more	0

(a) Treat the money-values as a continuous variable and estimate the 95 per cent confidence interval for the mean daily discrepancy rounded to the nearest 50 pence.

(b) The Chief Cashier believes that the discrepancy has a true mean of zero. Test this belief at the 0.1 significance level.

(Note that this assignment introduces a complication in the alternative hypothesis such that the mean may be either side of the H_0 value. In previous cases we have considered only instances of 'greater than' or 'less than' but here the appropriate hypothesis is 'not equal to'. Consequently, the area of significance is divided equally between two tails of the normal distribution, five per cent in each tail, which requires the reader to use critical Z values other than those used in earlier one-tail tests. Here five per cent in each tail indicates a Z value of ± 1.64.)

A4.7 In an advertising campaign, the copy design team are in dispute over the effectiveness of a particular newspaper display. One group says that the advertisement is controversial and forces the reader to take further notice of the description of the product. Another group claims that the buying public is immune to advertising shock because it has been used so frequently in recent years: they say that readers will recognize the attempt to stun them and will be repelled.

It is agreed that a trial should be arranged with randomly selected members of the public to assess the effectiveness of the advertising copy. One hundred shoppers in a large city-centre complex are invited to sit in a booth one at a time and to view the advertisement on an illuminated screen. Eighty of them say that they found the display to be visually interesting but only 18 felt impelled to buy the product.

(a) Establish a 95 per cent interval estimate for the proportion of the general public who will be impelled to buy from the advertisement.

(b) It is agreed by the two groups that if one-quarter of readers are attracted to purchase the product, then the advertisement is worth printing. Assess the evidence from the trial and advise the team whether or not the agreed condition has been met.

(c) After redesigning the advertisement, another random trial of 76 shoppers in a different location yields the following data:

	Yes	No
Do you feel that you must read this advertisement?	47	29
Are you attracted to the idea of the product mentioned?	28	48
Would you buy the product mentioned?	22	54

Discuss the view that the new advertisement is better at attracting actual purchasers than was the original.

A4.8　A pharmaceutical company has set up a research team to investigate the condition of insomnia, the inability to sleep restfully. A preliminary finding suggests that insomniacs are lonely people and that companionship, even in the form of pets, could greatly improve their condition. Two random groups of sufferers are selected from the records of general practitioners known to the company, and treated as follows:

Group A　Number in sample:　150
　　　　　Treatment:　　　　weekly discussion and glucose tablets passed off as the latest drug treatment
　　　　　Result:　　　　　41 greatly improved
　　　　　　　　　　　　　97 slightly improved
　　　　　　　　　　　　　12 no improvement

Group B　Number in sample:　200
　　　　　Treatment:　　　　latest drug sent through the post; strictly no communication with patients
　　　　　Result:　　　　　　44 greatly improved
　　　　　　　　　　　　　108 slightly improved
　　　　　　　　　　　　　　48 no improvement

(a) For a drug to be considered worthwhile for clinical use, it must be beneficial to two-thirds of patients. Assess the treatments and results for the two groups as shown by the proportions of improvement.

(b) Establish 90 per cent interval estimates for both groups' treatments, stating the proportion of insomniacs in the entire population who could be expected to benefit under either. (The reader should decide what is meant by 'benefit' in this context.)

(c) Decide which of the two treatments is most beneficial and discuss the problems of convincing the company to adopt it. In particular, comment upon the views of the Marketing Director that, '90 per cent confidence only means that you hold the opinion strongly — why should I believe you?' Also, criticize the treatment of Group A as it might impinge upon the National Health Service, if promoted by the company.

5—Resource Allocation

5.1 INTRODUCTION AND OBJECTIVES

5.1.1 The Subject of the Chapter

This chapter builds upon the simple graphwork and equations introduced in Chapter 1. Here we are concerned with the best use, or allocation, of the scarce resources available to an organization. These comprise any of the inputs to a production process and include raw materials, machines, labour and time. Time is a crucial resource since each productive day is limited to 24 hours, or 1440 minutes or three eight-hour shifts. There is no possibility of increasing this input and the consequences of this fact are important for the business analyst.

The methods introduced in this chapter fall under the general heading of *linear programming* and most texts will include such a reference in an index. The word 'linear' simply means that the relationship between input and output takes the form of a straight line and this chapter analyses ways of using the relationship to achieve desirable goals, such as profitability or the reduction of costs.

5.1.2 Objectives

1. To construct a linear model of the economic allocation problem in business.
2. To define the objective function in a production process.
3. To identify feasible solutions to the resource allocation problem.
4. To identify the optimum allocation of resources.
5. To arrange the resource allocation problem in a form suitable for computer solution.

5.2 BASIC PROBLEM DATA

A company manufactures two products which we shall call by codenames A and B. Both products are to be processed through two machine shops, one process after the other. Each item A spends 2 hours in the first machine shop and then 1 hour in the second. Each item B spends 5 hours in the first machine shop and then 6 hours in the second. The first machine shop is available for 70 working hours per week but the second for only 48 hours because of manning difficulties. Each A costs £80 in all to produce and each B costs £70. When sold by the company, each A yields a revenue (price) of £100 and each B a revenue of £125. The company has an objective of obtaining maximum revenue (weekly takings) from its sale of the two products. However, there is pressure from a sector of management to change the firm's objective to that of gaining the maximum profit from sales of the two products. An added complication lies in a contract to which the firm is a party whereby they must supply ten units each week of product A to a particular customer. The penalty for failure under the contract is sufficiently high that the company do not contemplate ever doing so.

5.3 RESOURCES ARE SCARCE BY DEFINITION

5.3.1 The Economic Problem

Whenever a machine (or man or land) is being used for one purpose, it cannot be used for anything else. If there are two or more uses to which the machine may be put, then we come up against the economic problems of scarcity and choice. The first machines are available for processing for 70 hours each week. Two products are to be processed: Product A requires 2 hours per item and Product B requires 5 hours. What numbers of the two products may be processed on these machines each week?

Clearly, processing 20 As and 20 Bs is not possible because that would take 140 hours of machine time; thus:

$$\begin{array}{lll} \text{Time on Product A} & 20 \times 2 \text{ hours} = & 40 \text{ hours} \\ \underline{\text{Time on Product B}} & \underline{20 \times 5 \text{ hours} =} & \underline{100 \text{ hours}} \\ \text{Total time used} & & \overline{140 \text{ hours}} \end{array}$$

However, 10 As and 10 Bs are possible and this combination would take just 70 hours of machine time. Another combination which uses exactly the available 70 hours is 5 As and 12 Bs. Another is 20 As and 6 Bs. The student should check that these combinations are possible.

To permit a mathematical analysis, let us say that the firm decides to process x units of Product A and y units of Product B in a week (x and y are *variables*, in the sense that they can each take one of a range of values). Then the total machine time used that week is given as follows:

$$\begin{array}{lll} \text{Time on Product A} & x \times 2 \text{ hours} = & 2x \text{ hours} \\ \text{Time on Product B} & y \times 5 \text{ hours} = & 5y \text{ hours} \\ \text{Total time used} & & 2x + 5y \text{ hours} \end{array}$$

Now, it is known that the total time used cannot exceed 70 hours and we may write the problem:

$$2x + 5y \text{ cannot exceed 70 hours}$$

or

$$2x + 5y \leqslant 70$$

In addition, we know that Products A and B will be processed by more than one machine shop. In the second, each A takes 1 hour, each B takes 6 hours and the machine shop is available for 48 hours each week. Then using the same argument as before:

$$x \text{ units of Product A take } x \text{ hours}$$
$$y \text{ units of Product B take } 6y \text{ hours}$$
$$\text{Total time used is } x + 6y \text{ hours}$$

For the second machine shop, the economic problem can be written:

$$x + 6y \leqslant 48 \text{ hours}$$

If there were other machines used in the production of Products A and B each would yield a similar inequality statement, one for each machine.

Note that a possible combination of units in one machine shop may not be possible in another. For example, as we saw above, 10 As and 10 Bs are possible on the first machines but not on the second. Conversely, 36 As and 2 Bs are possible on the second machine but not on the first. The reader should check these figures.

5.3.2 Drawing the Economic Problem

As we saw in Chapter 1, a straight line on a graph can also be represented by an equation. Similarly, any equation can be drawn on a graph. But what about an inequality? There is no problem so long as we remember that an inequality permits any combination up to a certain maximum and that combinations below the maximum are shown on a graph but not as a line.

Consider the constraint imposed by the 70 hours available for the first machine shop. If no As were processed, then all the time would be allocated to Bs and the maximum output from the machine shop would be 14 units of B. From the inequality this is seen as follows:

$$2x + 5y \leqslant 70$$
$$\text{let } x = 0, \quad \text{then } 5y \leqslant 70$$
$$y \leqslant 14 \text{ (i.e. } y \text{ cannot exceed 14)}$$

Thus one extreme combination is $x = 0$, $y = 14$. The other extreme is obtained by letting $y = 0$ (processing only As):

$$2x + 5y \leqslant 70$$
$$\text{let } y = 0, \quad \text{then } 2x \leqslant 70$$
$$x \leqslant 35$$

The other extreme combination is $x = 35$, $y = 0$. As the inequality is linear (contains no squared or higher terms) all other combinations will lie between these two. This is shown in Figure 5.1.

Any combination within the shaded area is feasible within the limited availability of the machines. Note that any combination lying below the upper boundary (the line $2x + 5y = 70$) is feasible but leaves the machine shop idle some of the time. For example, $x = 10$ and $y = 8$ is a possible combination but uses only 60 hours of machine time: for 10 hours each week the machine shop is idle or available for other work.

Now consider the graph of the second constraint arising from the other machine shop. Identify the extreme combinations as follows:

$$x + 6y = 48$$
$$\text{let } x = 0, \text{ then } y = 8; \quad \text{the extreme combination is } x = 0, y = 8$$
$$\text{let } y = 0, \text{ then } x = 48; \text{ the extreme combination is } x = 48, y = 0$$

This second inequality can now be superimposed on the graph to give Figure 5.2.

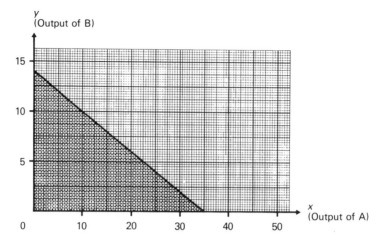

Figure 5.1   *The constraint of the first machines*

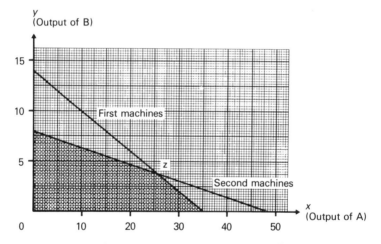

Figure 5.2   *The two processing constraints and the feasible region*

5.3.3   Keeping Track of Possible Combinations

The shaded area in Figure 5.2 indicates feasible combinations under *both* constraints. Any combination within that area is a possible combination for either machine shop. One particular combination, at the intersection marked Z uses all the available time in both machine shops, since Z lies on the upper boundaries of both. All other combinations involve one or other of the machine shops lying idle or available for other use.

It is worth noting that Figure 5.2 involves only the two constraints relating to the machine shops. However, we know that Product A is marketed in such a way that processing must involve at least 10 units per week: the firm has a long-standing contract to supply the 10 units per week. Therefore another constraint arises from this market feature which

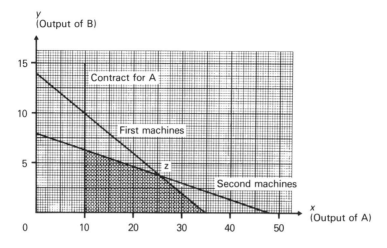

Figure 5.3   *Three constraints and the feasible region*

may be written:

$$x \geqslant 10$$

The $\geqslant$ symbol means 'greater than or equal to' under the same convention as for $\leqslant$. This market constraint may now be superimposed on the other two, to obtain Figure 5.3.

The new market constraint is different from the other two. Whereas the machine shops imposed upper values upon the output of A and B, the market contract imposes a *minimum* value below which the values are not feasible. Hence the feasible region is constrained from the left producing a smaller region.

Any combination of outputs of Products A and B from within the feasible region can be accommodated in the machine shops and will satisfy the contractual supply of A. Only the combination at the intersection marked Z fully uses the machine time and, to that extent, may be viewed as desirable. However, the selection of the best (optimum) combination depends upon the objectives of the firm. If maximum machine utilization is the objective, then combination Z is ideal; but we know nothing, as yet, about the profitability of Products A and B. It is quite possible that another combination yields maximum profit, leaving one machine idle or available for other use.

5.4   ACHIEVING THE OBJECTIVES OF THE FIRM

5.4.1   Getting the Most Out

The objective which the firm has set itself is the *maximization* of sales revenue. This objective presupposes that there is at least one constraint upon the activity of the firm and maximization really means 'maximization up to the limit of possibility'. In the example of Products A and B, maximization means processing up to, but not in excess of, the outer boundary of the feasible region.

We know that each Product A sells for £100 and each B for £125. Every time an A is sold, the firm receives £100, so that if x units of Product A are sold, the firm receives

£100x. Similarly, if y units of Product B are sold, the firm receives £125y. For any x, y combination sold in a week, the total revenue will be given by this relation:

$$R = £(100x + 125y)$$

It is this which the firm wishes to maximize and the objective is usually written as below. The notation should be interpreted to read, 'the maximum value of R which is calculated from $100x + 125y$'.

$$\max |R| = £(100x + 125y)$$

This relation is called the *objective function* since it states what is to be calculated and which value is sought: in this instance the maximum value within the feasible combinations of x and y. Note that it is assumed for simplicity that all production is sold, and that stocks are not increased. The situation when this is not true yields a more complex objective and is beyond the scope of this chapter.

An alternative maximization objective could be maximum profit where profit is defined crudely as sales revenue less production costs. If Product A costs £80 to produce, then its unit profit is (£100 − £80), that is, £20. If Product B costs £70 to produce, then its unit profit is £55. The profit (P) obtained from the sale of x units of Product A and y units of Product B can be written:

$$P = £(20x + 55y)$$

The objective function is therefore:

$$\max |P| = £(20x + 55y)$$

One combination of x and y will yield the maximum value of P and, as such, will satisfy the objective. It is found in section 5.5.4.

5.4.2   Keeping Costs Down

Before we go on to analyse the achievement of a maximization objective, it is worth while to consider the nature of the alternative, that is *minimization*. It is too glib to say that mini-mization of costs is an objective for a firm. Minimum costs are best achieved by ceasing pro-duction, closing down the firm and no longer spending money upon inputs at all! This is not the meaning of minimization. True minimization means stating an output target and then achieving it with least input cost. Alternatively, a firm may set itself the objective of mini-mizing the average unit cost per item of output regardless of type. Minimization objectives can become quite complicated but they all conform to the general definition, achieving a stated result with minimum cost, time or effort.

For simple minimization in our example, we could define the objective function like this:

x units of Product A cost £80x

y units of Product B cost £70y

Total cost (c)   £(80x + 70y)

The objective would be:

$$\min |c| = £(80x + 70y) \text{ subject to any stated output targets of the company}$$

5.5 FINDING THE BEST OUTPUT COMBINATION

5.5.1 Drawing the Objective Function

When the constraint inequalities were drawn upon a graph, the outer boundary was formed by the straight lines given by the 'equals' part of each of them. But the objective function is different in two respects. First, it is an equation, not an inequality, and as such is *not a region* but a single line. Second, we seek the maximum value of the objective function but it does not contain a statement of its own limitations, which each constraint inequality did do. Consider a sales value of £12 500 per week. This value is selected arbitrarily to be divisible by 100 and 125 to facilitate its drawing on a graph. Other values could be £62 500 or £25 000. Then we may state the objective equation as follows:

$$R = £12\,500 = £(100x + 125y)$$

We do not know that this is the maximum value of R, or even a possible value, until the xs and ys which could yield it have been discovered. This is done by similar arguments to those use in drawing the constraints. If no Product B were processed, then the entire sales revenue must derive from Product A. In that case, 125 units of Product A would be necessary to yield £12 500 per week, as follows:

$$R = 12\,500 = 100x + 125y$$
$$\text{let } y = 0, \text{then } 12\,500 = 100x$$
$$125 = x \text{ (output of Product A)}$$

Alternatively, if no Product A were processed, then Product B must be produced at a rate of 100 units per week:

$$R = 12\,500 = 100x + 125y$$
$$\text{let } x = 0, \text{then } 12\,500 = 125y$$
$$100 = y \text{ (output of Product B)}$$

Now that a pair of extreme values for x and y are available, the line corresponding to $R = £12\,500$ per week is drawn upon Figure 5.4.

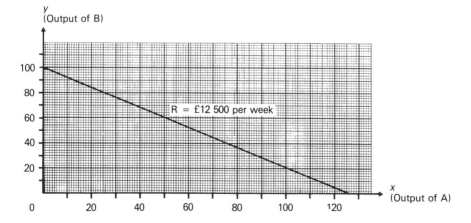

Figure 5.4   *The revenue line for £12 500*

Although we know only the end points of the line, the R equation is linear so that all other combinations yielding £12 500 per week are given by intermediate points. The student should check this by using another point, say $x = 50, y = 60$.

There is one obvious difficulty for the company if it plans to obtain sales revenue of £12 500 per week from Products A and B: the line in Figure 5.4 does not fall within the feasible region at any point. Simply, it is not possible for the company to sell so many units because it has not the resources to make them.

Consider Figure 5.5 in which the line of $R = £12\,500$ is superimposed upon the

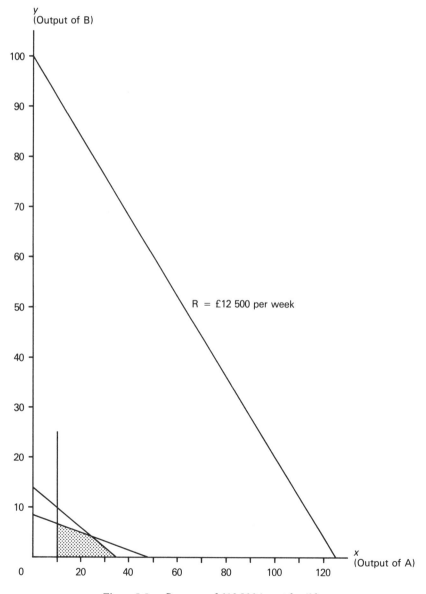

Figure 5.5   *Revenue of £12 500 is not feasible*

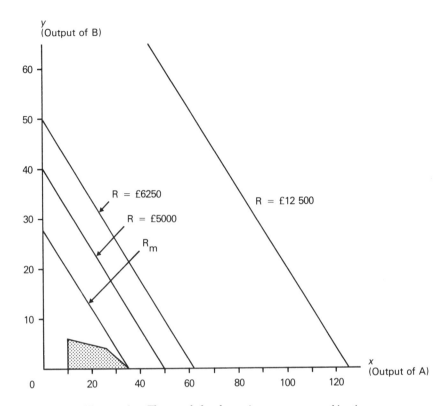

Figure 5.6 *The search for the optimum output combination*

constrained feasible region of Figure 5.3. We can see that a much lower sales value must be assumed for R if its line is to fall in the feasible region. The object now is to find that value of R which is just small enough to fall into the feasible region and is thus the maximum possible value.

Perhaps the search for the optimum value of R is most easily described by selecting a lower value and then noting the effect upon its line. Let $R = £5000$ per week, then the extreme values are as follows:

On the x axis: $y = 0$ and $x = 50$
On the y axis: $y = 40$ and $x = 0$

This line is shown in Figure 5.6 and it is clear that this R value is much closer to the feasible region. Even so $R = £5000$ is still not the *maximum possible* weekly sales value. However, the effect of reducing the arbitrary R value has been a shift of the objective line towards the origin of the graph, parallel to the first we considered. This will occur with any other lower R value while any increased R value will result in the line moving outward in a parallel manner. One line, marked R_m on Figure 5.6 is parallel to all other objective lines and just coincides with the feasible region at $x = 35$, $y = 0$. This point corresponds to a weekly production of 35 units of Product A and none of Product B. This combination is both feasible and lies on the highest objective line, though as yet we do not know the R value.

If production is organized so that 35 units of Product A are the only output of the company, the sales revenue will be maximized with a value of £3500 per week calculated as follows:

$$R_m = \pounds(100x + 125y)$$
$$= \pounds(100 \times 35) \text{ if } y = 0$$
$$R_m = \pounds3500 \text{ per week}$$

5.5.2   Left-overs and Idleness

The optimum allocation of resources need not imply that all resources are fully employed. The optimum relates to output, not to the actual use of resources, as our example shows. Here is a case of optimum allocation where two slightly surprising conclusions are reached.

1. Production of Product B should cease. This is *almost* intuitive when we consider the lengthy processing required for B, particularly upon the second machines. So heavy is the time input that it outweighs the fact that each B sells for £125 compared with only £100 for each A. At first glance the company may have decided to produce and sell as many as possible of B since it possesses the £25 revenue advantage. To do so would have yielded only £750 per week and is clearly non-optimal.
2. The second machine shop will be idle even though it is available for so few hours per week. This fact may be deduced from Figure 5.6 where we see that the optimum allocation lies on the boundary for the first 70-hour constraint but lies well within the boundary for that corresponding to the second machine shop. In numbers, 35 units of Product A use all 70 hours on the first machines but only 35 hours of the available time on the second, and so the second machines will be idle for 13 hours per week.

If the company were to change its objective to that of full employment for its machine shops, then the optimum allocation will change to point Z in Figure 5.3. Using whole numbers, Z corresponds to the values $x = 24$, $y = 4$ and under such a policy the weekly sales revenue would be given by:

$$R = \pounds(100x + 125y)$$
$$= \pounds(2400 + 500)$$
$$R = \pounds2900$$

which is less than the maximum we found of $R = \pounds3500$ but results in full employment of capital resources. A change in the objective, therefore, will generally affect the optimum allocation.

There need be no objection to fractional values of weekly output since they could refer to work-in-progress, but, for simplicity here, integers are desirable. It is important that the values lie inside the feasible region.

5.5.3   Maximum Profit as an Objective

In section 5.2, it was suggested that the company in our example was contemplating an alternative objective: that of maximum profit. We saw in section 5.4.1 that such an objective for these two products could be stated as:

$$\max |P| = \pounds(20x + 55y) \text{ per week}$$

Since this function is different from that for sales revenue, its lines on the x, y graph will also be different. The procedure for plotting it is the same. Select an arbitrary profit value of £1100 per week; then the extreme outputs of Products A and B are given as before. Note that this value is 20×55, taking these numbers from the P function. Therefore we know that this arbitrary £1100 is divisible by both 20 and 55.

$$P = 20x + 55y = 1100$$

$$\text{let } y = 0, \quad \text{then} \quad 20x = 1100$$

$$x = 55$$

$$\text{let } x = 0, \quad \text{then} \quad 55y = 1100$$

$$y = 20$$

The line of $P = £1100$ is shown on Figure 5.7, together with the maximum feasible profit P_m. We can see that the optimum allocation of machine time under this objective is at the intersection of the two machine constraints which we have previously identified as the point Z in Figure 5.3. In whole numbers output of 24 units of Product A and 4 units of Product B will yield a maximum profit of £700 per week, thus:

$$P_m = (20 \times 24) + (55 \times 4)$$

$$P_m = 480 + 220$$

$$P_m = £700 \text{ per week}$$

It is clear now that the profit-maximization objective yields the same optimum allocation as for the machine employment objective described in section 5.5.2. However, this result is merely coincidental and arises from the slope of the P line. There is no general rule

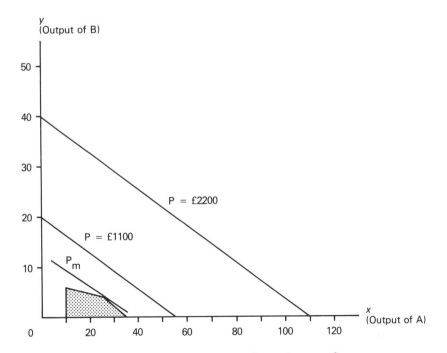

Figure 5.7   *Optimum output for maximum profit*

that maximum profit results in, or even coincides with, full employment of resources. Similarly, P_m does not coincide with R_m. Maximum profit of £700 is obtained from less than maximum income of £2900.

5.6   COMPUTER SOLUTIONS OF LARGER PROBLEMS

5.6.1   When to Use the Computer

The example studied in this chapter is simplified to help the introduction of ideas. However, even much larger allocation problems bear the same essential features, though their solutions are found more conveniently using a computer package.

The simplicity of our example arises from two features. First, there are only two variables (x and y) corresponding to the two products, whereas practically all firms are involved in making a wide range of products. This has an important effect upon the graph which we may wish to draw for such a company. Two products yielded a graph with two axes in two dimensions on a piece of paper. Three products would yield three axes in three dimensions which cannot easily be drawn or imagined. Figure 5.8 shows a simple three-dimensional graph for an imaginary three-product problem. It is generally agreed that drawing such a graph is often more confusing than helpful.

Obviously, for four products the graph cannot be drawn since there are only three dimensions available in space. Therefore, for four or more products, a special set of techniques is employed to search out optimum combinations and computer packages are readily available which perform the necessary procedures.

The second simplifying factor of our example lay in its few constraints. Most production processes involve many resource inputs and each one may impose a constraint, so that for complex products, such as motor vehicles or aeroplanes, the plotting of a graph

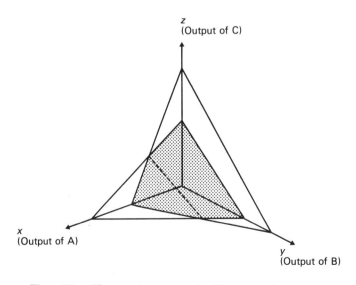

Figure 5.8   *Three products have a feasible space rather than area*

to show them all will be tedious, if not impossible. Fortunately computers do not tire and are ideally suited to manipulating large arrays of numerical data.

5.6.2 The Standard Form of the Problem

Before a linear-programming problem can be fed into a computer, it must be stated in a particular form. The exact form will vary according to the package, but all will share certain common elements.

For our example in this chapter, where the initial objective was sales revenue maximization, the standard form may be written thus:

$$\max |R| = 100x + 125y$$

$$\text{subject to } 2x + 5y \leqslant 70$$

$$x + 6y \leqslant 48$$

$$x \geqslant 10$$

Each constraint yields an inequality and each product yields a variable (x and y here). Since the computer deals basically with numbers, it is conventional in all packages to input just the numbers for the problem as shown below, where each number is situated in a column relating to its role in the problem. On many packages the operation column cannot be input direct and a variety of ways have been developed to overcome the difficulty. Students who wish to pursue this topic should consult the computer manufacturer's manual of application packages.

Objective	Product A (x)	Product B (y)	Operation	Resource limit
R	100	125		
	2	5	$\leqslant$	70
	1	6	$\leqslant$	48
	1	0	$\geqslant$	10

The computer package requires input of the array of numbers and the rules laid down in the manual must be adhered to.

ASSIGNMENTS

A5.1 An electronics company make two models of a stereo sound-mixing device, the Basic model and the Super. The components for both models are identical and there is sufficient supply for a total of 100 of the mixers to be made per month. The external finishes of the two models are different. There are labour and materials available for 60 Super models to be finished per month and it is generally reckoned that twice as many Basic models could be finished in the same time. In addition, there is a market constraint, whereby the firm agrees with its competitors (possibly illegally!) not to market more than 40 Super models per month. Each Basic model sells at £140 and each Super at £200.

(a) Show that the optimum combination for production of the two models is 80 Basics and 20 Supers.
(b) State the maximum sales revenue.

A5.2 A firm makes two kinds of roof-rack for motor cars, named Basic and De Luxe. Both pass through three production processes and take the following times:

	Process I	*Process II*	*Process III*
Basic	12 minutes	10 minutes	10 minutes
De Luxe	16 minutes	10 minutes	20 minutes

Processes I and III are available for 8 hours each day, while process II is available for 10 hours each day. Each Basic model yields a profit of £5.50 and each De Luxe model yields a profit of £9.50.

(a) State in any form you prefer the daily constraints upon the output of the two models.
(b) State the objective function if the firm's goal is to maximize daily profit.
(c) Deduce the output combination of the two models which satisfies the objective function.
(d) State the maximum daily profit and show that production process II will be lying idle for four hours each day.

A5.3 A small engineering company produces two different types of winch for use on tractors. Each winch goes through three production stages before it is ready for sale. Each type X winch requires 3 manhours on stage I, 1 manhour on stage II and 1 manhour on stage III. The corresponding figures for each type Y winch are 1, 1 and 2 manhours respectively. The weekly capacity of the three production stages are 180 manhours, 120 manhours and 135 manhours respectively.
    The firm makes £7 profit on each type X winch it sells and £9 on each type Y. The objective is to maximize total profit.
    Traditionally, the two types of winch have been produced in equal numbers. By formulating and solving a linear programme, show that the firm has been meeting its objective. State clearly any assumptions you make.

A5.4 A company makes and sells two models of a swivelling wall-mounted TV bracket under the names of Popular and Luxury which sell for £25 and £38 respectively. Both undergo three processes in manufacture and require machine time as follows:

Process	*Popular*	*Luxury*
Cutting	15 minutes	15 minutes
Assembling	15 minutes	20 minutes
Finishing	10 minutes	30 minutes

The equipment for each process is available for nine hours each day.

(a) State the daily constraints acting upon the production of the two models.
(b) State the objective function if the company intends to maximize daily output of brackets of both models.
(c) By drawing an appropriate graph, find the daily production of the two models which satisfies the objective.
(d) State the maximum daily output of brackets.
(e) State which (if any) of the processes are idle under this objective.
(f) Calculate the daily sales revenue under this objective.
(g) Show that this is *not* the maximum daily sales revenue.

A5.5 A clothing manufacturer makes, among other things, two types of shirt. One is a cheap sports shirt which yields a unit profit of £1 and the other is a high-grade dress shirt (complete with frilly front) which yields a unit profit of £3.50.

If the firm's equipment were given over entirely to the production of the cheap shirts they could make 5000 per week. The dress shirts each take five times longer to make.

For the cheap shirt, each length of material costs £2.00 and for the dress shirt, each length costs £6.00. The weekly budget for material purchase is £9000.

To maintain employment, the firm has agreed that ouput shall not fall below 1500 shirts each week, as a total of both types.

(a) State the constraints acting upon weekly production of the two shirts.
(b) State the objective function if the company intends to maximize weekly profit.
(c) Find the weekly production of the two shirts which satisfies the objective.
(d) State maximum weekly profit.
(e) In a time of economic recession, the firm decides to minimize costs by cutting output. Within the existing constraints, find the minimum cost output of the two shirts and state the minimum weekly cost.

A5.6 A firm is planning to reduce its output of an entire range of products. Two products in particular are made on a production line involving three processes.

Product A takes   20 minutes in process 1 at a cost of £5,
                 30 minutes in process 2 at a cost of £9.50 and
                 25 minutes in process 3 at a cost of £7.25.
Product B takes   50 minutes in process 1 at a cost of £3,
                 10 minutes in process 2 at a cost of £15 and
                 15 minutes in process 3 at a cost of £9.

It has been decided that each process must operate for at least 15 hours each week to prevent deterioration of the machinery and to maintain the employee-training programme.

(a) State the constraints upon production during a week's operation.
(b) State the objective function if the firm's goal is to operate at minimum processing cost.
(c) Find the combination of the two products which satisfies the firm's objective. State the processing cost for this combination.
(d) State which processes (if any) operate in excess of the 15-hour minimum, and by how long.

6—Business Forecasting: Part 1

6.1 INTRODUCTION AND OBJECTIVES

6.1.1 The Subject of the Chapter

No business, nor any administrative activity, exists just for today. All decisions and procedures must account for tomorrow and further into the future, and consequently all business people make forecasts. A shopkeeper must forecast the sales of various lines of merchandise; otherwise he would not be able to place reasonable orders with the wholesaler. A local authority must be able to forecast demand for bus services, school places, library usage and car parking: how else can plans be made which will accommodate the needs of the community? This chapter is about forecasting and uses past information to learn about the future. The methods employed and the arithmetic involved are both simple, as befits a first course. But the notion of forecasting, and the technique introduced here, is capable of extensive development in later studies, should the reader go further in business analysis. The material in this chapter answers three questions. First, what are business data like and how may they be studied? The answer will involve us in techniques known as *analysis of time-series by moving averages*. Second, how can business fluctuations be accounted for in planning? This will lead us to a consideration of *seasonal adjustment*, an idea frequently met in newspaper reports on unemployment or wage rises. Third, what will the future be like? The answer to this is one of *forecasting* proper, using data to make statements about the future.

6.1.2 Objectives

1. To understand the general nature of business data, especially those with regular or seasonal patterns of variation.
2. To be able to decompose a time-series into trend, seasonal and residual components by the method of moving averages.
3. To calculate and plot upon a graph the trend and the deseasonalized series.
4. To understand and use the concept of trend-extrapolation for forecasting purposes.
5. To reconstruct a time-series as a set of forecast values.
6. To question and evaluate the assumptions underlying these methods of analysis.

6.2   BASIC PROBLEM DATA

A car-hire company operates a coach trip service at weekends, offering mystery tours and visits to nearby seaside resorts. Recently, the service has suffered a decline and the owners contemplate its closure. To assess its viability a forecast of bookings is to be made for the next year. Records have been searched and the number of coach bookings in each quarter for a number of years has been totalled. The quarters commence in January, April, July and October.

Number of Bookings in Quarter
Year

	1	2	3	4	5	6	7
Quarter I	50	44	22	8	10	28	30
Quarter II	63	53	27	17	23	37	35
Quarter III	62	48	26	20	30	40	34
Quarter IV	48	30	12	10	24	30	20

6.3   THE PAST IS KNOWN, MORE OR LESS

6.3.1   Pictures of the Past

The booking data above are a series of numbers collected over time, describing a situation at a large number of past moments. In this case the description is simply a count of bookings. Even so, the table is a jumble of numbers and analysis of such a time-series starts with a visual impression from a graph. The data are shown in Figure 6.1. One point must be emphasized about the graph: each value is joined to the next by a short line but this should not be interpreted to mean that during those intervening times, bookings actually change. Of course, the only points on the graph which have numerical meaning are the four values each year: the short lines merely aid the visual impression.

   The recent history of the coach service can now be seen clearly. From Year 1 to Year 4 there was a steep decline in bookings which seemed to recover somewhat until Year 7 but finally suffered a further downturn. The worst quarter for bookings was the first in Year 4 when there were only eight in the three-month period. The best quarter in the later recovery was the third in Year 6. What will happen next is the question which we will attempt to answer.

6.3.2   Seasonal Fluctuations

Within the general movement in the data of Figure 6.1 we can see that each year displays a similar pattern of bookings. Typically, the first quarter's bookings are low for the year. For example in Year 1, they totalled 50 when the subsequent period totalled 63. Similarly, in Year 2, the comparison is between 44 and 53 respectively. The same pattern appears each year. In fact, the general appearance of the bookings graph is one of regular ups and downs, displaying distinct seasonal influences. First quarters, as we have seen, are relatively low for

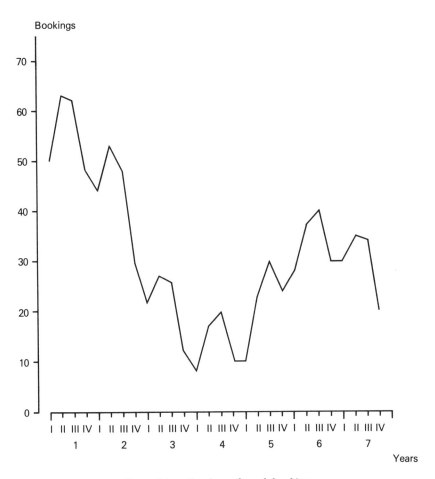

Figure 6.1   *Numbers of coach bookings*

the year; second and third are relatively high; the fourth is relatively low again. In the context of a coach trip operation, this is reasonable since excursions are less popular during the period between late Autumn and early Spring. Similar patterns often exist in the market performance of companies; within tourism it is to be expected but it is also observed in the fashion trade, in building construction, in the sale of vegetables and in milk production, to mention just a few. Sometimes the seasonality is directly attributable to climate in terms of sunshine and temperature. With other seasonal patterns, the cause may be traditional, as with the sale of Christmas cards, or economic, as with Stock Exchange prices. Whatever the reason, knowledge of the pattern permits forecasts to be made which take into account short-term fluctuation regardless of changes in the underlying long-term movements.

As an example of this possibility, the coach-booking data lead to the following approximate pattern, taking Year 4 as a model:

Mean quarterly bookings: 13.75
Quarter   I: 5.75 bookings below mean
Quarter II: 3.25 bookings above mean
Quarter III: 6.25 bookings above mean
Quarter IV: 3.75 bookings below mean

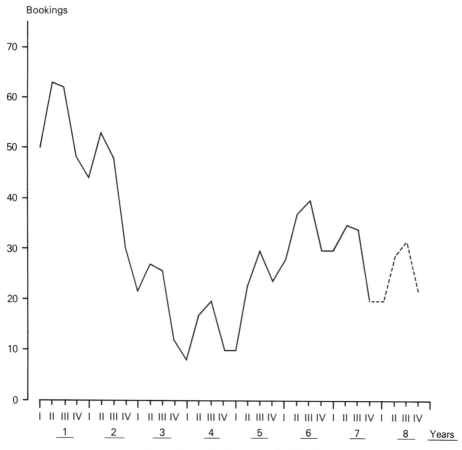

Figure 6.2   *Crude forecast for Year 8*

Consequently, if the mean of bookings for the next year after the end of the data is estimated, the detailed quarterly bookings may be forecast. Consider a simple approach to this procedure:

Year	Total bookings	Mean bookings
5	87	21.75
6	135	33.75
7	119	29.75
8	103*	25.75*

(The asterisk indicates a forecast made by continuing the decline in mean bookings between Year 6 and Year 7.)

Then a crude forecast of quarterly bookings may be made as follows:

Quarter	Seasonal effect	Mean for year	Forecast
I	− 5.75	25.75	20
II	+ 3.25	25.75	29
III	+ 6.25	25.75	32
IV	− 3.75	25.75	22

Although these forecasts have been derived by a simple averaging process, they do seem perfectly acceptable as we may see in Figure 6.2. At this elementary level, the fact that forecasts are *visually* acceptable is important and probably sufficient.

To rely upon simple averages in forecasting is a procedure obviously limited in its applicability for at least two reasons. First, in rapidly fluctuating data, the annual mean may vary in such a way as to prevent the easy 'continuing-decline' method above. Second, the seven years' data in our basic coach-hire problem contain twenty-eight values but there are only seven annual averages. The other data, in effect the other twenty-one items of information, are ignored by the method. To make forecasts, we really ought to use *all* the available data and an extension to the method is necessary to make that possible, as we shall see in section 6.4.

6.3.3   Where Are We Going?

Even the slightest glance at Figure 6.1 gives the impression that the coach-hire operation is experiencing difficult times. The partial recovery of Years 5 and 6 has not been maintained and, almost certainly, the immediate future will show continuing decline. This does not imply that the general trend will be downward forever: only that it seems unlikely to rise in the next year. In the previous section we estimated the trend by considering annual mean bookings for the last three years. Although it afforded a rough and ready analysis of general direction, no analyst would regard it as anything other than just that. To obtain a more general impression of trend in the bookings, we could draw a *free-hand curve* through the data and extend it in a way which seems to represent a likely future course. In Figure 6.3, the various dotted lines after Year 7 show how we may decide upon a 'preferred' estimate of trend. However, the concept of a general trend may be quite complicated and not restricted to just a few years. An alternative view is presented in Figure 6.4, where the word 'trend' is interpreted to mean a very long-term general tendency.

The question, 'Where are we going?' can be answered only by reference to a fundamental view of how important it is to consider a long-term analysis or even a very long-term one. As we shall see in section 6.4 there is often a convenient long term which suffices for analytical purposes but is still short enough to be translated into everyday up and down movements. Essentially, the view taken by the analyst will affect the nature of the forecast in a number of ways. First, it may limit the extent of forward looking in the forecast, since the longer the basis of the analysis, the more confident the analyst may feel in extending the trend from the known values. Also, the seasonality perceived in a time-series will depend upon the length of the assumed trend-period. Daily fluctuations may be quite important in a monthly view, but would hardly be worth considering if an annual analysis were to be carried out. Conversely, a five-year fluctuation from peak to peak, as may be observed in such economic variables as inflation rate or unemployment, will be analysed certainly without regard to daily or weekly changes, or perhaps even monthly or quarterly changes. As we shall see, such problems of analysis are often solved subjectively; that is, by a mixture of intuition and 'good practice'.

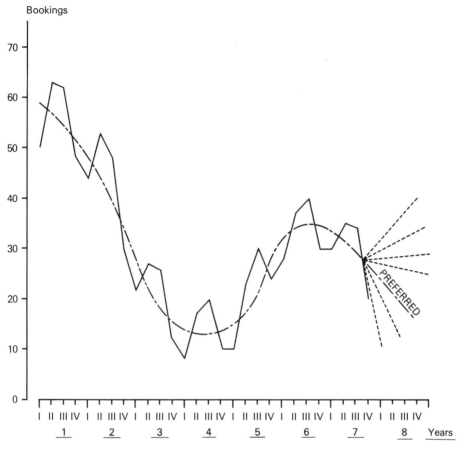

Figure 6.3   *Subjective view of the trend*

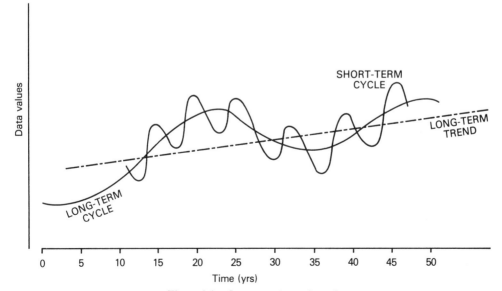

Figure 6.4   *Interpretations of trend*

6.4   DISSECTING THE PAST

6.4.1   The Sum of Experience

Any business data which fluctuate can be envisaged as being built up from components. As Figure 6.5 suggests, each value in a time-series represents an underlying trend combined with a regular (or seasonal) component, and probably also with an error component which reflects the uncertainty of business life.

The data value marked X in Figure 6.5 is greater than that marked Y; that is, it is higher up the vertical scale. Why is it greater? Partly because the general trend in the data is upwards as time passes; partly because X occurs at a different season than does Y in the sense that they are at opposite stages in a cycle. In addition, we ought perhaps to admit that the difference given by $(X - Y)$ includes the random component mentioned above. If such a model is adopted then we may construct an equation as follows:

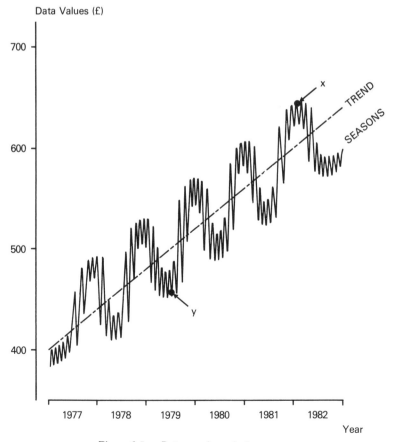

Figure 6.5   *Data equal trend plus season*

$$\text{Actual data} = \text{Trend value} + \text{Seasonal effect} + \text{Random error}$$

or symbolically,
$$\text{Data} = T + S + R$$

The purpose of time-series analysis later in this chapter is to *explain* data, from which it may be possible then to *forecast* on the basis of simple assumptions. For example, point X in Figure 6.5 is about thirty months later than point Y. Ignoring seasonal influences, we would predict X as taking the value £600. From the top of a cycle to the trend is apparently about £35. Thus we would predict X as being about £635 per month, the 'about' indicating the random error since no analyst would insist on a spot value being exactly correct.

6.4.2 Getting Rid of the Ups and Downs

The determination of trend requires removal of seasonal and random influences from data. Symbolically we are subtracting S and R from the data, as follows:

$$\text{Trend} = \text{Data} - \text{Seasonal effect} - \text{Random error}$$

$$T = (T + S + R) - S - R$$

The problem, clearly, is to remove S and R, and this is accomplished by the method of moving averages which is an extension of the simple averaging method used in section 6.3.2. Instead of calculating only one average for each year, giving seven for the coach-booking data, we shall consider successive four-quarter periods. Thus we shall consider a whole year of data throughout, but each year will start at a successively later quarter. For the basic problem data we could calculate a moving average as follows:

First four values (50, 63, 62, 48): total 223: mean 55.75
Next four values (63, 62, 48, 44): total 217: mean 54.25
Next four values (62, 48, 44, 53): total 207: mean 51.75
Next four values (48, 44, 53, 48): total 193: mean 48.25

And so on, for successive four-quarter periods. If the reader plots these values on Figure 6.1, it will be seen that averaging over a full annual cycle has removed the seasonal component. However, a major problem arises in graphing such moving averages: at what instant in time shall a moving average be plotted to represent the year from which it is calculated? It seems reasonable to plot each at its mid-year point but, because years are defined by four quarters, the mid-year point is between the second and third quarters. This is not a convenient moment in time since the moving average cannot be compared directly with any actual data value. For this reason a slight modification is employed in calculating the moving average, in which the simple four-quarter means are further averaged by a 'centring' procedure. A second benefit derives from the extra averaging applied to the data which further rids the data of seasonal effects. The centred-sum procedure can be shown in principle as follows:

Year	Quarter	Data	Moving total	Centred sum	Moving average
1	I	50	—	—	—
	II	63	223	—	—
	III	62	217	440	55
	IV	48	207	424	53
2	I	44			
	II	53			
			etc.	etc.	etc.

Table 6.1 *Calculation of the moving average.*

Year	Quarter	Coach bookings	Moving annual total	Centred sum	Moving annual average
1	I	50	–	–	–
	II	63	223	–	–
	III	62	217	440	55
	IV	48	207	424	53
2	I	44	193	400	50
	II	53	175	368	46
	III	48	153	328	41
	IV	30	127	280	35
3	I	22	105	232	29
	II	27	87	192	24
	III	26	73	160	20
	IV	12	63	136	17
4	I	8	57	120	15
	II	17	55	112	14
	III	20	57	112	14
	IV	10	63	120	15
5	I	10	73	136	17
	II	23	87	160	20
	III	30	105	192	24
	IV	24	119	224	28
6	I	28	129	248	31
	II	37	135	264	33
	III	40	137	272	34
	IV	30	135	272	34
7	I	30	129	264	33
	II	35	119	248	31
	III	34	–	–	–
	IV	20		–	–

The full calculation is shown in Table 6.1 and it may appear a daunting procedure for the reader to undertake such analysis. In fact, it is simple arithmetic and there is a trick to finding the moving total. Once the first total is obtained, the next is an adjustment involving the addition of the next data value in the series and the subtraction of the trailing value. The reader merely covers up three values and adjusts by the difference of the numbers to be added or subtracted. In our coach-booking example, the first annual total is 223 and the next is equal to $223 + 44 - 50$ which is $223 - 6$, i.e. 217 as the table shows. The moving average is one-eighth of the centred sum since eight original values (coach bookings) comprise the sum itself.

As we saw in the simple averaging example above, the essential feature of a trend is its ability to portray the general movement within data, without regard to seasonal variation.

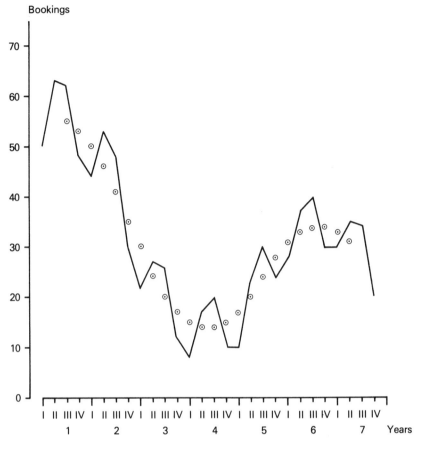

Figure 6.6 *The trend in coach bookings*

That the centred moving average possesses such an ability is shown in Figure 6.6. It passes through the succession of annual cycles and gives a clear impression of direction. Of particular interest is the last section, in Year 7, where we can see that a downturn has indeed occurred. One other noticeable feature which arises from the procedure of calculation is that two quarters of the trend have been 'lost' from the front of the time-series and another two from the rear. A whole year is missing from any comparison between data and trend; it is unavoidable. Even so, a basis has been obtained for further analysis of the data: we have obtained *T*.

6.4.3   The Four Seasons

By the definition of the trend in the previous section, any numerical difference between data and trend must represent the remaining components—seasonality and random errors. For example, the coach bookings deviate from trend as we have seen and a list of deviations may be obtained as in Table 6.2. The column headed 'Deviation' is calculated by subtracting the

Table 6.2   *Removal of trend from the data.*

Year	Quarter	Coach bookings $(T + S + R)$	Moving annual average (T)	Deviation $(S + R)$
1	I	50	–	–
	II	63	–	–
	III	62	55	+ 7
	IV	48	53	– 5
2	I	44	50	– 6
	II	53	46	+ 7
	III	48	41	+ 7
	IV	30	35	– 5
3	I	22	29	– 7
	II	27	24	+ 3
	III	26	20	+ 6
	IV	12	17	– 5
4	I	8	15	– 7
	II	17	14	+ 3
	III	20	14	+ 6
	IV	10	15	– 5
5	I	10	17	– 7
	II	23	20	+ 3
	III	30	24	+ 6
	IV	24	28	– 4
6	I	28	31	– 3
	II	37	33	+ 4
	III	40	34	+ 6
	IV	30	34	– 4
7	I	30	33	– 3
	II	35	31	+ 4
	III	34	–	–
	IV	20	–	–

trend (as the moving annual average) from the data. Symbolically, we subtract T from $T + S + R$ to yield $S + R$, which is the remaining component due to seasonal and random influences. The plus and minus signs indicate whether or not the data are above trend (with a + sign) or below it (with a – sign).

Also noticeable in Table 6.2 is the regularity of the seasonal influence: the plus and minus signs. They occur in pairs so that Quarter II and Quarter III each year are clearly above trend, and the other two are below. This confirms the impression already gained from Figure 6.6 and from the original table of coach bookings. Even so, these deviations from trend are not the seasonal variations we desire to isolate since they contain also R, the random element in the data. This fact may be inferred by consideration of each of the first quarters, as follows:

Year	1	2	3	4	5	6	7
First quarter deviation		– 6	– 7	– 7	– 7	– 3	– 3

Since we have adopted a model which states that S is a constant added to or subtracted from the trend, the differences in these values may be attributed to R. To eliminate R, we must make a simple assumption: that over a long period of time the mean value of R will be zero, which raises a major difficulty. Do the data values in the coach-booking series constitute a long period of time? The answer must be that they probably do not. Most business analysts would expect at least fifty data values for the assumption to be justified. For our purposes, we must make the assumption and take it to be valid, despite the relative paucity of data: only by doing so can we progress to a fuller analysis of this market. Symbolically, we are assuming for each quarter that:

$$\text{Mean } (S + R) = S + \text{Mean } (R)$$

$$= S + \qquad \text{since Mean } (R) = 0 \text{ over a long period}$$

$$= S$$

As we shall see, a slight residual error occurs for the data available but it is sufficiently small to be immaterial in terms of real-life coach bookings.

The process of isolating each S component is accomplished in Table 6.3. Again, the regularity of the plus and minus signs is apparent in the columns and is clearly an important feature of the seasonal means. The conclusions to be reached are that each Quarter I is 5.5 bookings below trend, each Quarter II is 4 bookings above trend, each Quarter III is 6.3 bookings above trend and each Quarter IV is 4.7 below trend. Note that these are calculated to one place of decimal fractions, which introduces a small rounding error at the same time as being unrealistic: fractional bookings cannot occur. However, if the data had been continuous in nature, such as money or time, the fractions would have meaning and should be calculated to a reasonable degree of precision.

Table 6.3   *Calculation of seasonal components*

Year	Quarter			
	I	*II*	*III*	*IV*
1	−	−	+ 7	− 5
2	− 6	+ 7	+ 7	− 5
3	− 7	+ 3	+ 6	− 5
4	− 7	+ 3	+ 6	− 5
5	− 7	+ 3	+ 6	− 4
6	− 3	+ 4	+ 6	− 4
7	− 3	+ 4	−	−
Totals	− 33	+ 24	+ 38	− 28
Means	− 5.5	+ 4	+ 6.3	− 4.7
Rounded	− 5	+ 4	+ 6	− 5

The residual error arising from R can be seen in Table 6.3 where the sum of the four quarterly deviations is not zero. If our model were a perfect description of the series and the R assumption were valid, then all above-trend values would be cancelled by all below-trend values. This is not the case here since the negatives total − 10.2 (rounded) whereas the positives total + 10.3 (rounded). However, the discrepancy is very small and we could accept it without its casting doubt upon the model. If the net R effect is not so small, then each seasonal mean must be adjusted to preserve a near-zero position in total.

In conclusion, the seasonal components in the series can be summarized as follows. It seems reasonable to round off the values to the nearest whole number, and the half rounded downwards. (It is widely adopted as a convention that halves are rounded to yield the odd number, rather than the even one.)

Quarter	I	II	III	IV
Quarterly component (S)	− 5	+ 4	+ 6	− 5

We are now in a position to 'dismantle' the coach-bookings data and then to use the components for forecasting.

6.4.4   The Real Coach Bookings

If coach bookings are defined as $T + S + R$, and if S can be subtracted, then we can obtain just $T + R$ by doing so. Such a series of values is usually referred to as *seasonally adjusted* data since it represents what would have happened if there were no seasonal component.

Table 6.4   *Seasonal adjustment of the data.*

Year	Quarter	Coach bookings $(T + S + R)$	Seasonal component (S)	Seasonally adjusted bookings $(T + R)$
1	I	50	− 5	55
	II	63	+ 4	59
	III	62	+ 6	56
	IV	48	− 5	53
2	I	44	− 5	49
	II	53	+ 4	49
	III	48	+ 6	42
	IV	30	− 5	35
3	I	22	− 5	27
	II	27	+ 4	23
	III	26	+ 6	20
	IV	12	− 5	17
4	I	8	− 5	13
	II	17	+ 4	13
	III	20	+ 6	14
	IV	10	− 5	15
5	I	10	− 5	15
	II	23	+ 4	19
	III	30	+ 6	24
	IV	24	− 5	29
6	I	28	− 5	33
	II	37	+ 4	33
	III	40	+ 6	34
	IV	30	− 5	35
7	I	30	− 5	35
	II	35	+ 4	31
	III	34	+ 6	28
	IV	20	− 5	25

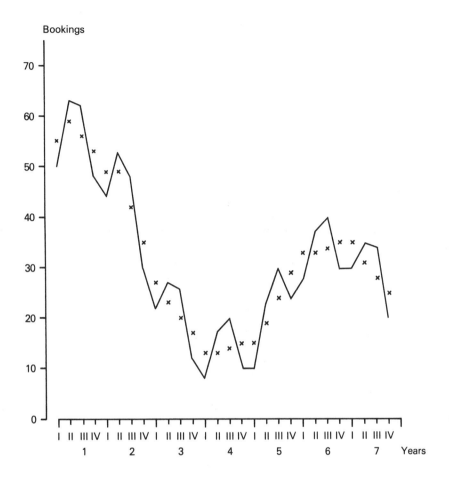

Figure 6.7 *Seasonally adjusted coach bookings*

It permits us to compare values at different moments in time without the seasons causing confusion. For example, Year 1, Quarter IV has 48 bookings, and so has Year 2, Quarter III. The fact that they are equal does not mean there has been no change in the market, but that the seasonal influence has overridden 'real' bookings. A proper comparison requires that seasonal influences be removed. This is accomplished in Table 6.4: the column headed 'Seasonal component (S)' has the rounded values from the previous section, repeated in groups of four throughout the seven years of data. When S is subtracted from the data, what remains is the underlying trend (T) and the unpredictable random component (R). Note that subtraction of a negative S results in addition, of course.

Most official statistics are presented in seasonally adjusted form, since only then can direct comparisons be made. As Figure 6.7 shows, seasonally adjusted data superficially look like the trend but they are not the same since they include the random market disturbance. It is now clear that the coach-booking business suffered a real decline from Year 1 to Year 4 and then experienced a real recovery until the end of Year 6, after which another real decline set in. The word 'real' may be interpreted to mean 'not due to short-term influences': the shape of the graph reflects fundamental changes in the circumstances of the business.

6.5   THE FUTURE COULD BE LIKE THE PAST

6.5.1   Extrapolation

Forecasting is doomed to failure if it is expected to yield spot predictions of future values. The best that should be expected of it is 'a view of the future' in the sense that it should provide a general foundation upon which plans may be based. Any method of forecasting primarily must be reliable: it should be applicable in a wide range of circumstances and yield similar estimates under similar conditions. Accuracy is also important but secondary because the search for it is generally thought to be fruitless. By its nature, forecasting requires a philosophy which accepts that the future will, in all important respects, be like the past. If it is, we can forecast. If it is not, then the uncertainty swamps any analysis we may have performed. This chapter, indeed this book, is based on the assumption that such a philosophical approach is valid.

Since data have been defined symbolically as $T + S + R$, a simple forecast can be obtained by reversing the dissection process. A future data value for the coach bookings may be constructed as follows:

$$\text{Forecast bookings} = T^* + S^* + R^*$$

Here the asterisk indicates 'the expected value of'. For R^* we would expect zero, since that was a basic assumption behind the analysis of data. For S^* we have the seasonal components calculated in section 6.4.3. For T^* we need an estimate and Figure 6.8 suggests one method of obtaining it. Within the infinite possibilities of the future, some trends are more credible than others and one in particular is most acceptable: it is marked by a dotted line.

Such a process of extending the trend outside the time-range of the data is called *extrapolation*. The estimates of future trend in this case are 28, 25, 22 and so on. From these, future bookings may be forecast by reversing the data dissection as in Table 6.5. By adding the regular seasonal component to estimated trend we obtain forecasts for the following year, Year 8. Note that the first two 'forecasts' correspond to known coach bookings: 34 in Year 7 Quarter III and 20 in Year 7 Quarter IV. Table 6.5 'forecasts' these to be 34 bookings and 20 bookings respectively, which lends validity to the model we have used.

The forecasts for Year 8 are as follows:

> Year 8   Quarter   I   17 bookings
> Quarter   II   23 bookings
> Quarter III   22 bookings
> Quarter IV   8 bookings
> Total bookings for the year: 70 bookings

If we now add the forecasts to the graph of the original series, we can see exactly how our method has performed. Figure 6.9 gives a good visual impression and above all else looks credible! This is not an unimportant feature especially in communication with management, when impressions count for so much.

6.5.2   Important Questions

The assumptions upon which the moving average method of forecasting is based are simple but sweeping. Two in particular must be borne in mind and questioned:

1. That seasonal variations are constant. It could be that the passage of time affects a business such that the heights of each peak and the depths of each trough change. If that were to happen, we would not be able to adopt a group of S values as constants to be added to trend. The reader should consider again the deviations in Table 6.3 and ask the question, 'Do they seem to have the same general magnitude in Year 1 and Year 7?' If the answer is a quite definite 'No', then the method is in doubt.

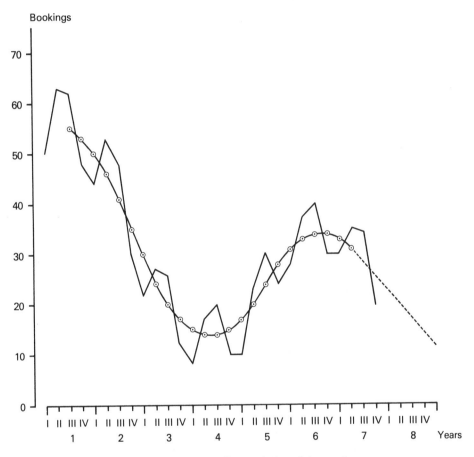

Figure 6.8 *Extrapolation of the trend*

Table 6.5 *Reconstructing for forecasts*

Year	Quarter	Estimated trend	Seasonal component	Forecast bookings
7	III	28	+ 6	34
	IV	25	− 5	20
8	I	22	− 5	17
	II	19	+ 4	23
	III	16	+ 6	22
	IV	13	− 5	8

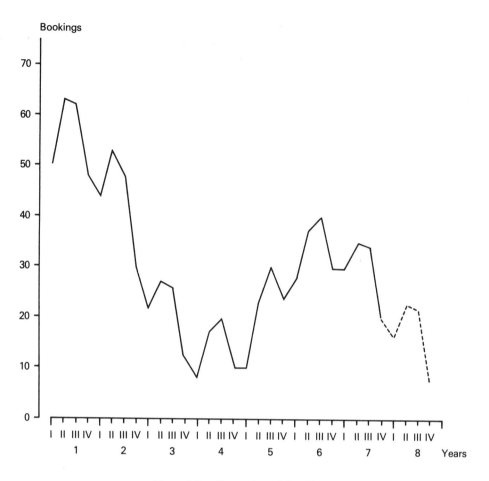

Figure 6.9   *Forecast coach bookings*

2. That trend will continue to behave as it did in the past. This is equivalent to saying that the future will contain no surprises or catastrophies. Really, such an assumption should be made only if the past has been regular and more or less free from shocks. This is a true weakness of all forecasting: it works for data which are easy to forecast! Unfortunately, the forecasts businesses want for difficult situations, not easy ones.

Finally, there is one major difficulty in all averaging methods: it is deciding the period of time over which the series is to be smoothed. In the basic problem data above, a one-year period was obviously the most appropriate. However, some data do not display regular fluctuations, so that one year does not cover a whole cycle. It is most important to average over a cycle and so eliminate each cycle's variation. When a clear cycle does not present itself, the analyst must experiment until a suitable degree of smoothing is obtained in the trend. There is an assignment at the end of the chapter which exemplifies this difficulty.

Smoothing a series over a whole cycle means taking four quarters in the moving total when data are available in quarterly form. If they are in the form of monthly values, the moving total should include twelve values. Otherwise the basic method is the same. The last assignment at the end of the chapter gives an example of such data.

ASSIGNMENTS

A6.1 A seaside gift shop is to be sold, and the auctioneer's prospectus is required to state 'typical quarterly turnover' and give an estimate of the total turnover in the four quarters of 1983. The following data are available:

	Quarters			
	I	II	III	IV
1979	22	34	32	18
1980	18	28	28	16
1981	14	22	20	12
1982	16	22	24	16
1983	16	24		

(Turnover × £1000)

(a) Decompose this series by moving averages and state the seasonal components.
(b) Plot the data on a time-series graph together with the trend component.
(c) State the information you would make available for the prospectus, commenting upon the validity of the phrase 'typical quarterly turnover'.

A6.2 An estate agent is concerned that his business is failing because of local slum clearance work. He decides that he will wind up the business unless he seems able to sell thirty houses over the next year. He has the following data on quarterly sales:

Year	*Quarter*	*Houses Sold*
1978	I	12
	II	24
	III	22
	IV	8
1979	I	8
	II	18
	III	18
	IV	6
1980	I	4
	II	12
	III	10
	IV	2
1981	I	6
	II	12
	III	14
	IV	6
1982	I	6
	II	14

(a) Obtain the seasonal components for house sales and deseasonalize the data. Hence compare the lowest quarterly sales (in 1980) with the 'real' trough in the house market.
(b) Do you believe that this estate agent will decide to close his business?

A6.3 A financial analyst is asked by a client to investigate the changing price of a particular company share. He obtains the following information for the first Thursday in each of January, April, July and October.

	Month			
	Jan	Apr	July	Oct
1979	91	94	103	95
1980	99	102	109	101
1981	104	105	113	103
1982	106	107	114	104
1983	106	107	114	103

(Pence per share)

(a) Explain the assumptions that must be made regarding the other eight months' data each year, if this series is to be smoothed by moving averages.

(b) Forecast the price of this share on 1 January and 1 April 1984.

(c) Explain the problems in forecasting the price on 15 March or 21 April 1984.

A6.4 (In this assignment, the difficulty is that of deciding the averaging period. The reader should experiment with more than one period; if an odd time-period is chosen the centring of the sum is unnecessary, in which case the moving total will be divided by the odd number of the averaging period. Awkward fractions should be rounded to one place of decimals.)

A forestry corporation is planning to develop and sell dwarfed varieties of wood-land trees such as oak, walnut and poplar. A team of scientific and commercial analysts is sent to a number of Scottish islands to investigate growing conditions. Of particular concern is the annual rainfall which must have a mean of 135 centimetres if the young saplings are to thrive. Rainfall data for the last twenty-eight years are available:

Year	1954	1955	1956	1957	1958	1959	1960
Rainfall (cm)	137	142	154	129	139	136	152

Year	1961	1962	1963	1964	1965	1966	1967
Rainfall (cm)	141	150	140	128	138	156	131

Year	1968	1969	1970	1971	1972	1973	1974
Rainfall (cm)	139	135	139	155	136	139	136

Year	1975	1976	1977	1978	1979	1980	1981
Rainfall (cm)	160	127	160	151	150	142	136

(a) Plot the rainfall data on a graph, inspect the peaks and troughs, and decide the number of years needed to make up an averaging cycle.

(b) Calculate the moving average using your cycle period and plot it on the graph.

(c) Is the average rainfall sufficient for the saplings to thrive?

(d) Increase your cycle period by one year and perform the analysis again. Discuss the relative performance of the calculations.

(e) How confident would you feel about forecasting rainfall for the next three years? (Hint: try to establish the pattern of regular variations above the moving average.)

A6.5 (In this assignment, the calculation will be lengthy. The data cycle is twelve months and smoothing must be accomplished by moving totals over that period.)

The number of wedding rings sold by a jeweller in each month over a number of years is given below. The manager believes that there is an upward trend in sales.

	Year			
	1980	1981	1982	1983
Jan	16	19	15	18
Feb	21	20	26	24
Mar	47	46	48	49
Apr	39	38	39	41
May	16	15	17	18
June	22	24	24	27
July	30	34	31	31
Aug	28	31	26	32
Sept	51	48	51	54
Oct	41	41	37	35
Nov	16	14	10	15
Dec	30	36	34	31

(Rings per month)

(a) Plot these data on a graph and superimpose upon them the annual trend.

(b) Obtain the monthly variations and deseasonalize the data.

(c) Compare the general appearance of both the trend and the seasonally adjusted data. Discuss the major differences and what they mean in terms both of the data and the method.

(d) Do you believe that the manager is correct about the trend?

(e) Forecast the next six months' sales of rings.

7—Business and Economic Changes

7.1 INTRODUCTION AND OBJECTIVES

7.1.1 The Subject of the Chapter

If there is one aspect of business life that is ever present, and which makes planning so difficult, it is its variability. Everything seems to change: prices, quality, output, demand, efficiency and profitability. It is important for the analyst to be able to measure such changes, partly to keep track of what has been happening and partly to form a base of data from which to plan the future.

The changes to be analysed in this chapter refer specifically to prices and costs, although the method can be applied quite easily to quantities. In technical terms, these methods are usually referred to as *index numbers*. They are widely used in business and official statistics, and even the most junior analyst ought to be acquainted with them.

7.1.2 Objectives

1. To understand the need for composite measures of change and apply simple percentage calculations to the problem.
2. To calculate price-relatives and consider difficulties in their aggregation.
3. To understand the need for a system of weights in aggregating price-relatives and to derive them from available data.
4. To calculate an all-item index with simple weights, base quantity weights and current quantity weights.
5. To be able to convert a fixed-base index to a chain-base index and vice versa.
6. To be able to rebase an index at a different moment in time.

7.2 BASIC PROBLEM DATA

The Chairman of the Board of a company has heard that a group of shareholders is planning to raise embarrassing questions about the low interim dividend paid in the first half-year. He decides to incorporate in his 1983 Annual Report a statement about rising costs and asks the Financial Director to investigate ways of presenting the information. Eventually, a financial assistant is set to work upon the problem and the following data are obtained:

Item	1981 Unit cost	1982 Unit cost	1983 Unit cost	Total cost 1983
Direct labour[a]	£3 per hour	£3.30 per hour	£3.60 per hour	£200 000
Administration[a]	£100 per month	£106 per month	£112 per month	£100 000
Materials	£125 per ton	£150 per ton	£180 per ton	£550 000
Equipment	£3600 per unit	£4000 per unit	£5000 per unit	£ 50 000
Power	4.8p per unit	5.4p per unit	6.0p per unit	£100 000

([a]typical employee in this sort of work)

He is charged with the job of finding out, 'How much have our costs risen recently?'

7.3   MEASURING THE CHANGES

7.3.1   Choose a Starting Year

The very idea of change implies that a base has been established from which changes may be measured. It seems reasonable with the data in the basic problem to regard 1981 as the *base year* since it is the first. However, this need not be the case, as we shall see later.

Clearly, the unit cost of all the items have risen throughout the period 1981–1983, probably as a reflection of the general trend of inflation within the economy at large. From the point of view of the Chairman, a two-year increase will be more dramatic than one, and so to base the 1983 increases on 1981 would be a good idea.

Having selected a base year, the real problem is that of measuring the rate of change. Direct labour costs rose by 30 pence per hour between 1981 and 1982, which is a 10 per cent rise. In the next year it rose again by 30 pence per hour, resulting in a 60 pence or 20 per cent rise over the two years 1981–1983. However, the 30 pence increase in 1982–1983 did not represent a 10 per cent increase, since 30 pence is only about nine per cent of £3.30. Here we see the importance of the base year: to give a consistent picture of increases we require a single basis for comparison. (There is an exception to this rule which will be considered later.) Using this approach we may construct Table 7.1 to show changes in unit cost over the two-year period.

It is clear from Table 7.1 that materials have risen most rapidly in cost and administration least rapidly. For example, the £55 increase in materials' unit cost is expressed as a percentage in the usual way:

$$\text{Percentage increase} = \frac{£55}{£125} \times 100 = 44\%$$

Similarly, equipment has increased by a percentage given as follows:

$$\text{Percentage increase} = \frac{£1400}{£3600} \times 100 = 39\% \text{ (rounded)}$$

The question to be answered now is, 'What has been the overall rate of cost increase suffered by the company since 1981?' There is no simple answer unless we are prepared to accept a vague statement such as, 'Somewhere between 12 per cent and 44 per cent'. Of

Table 7.1   *Percentage increases in prices*

	1981	1982			1983		
Item	*Base-year unit cost*	*Unit cost*	*Increase since 1981*	*Per cent increase*	*Unit cost*	*Increase since 1981*	*Per cent increase*
Direct labour	£3 per hour	£3.30	30p	10	£3.60	60p	20
Administration	£100 per month	£106	£6	6	£112	£12	12
Materials	£125 per ton	£150	£25	20	£180	£55	44
Equipment	£3600 per unit	£4000	£400	11[a]	£5000	£1400	39[a]
Power	4.8p per unit	5.4p	0.6p	12.5	6.0p	1.2p	25

[a]These numbers are rounded.

course, a different approach would be to compare total expenditure in each year, but to do so would fail to identify cost increases in individual items and, presumably, there is something to be gained by blaming low dividends on material, equipment and power. The fact that administration has risen least rapidly is a point worth including in any analysis.

7.3.2   A Measure for Change

Since 1981 is the base year, we will let unit costs that year be called 100 for each expenditure item. In other words, the £3.00 per hour for direct labour is to be called 100; the £100 per month for administration is to be called 100 and so on. This is to be interpreted to mean that base-year unit costs are 100 per cent of base-year unit costs. Sometimes the 100 will correspond to an actual amount of £100 (as with administration) but generally it merely represents a starting point.

  If base unit costs are shown as 100, then later unit costs can be shown on the same scale. The 1982 unit cost of direct labour will be 110 since it is 10 per cent higher than the base value. Such a value is called the *price-relative for direct labour* and may be calculated as follows:

$$\text{Price-relative} = \frac{1982 \text{ unit cost}}{1981 \text{ unit cost}} = \frac{£3.30}{£3.00} \times 100 = 110$$

Similarly, the price-relative for power in 1982 may be calculated as follows:

$$\text{Price-relative} = \frac{1982 \text{ unit cost}}{1981 \text{ unit cost}} = \frac{5.4}{4.8} \times 100 = 112.5$$

Notice how these values agree with the percentage increases given in Table 7.1. For power, the price-relative is interpreted to mean that in 1982 unit power costs were 112.5 per cent of 1981 unit power cost. For each item of expenditure, the price-relatives for 1982 and 1983 are given Table 7.2. As a general principle, the price-relative for any item is given by:

$$\text{Price-relative} = \frac{\text{current unit cost in year under consideration}}{\text{base unit cost}} \times 100$$

  Table 7.2 reinforces the impression gained from Table 7.1 that materials and equipment have increased most rapidly in cost. It is easy and convenient to think of price-relatives as percentages of base-year costs, even though conventionally the percentage sign is omitted.

Table 7.2   *Price-relatives based on 1981*

Item	1981 price-relatives	1982 price-relatives	1983 price-relatives
Direct labour	100	110	120
Administration	100	106	112
Materials	100	120	144
Equipment	100	111[a]	139[a]
Power	100	112.5	125

[a]These numbers are rounded.

7.3.3   Combining a Number of Changes

If the search is for a single figure to represent cost inflation in the Annual Report, the price-relatives must be combined in a way that reflects the value of each of them. The easiest way would be simply to find the mean price-relative in each year: to find the 'average cost increase'. Thus for 1982, the mean price-relative is the sum $(110 + 106 + 120 + 111 + 112.5)$ divided by 5, to yield 112 rounded to a whole number. For 1983, the mean price-relative is found to be 128, by the same procedure. Table 7.3 summarizes the calculations so far and gives the mean price-relative its usual name of 'index'; in this case the index is a crude average. From Table 7.3 the conclusion could be drawn that, on the whole, taking all expenditure items into account, the costs for the company rose by 12 per cent in the year 1981–1982 and by 28 per cent over the period 1981–1983. As a matter of interest, we may also say that costs rose by about 14 per cent in the year 1982–1983 since the index rose by 16 points from 112 as follows:

$$\text{Percentage increase} = \frac{128 - 112}{112} \times 100$$

$$= \frac{16}{112} \times 100$$

$$= 14.3\%$$

Table 7.3   *Mean price-relatives*

Year	1981	1982	1983
Crude index of costs	100	112	128

There are unsatisfactory features about the information in Table 7.3. It is true that equipment unit cost has risen considerably and, no doubt, this will have contributed to the index values. However, although unit cost of equipment is the second most rapid increase, and per item is by far the most expensive, it has not constituted a major purchase by the company in 1983. Indeed, equipment purchase is by far the smallest item of expenditure at £50 000 out of a budget of £1 million. By contrast, materials have not only risen most rapidly in unit cost, they also constitute the largest single category of expenditure at £550 000 in 1983. The administration unit cost has risen least rapidly and constitutes a moderate proportion of total expenditure, in excess of both power and equipment. What we are seeing here are differences in the 'importance' of each item as regards the company's total costs of operation. It seems reasonable to say that an 'important' item which carries a high price-relative is of greater concern than an 'unimportant' item carrying the same price-relative. Clearly, to answer the question posed to him, the financial assistant must obtain a more balanced approach to these two aspects of price-relative and importance. There is a need for a system of weights to be attached to the price-relatives and a clue as to their nature lies in the basic data of section 7.2.

7.3.4   How Important is Administration?

Of the £1 million spent by this company in 1983, £100 000 was used to pay administrative staff. Another way of considering the same information is that 10 pence in every £1 went on staff. Similarly, 20 pence went on labour, 55 pence on materials, 5 pence on equipment and 10 pence on power. The relative importance of the items can now be assessed easily. The least important item of expenditure was equipment, even though the unit cost was by far the greatest and the 1981–1983 price-relative was second highest. Here is a better basis for averaging (or aggregating, as it is often called) the price-relatives. The calculation is in every way similar to that for the arithmetic mean except that weights are used instead of frequencies, as shown in Table 7.4. The product of price-relatives (p) and weights (w) in each year is divided by the total weight which will be 100 when percentages are used as weights. The formula for this weighted aggregate in Year n is given by I_n as follows:

$$I_n = \frac{\Sigma(p \times w)}{\Sigma w}$$

(Note: the Σ sign indicates the sum over all items, as used previously.)

Table 7.4   *Weighted-aggregate index*

		1981		1982		1983	
Item	*Weight (w)*	*Price relative (p)*	*p × w*	*p*	*p × w*	*p*	*p × w*
Direct labour	20	100	2000	110	2200	120	2400
Administration	10	100	1000	106	1060	112	1120
Materials	55	100	5500	120	6600	144	7920
Equipment	5	100	500	111	555	139	695
Power	10	100	1000	112.5	1125	125	1250
Totals	100		10 000		11 540		13 385
All-item cost index		100		115.4		133.9	

The weight system has had a marked effect upon the aggregated price-relatives, by raising them above the crude values in Table 7.3. Clearly, the heavy weight attached to materials, when combined with the rapid cost increase has overridden the smaller cost increases in labour and administration. From the point of view of the Chairman of the Board, the effect of weighting has been highly satisfactory. It has shown that, for the business as a whole, costs rose by over 15 per cent in the year 1981–1982 and by nearly 34 per cent in the two years 1981–1983. These facts may help forestall shareholder criticism since, by implication, profits are under pressure.

As a conclusion to this analysis, it is worth stating the sort of information that the financial assistant should produce for the Financial Director. First, the relative importance of each item is of interest, especially since it shows that materials constitute the major expenditure and that administration is much less important. Second, the cost increases for the five items should be given, possibly in the form given in Table 7.5. Finally, the aggregate cost index should be given to show the overall effect.

Table 7.5   *Information for the Chairman*

Item	Total cost 1983	Unit increase 1981–82	Unit increase 1981-83
Direct labour	£200 000	10%	20%
Administration	£100 000	6%	12%
Materials	£550 000	20%	44%
Equipment	£ 50 000	11%	39%
Power	£100 000	12.5%	25%

Year	1981	1982	1983
Overall cost index	100	115.4	133.9

As a matter of terminology the aggregate cost index calculated in this section is sometimes referred to as the all-item index, or sometimes as the weighted aggregate. Both names are good descriptions of what is meant.

7.4   THE COST OF LIVING INDEX

Every month the Central Statistical Office publishes data on wages and prices, so that trade unions, newspapers and the broadcasting services can inform the population at large. Of particular interest to business people, and the private individual, is a single figure correctly named the Retail Prices Index. It is known commonly as the 'cost of living index' since that is the interpretation usually placed upon it: it measures how inflation affects the living standards of private households. It is an aggregated price-relative and is presented in the form of a table published in the *Monthly Digest of Statistics*. This publication is one through which every business person should browse from time to time.

A number of interesting features are apparent in the Retail Prices Index. First, the choice of base year; 1974 was a year when the previous index rose to values around 200 and most analysts, let alone private individuals, tend to lose track of the annual rate of change when this happens. The index was rebased in 1974 to start again at 100. Secondly, the weights attached to the various categories of household expenditure represent their import-ance within family budgets. For example, food has a weight of 230 out of a total of 1000, indicating that about 23 per cent of household expenditure is upon all items of food con-sumed in the home. Such information for each category is obtained by regular social research resulting in the annual publication *Family Expenditure Survey* (HMSO). The reader should consider the various weights given for 1980–1981 and be sure that their meaning is clear: see Assignment 7.4.

7.5 WAYS ROUND THE WEIGHTING PROBLEM

7.5.1 Disagreement Over Weights

It is not always easy to assign weights to price-relatives in the way that we have seen earlier in the chapter. The concept of importance has so many different interpretations that weights approved by one group of analysts may seem inappropriate to others. For instance, the Retail Prices Index (RPI) applies its categories to a typical household and is consequently inapplicable to certain households such as pensioners, large families with many children, the disabled, the unemployed, families on low incomes or the aristocracy. Each of these groups will have expenditure patterns other than those suggested by the RPI weights. Pensioners probably spend far more than 23 per cent of their incomes on food, for example. To raise pensions in line with the RPI could result in pensioners' being worse off if food prices rise more rapidly that the all-item index. Similarly, altering unemployment or sickness bene-fits in accordance with the RPI may not have the desired effect since the recipients presum-ably do not spend the typical proportion of their incomes upon restaurant meals or trans-port. In short, untypical groups experience different weightings within their expenditure patterns.

In terms of the basic problem data a similar difficulty may arise. Relating weights to current total expenditure could give a false impression: the expenditure upon each item will have changed over the years and so will the importance of each. In the early years of the company's operation equipment purchase would have constituted a major expenditure, not the mere five per cent which it became in 1983. The weighting will have changed and some account must be taken of changing circumstances.

7.5.2 How Much More Are We Spending? (Part 1)

This is the question behind index number construction and it could be answered simply by reference to total expenditure in two years as follows:

$$\frac{\text{Expenditure}}{\text{Index}} = \frac{\text{Total current expenditure}}{\text{Total base expenditure}} \times 100$$

Such an index may be of limited interest but it measures only the growth of the total cash outflow: it says nothing about the effects of inflation upon the prices of inputs. After all, an increase in the Expenditure Index could be explained entirely by expansion in the market, not by inflation at all.

It seems obvious that an index number of costs must relate to a certain volume of output or another measure of business operations. One question that could be asked to yield an appropriate measure is linked to *Laspeyre's Index:* 'How much more are the base-year quantities costing this year than they would have done in the past? The answer depends on base-year quantities of items or people in the firm's total expenditure. In the basic problem data, there is a requirement for more information: we need to know the numbers of people, machines and purchases for the base year of 1981. These are given in Table 7.6.

Table 7.6   *Quantities purchased in 1981*

	1981		1982	1983
Item	*Unit cost*	*Number 'bought'*	*Unit cost*	*Unit cost*
Direct labour (hrs)	£3	40 000	£3.30	£3.60
Administration (monthly salaries)	£100	750	£106	£112
Materials (tons)	£125	3050	£150	£180
Equipment (units)	£3600	40	£4000	£5000
Power (units)	4.8p	1 500 000	5.4p	6.0p

The actual cost of operation in 1981 was the sum of the costs for each expenditure item as follows:

Item	*1981 cost (£)*
Direct labour	120 000
Administration	75 000
Materials	381 250
Equipment	144 000
Power	72 000
	£792 250

Now consider what such an operation would cost at 1982 prices. This time the costs are notional since they were not actually incurred: we apply the *base-year quantities at 1982 prices* to yield £910 000 as follows:

Item	*1982 cost (£)*
Direct labour	132 000
Administration	79 500
Materials	457 500
Equipment	160 000
Power	81 000
	£910 000

For 1983 the total notional cost of the 1981 operation can be calculated as £1 067 000, which the reader should check from Table 7.6. At a fixed level of activity the company would have been faced with total expenditure as in Table 7.7. Also, each can be expressed as a percentage of the base value to give Laspeyre's Index (I_n) for any particular year (Year n) after the base year (Year o):

$$I_n = \frac{\Sigma(p_nQ_o)}{\Sigma(p_oQ_o)} \times 100$$

By reason of its weighting system, Laspeyre's Index is often referred to as a 'base quantity weighted index'.

Table 7.7   *Base quantity weighted aggregate: Laspeyre's Index*

	1981	*1982*	*1983*
Cost of 1981 quantities	£792 250	£910 000	£1 067 000
Laspeyre's Index	100	114.9	134.7

It is apparent that Laspeyre's Index gives a slightly different assessment of rising costs than did the aggregated index of section 7.3.4. It answers the particular question about 'the original quantities'. If anything, it has tended to overestimate the cost increase for equipment since in 1983 only £50 000 was actually spent on this item, although Laspeyre's calculation would give it the value £200 000. On the other hand, Laspeyre's calculation for administration would give £84 000 in 1983 (that is, 750 salaries at £112) whereas actually it cost £100 000. Similarly, in 1983 direct labour costs an actual £200 000 but Laspeyre's method assesses it on the basis of £144 000 (that is, 40 000 manhours at £3.60).

Despite this weakness in Laspeyre's method, the index is commonly used in official publications and for inflation accounting. It has the two benefits of being easy to understand and easy to calculate. There is an assignment at the end of the chapter which will use Laspeyre's Index.

7.5.3   How Much Are We Spending? (Part 2)

Since Laspeyre's Index considers only original quantities, it suffers from being always out of date as regards its weighting system. Old quantities are never as useful as current ones since the latter are a better reflection of how the business is performing. There is a second index which uses current quantities as weights: it is widely known as *Paasche's Index*. Because of its structure, it is sometimes referred to as a 'current quantity weighted index'. In terms of a formula, Paasche's Index (I_n) for Year n with base in Year o is given by:

$$I_n = \frac{\Sigma(p_nQ_n)}{\Sigma(p_oQ_n)} \times 100$$

The top summation is total cost in Year n, the current year. The bottom summation gives total cost in the base year if current quantities had been bought. Consequently, this index is answering another question, 'How much more are these quantities costing than they would have done in the base year?' The calculation of Paasche's Index is more lengthy but not difficult and should be carried out by the reader as an exercise. More information is needed concerning quantities in each year and these are given in Table 7.8.

Table 7.8   *Quantities purchased each year*

Item	Units	Quantities		
		1981	*1982*	*1983*
Direct labour	manhours	40 000	48 000	55 556
Administration	salaries	750	825	893
Materials	tons	3050	3060	3057
Equipment	units	40	60	10
Power	units	1 500 000	1 600 000	1 666 000

Calculation should produce the values in Table 7.9. The essential differences between Laspeyre's and Paasche's indices are apparent in the annual values. Both are based upon 1981, but Laspeyre's exceeds Paasche's for 1982 and for 1983. As we have seen this is due to Laspeyre's weights being fixed in 1981 whereas Paasche's weights alter with each year's quantities.

Table 7.9   *Calculation of Paasche's Index*

	1981	1982		1983	
	$p_{81}Q_{81}$	$p_{82}Q_{82}$	$p_{81}Q_{82}$	$p_{83}Q_{83}$	$p_{81}Q_{83}$
Direct labour	£120 000	£158 400	£144 000	£200 000	£166 668
Administration	£ 75 000	£ 87 450	£ 82 500	£100 000	£ 89 300
Materials	£381 250	£459 000	£382 500	£550 000	£382 125
Equipment	£144 000	£240 000	£216 000	£ 50 000	£ 36 000
Power	£ 72 000	£ 86 400	£ 76 800	£100 000	£ 80 000
Totals	£792 250	£1 031 250	£901 800	£1 000 000	£754 093

Paasche's Index	100	114.4	132.6

Overall, regardless of the means whereby an index is calculated, we now have an impression that the company in the basic problem has suffered cost increases of the order of 15 per cent in the period 1981–1982 and more than 30 per cent in the period 1981–1983. By itself, such information would be of help to the Chairman and interesting to shareholders. The actual expenditures each year are of concern only in relation to the changing pattern of costs over the period. In fact, these total costs have not risen consistently over the period, as Table 7.9 shows, varying from £792 250 in 1981 to £1 031 250 in 1982 and back to £1 million in 1983. The Chairman would be less than keen to have such information emphasized!

7.6   OTHER WAYS WITH INDEX NUMBERS

7.6.1   Taking One Year at a Time

The weighted aggregate index in Table 7.4 showed values of 100, 115.4 and 133.9 for the years in question. These may be interpreted as showing a 15.4 *per cent* increase in the first period of 1981–1982 and an 18.5 *point* increase in 1982–1983. To be of immediate use, this point increase should be presented as a percentage. An 18.5 point increase is a 16.0 per cent increase on 115.4 as follows:

$$\frac{(133.9 - 115.4)}{115.4} \times 100 \; = \; \frac{18.5}{115.4} \times 100 \; = \; 16.0\%$$

Therefore, a different kind of index could be constructed to show the increase year by year. Each value would then be based upon each preceding year. Instead of a fixed base year, it is an index with a chain of base years, one after the other. For this reason such an index is called a *chain-base index* and may be calculated simply by dividing each value by its predecessor, expressing the quotient as a percentage. For Laspeyre's Index in Table 7.7, the alternative chain-base values are as in Table 7.10. The calculation is made as follows:

$$\frac{\text{Chain-base}}{\text{value}} = \frac{\text{Fixed-base value for year}}{\text{Fixed-base value for previous year}} \times 100$$

Thus each chain-base value shows the increase from one year to the next. For this reason, 1981 has none: we have insufficient information to calculate the increase in 1980–1981.

Table 7.10   *Chain-basing Laspeyre's Index*

	1981	1982	1983
Laspeyre's Index	100	114.9	134.7
Chain-base index	–	114.9	117.2

As a broader example of the chain-base principle, Table 7.11 gives a longer series, the calculation of which the reader should confirm using the above formula. Note that the base year for the fixed-base series need not be within the available period.

Table 7.11   *Chain-basing an index*

	1974	1975	1976	1977	1978	1979	1980	1981	1982	1983
Fixed-base index 1970 = 100	136.4	151.3	165.6	186.8	212.0	242.1	271.4	300.7	330.2	353.9
Chain-base index	–	110.9	109.5	112.8	113.5	114.2	112.1	110.8	109.8	107.2

One feature of the fixed-base series in Table 7.11 is of particular interest. The values after 1976 or 1977 fail to convey a clear meaning as regards the rate of change because of the magnitude of the numbers. The purpose and advantage of the chain-base index lie in its ability to show year-on-year increases: thus from 1978 to 1979 there was a 14.2 per cent increase. That is, with 1978 = 100, 1979 = 114.2.

7.6.2 Choosing a New Base Year

Another aspect of the fixed-base index in Table 7.11 is that 1970, the base year, is too far in the past for an immediate impression to be gained. What is required is a new starting year closer to the end of the data. This is accomplished simply by *rebasing the series*. Let us decide to rebase Table 7.11 at the year 1980: that year's index will become 100.

The rebasing calculation answers the question, 'What must be done to the 1980 value to make it 100?' The answer is, 'Divide it by 2.714', and that is what should be done to the entire series to yield Table 7.12. Now 1980 is recognizably the base year and the 1983 value has a meaning more easily comprehended.

Table 7.12   *Rebasing an index at 1980*

	1974	1975	1976	1977	1978	1979	1980	1981	1982	1983
Fixed-base index 1970 = 100	136.4	151.3	165.6	186.8	212.0	242.1	271.4	300.7	330.2	353.9
Fixed-base index 1980 = 100	50.3	55.7	61.0	68.8	78.1	89.2	100.0	110.8	121.7	130.4

Notice in Table 7.12 that values prior to the 1980 base value are below 100, indicating that they represent years during which the series was always rising. Conversely, the post-1980 values rise above 100, indicating that increases are continuing. Rebasing of this type is common, even necessary, in official indexes and the Central Statistical Office does it from time to time.

ASSIGNMENTS

A7.1   A household spends money on five categories of essentials, as shown in the table.

Item	1980 price	Current price	Units	Total 1981 expenditure
Food	£90	£128	Total for month	£1560
Heating	$3\frac{1}{2}$p	5p	Per unit of electricity	£1300
Travel	$10\frac{1}{2}$p	18p	Per mile	£ 780
Clothing	£29	£46	Total for month	£ 520
Housing	£15	£25	Weekly rental	£1040

(a) Deduce a system of weights that describes the importance of each item.
(b) Calculate the all-item index for the current year with 1980 as the base.
(c) Explain what is meant by the index number you have found.

A7.2   A company assembles bought-in parts into larger mechanical structures. The costs of the parts have been changing and the Purchasing Department draw up the following table:

Part	Total cost this year	Unit price 1980	Unit price 1982
A19/2	£ 500	£ 3.00	£ 3.30
A26/4	£1500	£ 2.00	£ 4.00
A27/8	£ 900	£ 5.50	£ 4.50
B11/6	£ 700	£11.25	£14.00
B17/2	£2500	£ 6.10	£ 7.00
B17/3	£1200	£14.50	£ 6.00
C22/8	£ 800	£ 0.75	£ 0.90

(a) Deduce the weight that may be adopted for each part and calculate the all-item index for 1982 with 1980 = 100.
(b) During the previous five years the company's purchasing costs had risen according to the following index series:

1977	1978	1979	1980	1981
100	108	119	129	136

Extend this series to include the 1982 index, maintaining the 1977 base.
(c) Rebase the whole series at 1979.

A7.3   In 1979 a particular household spent the following sums upon gardening:

Item	Spade	Trowels	Pkts seeds	Onion sets	Balls of string
No. bought	1	2	12	100	5
Unit price	£5.00	£1.50	10p	2p	20p

In 1982 the same household found it necessary to spend the following sums upon gardening:

Item	Spade	Trowels	Pkts seeds	Onion sets	Balls of string
No. bought	0	1	8	75	3
Unit price	£11.00	£2.00	30p	7p	50p

(a) Calculate Laspeyre's Index for this household's gardening expenditure and explain its meaning.
(b) Calculate the *actual expenditure* in both years. Explain the conflict between these actual sums and the information given by the answer to (a).
(c) Paasche's Index for the same data yields a value of 253.4. Explain why this value is different from that given in the answer to (a).

A7.4   Consult the latest issue of the *Annual Abstract of Statistics* in the library and inspect the Index of Retail Prices. Answer the following:

(a) What is the base date for the most recent section of the series?
(b) Why is the weight in each category changed every year?
(c) Why does this publication list annual averages for index values?
(d) Which category's prices have risen most rapidly since the last base date?

(e) Which category's prices have risen most rapidly in the past two years?

Also, convert the past five years of the series to chain base, explaining what is shown by it.

A7.5 Consult the latest issue of *Financial Statistics* (HMSO) and inspect the table entitled 'Company security prices and yields'. Answer the following:

(a) What is the base date for the Financial Times Index of Industrial Ordinary Shares?
(b) What is the base date for The Times Index of Industrial Ordinary Shares?
(c) Do the various indexes of ordinary share-prices agree about the peak and trough in values over recent years?
(d) Is there one series which gives a better impression of month-to-month variation in share prices?

A7.6 (a) In a certain country, retail prices rise every month for a year at the following rates:

Jan, Feb, Mar each at $1\frac{1}{2}\%$	Apr, May, Jun each at $1\frac{1}{4}\%$
Jul, Aug, Sep each at 2%	Oct, Nov, Dec each at $1\frac{3}{4}\%$

(i) Present this information as a twelve-value chain-base index.
(ii) Convert your index to a fixed base at January = 100.

(b) Rebase the following index at 1980 = 100:

1975	1976	1977	1978	1979	1980	1981	1982
105	112	107	102	97	96	99	104

(c) The following series is chain based.

1979				1980				1981				1982	
I	II	III	IV	I	II	III	IV	I	II	III	IV	I	II
101	104	109	112	107	103	101	99	97	96	98	102	108	112

(i) Convert this index to fixed base with 1979 I = 100.
(ii) Rebase the fixed-base index at 1980 IV = 100.

8–The Accountant Provides Information

8.1 INTRODUCTION AND OBJECTIVES

8.1.1 The Subject of the Chapter

All businesses use money to keep track of transactions and to measure effectiveness. A company, whether it is involved in the business of producing or buying and selling goods or providing services, must be able to show that the transactions are beneficial in some way. That is, that the money-values of the purchases and sales or services, after the costs of business activities have been deducted, create a worthwhile surplus in the company's account.

To gauge the effectiveness of its operations we must look at the company's method of trading. For example, excessive use of credit trading could be interpreted as a weakness ('promises are worth less than cash'). In addition, we must examine the size of the net profit in relation to the scale of operations. If two firms each obtain a net profit in one year of £20 000, one being a one-man window-cleaning business, the other a large construction company with millions of pounds of turnover, what would be regarded as a good income for the former would scarcely be regarded as a profit at all by the latter.

These weaknesses, or strengths, are exposed by the company's accounts. The business analyst needs to be able to interpret a set of accounts. This chapter will deal with the basic concepts and methods of book-keeping. It will introduce methods for analysing two questions: 'What is the business worth?' and 'Is this business effective?' We shall consider the purpose and creation of a trading account and of a balance sheet. We shall also cover the interpretation of those data to assess the acceptability of performance.

8.1.2 Objectives

1. To understand the nature of the accounting equation between sources of funds and their application.
2. To be able to construct a trading and profit and loss account, and interpret it from the point of view of a participant.
3. To be able to construct and interpret a balance sheet.
4. To calculate a variety of financial ratios relating to liquidity, profitability and return, as if for an intending investor.

8.2 BASIC PROBLEM DATA

Nufoods Limited is a company pioneering the manufacture and sale of animal foodstuffs derived from bacteria grown on useless waste from the oil industry. The European Regional Fund provides a large proportion of the finance for Nufoods and also undertakes to distribute the entire production of the foodstuffs throughout the EEC at a guaranteed price of £140 per metric tonne. The Fund has provided £300 000 at an interest rate of eight per cent payable annually. A further £600 000 has been raised by the issue of ordinary shares which pay a dividend to holders depending upon profits.

At the beginning of the year, Nufoods has a stock of raw material valued at £28 200 and at the end a stock valued at £16 000. During the year it had purchased £142 000 worth of raw material and sold 3300 tonnes of the processed foodstuffs. Wages and salaries had cost £79 200, administration expenses £14 400, packaging £21 550, electricity £25 650, local rates £2500 and insurance premiums £1750. The buildings and plant were valued at £500 000 and are assumed to depreciate annually by 10 per cent of valuation. The firm also had £50 000 invested in government securities which yielded six per cent annually. Tax is payable on annual profit at the rate of 40 per cent.

8.3 SOURCES AND USES OF FUNDS

8.3.1 Current and Capital Funds

The various sums of money that have passed through the hands of the Nufoods management seem to fall into two categories. One category consists of expenditure which occurs daily or weekly, certainly regularly, to pay for the activities of the firm in processing raw materials and packing the final product. These include wages, raw materials, administration and electricity. Such expenditures are called *current* expenditures because they occur at short intervals. Similarly, the company receives current benefits from its activities, such as sales income at £140 per tonne. Consequently, part of the accounting procedure must be related to these everyday inflows and outflows of money.

The other category of flows is the once-and-for-all kind, when repetition is not planned or expected in the foreseeable future. This happens when a company borrows money to build a factory or set up a production plant. These sums of money change hands just once during the life of the business. This can be seen most clearly in the case of ordinary shares, where the shareholders lend to the firm and never expect to receive the money back until the firm is wound up or taken over by another, or until they sell the shares on the Stock Exchange. This conversion of money into fixed industrial assets is an example of *capital creation* and the sums are usually referred to as 'capital' for that reason. The second part of the accounting procedure must be able to assess the state of the company in terms of what it borrowed and what it now has by way of buildings, plant and cash in a bank account. Such an account is called a balance sheet and we shall construct one later for Nufoods.

8.3.2 The Costs of Materials

Since Nufoods is concerned primarily with petroleum waste, we ought to consider the profitability (or otherwise) of the material itself. We do not know yet the cost of materials in one tonne of the foodstuffs so we must start by asking a particular question, 'What is the cost of the materials used in the goods sold this year?' Then we ask, 'Has a profit been made on processing and selling the materials?' We shall construct a trading account to show what value of materials has been used in the year. Simply, this value is the total of purchases and any change in stocks. If stocks have risen, then not all purchases have been converted into saleable foodstuffs. Since stocks have fallen in value, we know that final output exceeds purchases by the difference in stocks. Also, we know that sales were 3300 tonnes at a price of £140, so we may now construct a double-column account as follows to calculate the gross surplus on materials processed. Conventionally, the left-hand column shows debits (outflows) and the right-hand column shows credits (inflows).

Example 8.1

Trading Account Year 1

	£		£
Opening stock	28 200	Sales	462 000
Purchases	142 000		
	170 200		
less Closing stock	16 000		
Cost of materials in sales	154 200		
Gross profit	307 800		
	462 000		462 000

It can be seen now that the 3300 tonnes of foodstuffs sold for £462 000 and contain £154 200 of raw materials. The figure for gross profit is calculated by finding the sum which would make both columns equal in total; this is then inserted in the debit side. This is a convention that may cause confusion but it simply preserves the balance between the sources of money (sales) and its applications (paying for materials). The gross profit is now available to pay for other applications involving labour, power and packaging.

The trading account also shows us two facts of interest in the economics of this production process. First, the 3300 tonnes of foodstuffs contain £154 200 of materials so that each tonne must contain £46.73 of materials. Second, since each tonne sells for £140, the explanation for the large surplus is easy to see: materials amount to about only one-third of the sale value of the final product.

8.3.3   Is There an Overall Profit?

In Nufoods as a whole, there are more activities than the conversion of petroleum waste. The company has investments, an administrative structure and other expenditures which are not directly attributable to production. To pay for all these, there is the materials gross surplus and investment income. Another current account is required to assess the overall profitability of the company: it is usually referred to as a profit and loss account. Once again, the left-hand column shows debits and the right-hand column shows credits. The pretax profit figure makes the two columns balance. Note that a convention is applied to debits such that essential expenditures requiring immediate cash payment are placed near the top of the list: the items at the bottom are those which do not require immediate settlement. For the time being we shall assume that Nufoods operate on a cash basis rather than running up debts to suppliers.

Example 8.2

Profit and Loss Account

	£		£
Wages and salaries	79 200	Gross profit	307 800
Rates	2 500	Investment income	3 000
Loan interest	24 000		
Electricity	25 650		
Insurance	1 750		
Administration	14 400		
Packaging	21 550		
Depreciation	50 000		
	219 050		
Pretax profit	91 750		
	310 800		310 800
Tax provision	36 700		
Net profit	55 050		
	91 750		

The investment income is six per cent of the £50 000 invested in government securities. The figure for depreciation can seem a mystery to the newcomer since the company has not actually spent £50 000 on maintaining the plant. That is not important; the plant will wear out and be valued at the year's end as only £450 000. Somehow this loss of productive capacity must be counteracted and at some future time replacements obtained. The company must therefore make provision by setting aside sums of money rather than distributing all the profit to the shareholders. Depreciation may be represented in reality as cash in a replacement fund or as increased stocks or materials: in fact, anything that can be converted easily into a source for the replacement of the worn-out plant. Depreciation, therefore, is a true cost which reduces profit. We shall see it again in the capital account.

From Example 8.2, the pretax profit is £91 750, which is a considerable reduction on the gross profits. This shows the importance of the activities other than material-processing in the manufacture of the foodstuffs. The cost of items other than materials for the 3300 tonnes can be calculated as £66.38 per tonne, which with the material cost of £46.73 per tonne yields a total unit cost of £113.11 per tonne made, packed and sold. Since the foodstuffs sell for £140 per tonne, there is a profit of £26.89 per tonne on its manufacture. There is also a small unit contribution obtained from the investment income equal to £0.91 per tonne so that the pretax profit of £91 750 represents an overall unit profit of £27.80 per tonne.

The account also shows the company's liability to taxation. Only £55 050 is available for distribution to the owners of the company, in this case the shareholders, the rest going to the Exchequer. It is worth noting that £55 050 distributed to 600 000 shares represents almost exactly 9.1 pence per share for this year: that is, a dividend of 9.1 per cent. Such considerations will be investigated later in the chapter since they are a measure of Nufoods' effectiveness as a company. Of course, if total cost exceeded total income, then the profit and loss account would show a negative value against profit and so be called a loss. Tax would not then be paid but neither would shareholders receive any dividends. Hence, the profit figure is a measure of the worth of the Nufoods company in the eyes of the shareholders who may rely upon it for their incomes.

8.3.4   What is the Company Worth?

This question has a variety of meanings but we shall consider only two. It could mean, 'What must be paid to buy the company as a going concern?' Or it could mean, 'What sum of money would be required to pay off the company's debts?' Both are aspects of the same problem because Nufoods' debts have been converted into Nufoods' assets such as plant and stock. If a sum of money can buy the assets, it could also settle debts which created them.

At the commencement of Nufoods' activities, it was indebted to the European Regional Fund and to shareholders. The firm's liabilities, as they are called, total £900 000. This sum has been spent upon buildings, plant and an initial stock of raw materials. We may show this balance between source and application on a balance sheet as in Example 8.3, which also shows that not all the money has been used for creation of assets. By convention, assets which may be changed daily are named 'current assets' and those which are not are named 'fixed assets'. Investments are intermediate in this respect since they take some time to change into cash but not as long as buildings. A similar distinction applies to liabilities but at the commencement Nufoods has only long-term debts.

It is apparent that Nufoods has not really set up its manufacturing process to the limit of its funds since nearly one-third of its borrowing has been retained in a bank account as cash. The figure for cash makes the balance in the account and can be checked against the company's bank statement. Perhaps during the first year of operation it will use its funds more rationally in purchasing, making and selling. Such is not the case, as we can see from Example 8.4. The pretax profit of £91 750 is added to the liabilities of Nufoods because part of it must soon be paid to the Exchequer and the rest must be made available for the shareholders. These two items are current liabilities since they may be expected to change in the near future. The result of the profitable activity has been to increase the cash in Nufoods' bank account; no new plant has been purchased. Nufoods seem not be taking full advantage of the availability of cash.

Example 8.3

Balance Sheet: Start of Year 1

Liabilities	£	Assets	£
Loan	300 000	Fixed:	
Shares	600 000	Building and plant	500 000
		Investments	50 000
		Current:	
		Stocks	28 200
		Cash	321 800
Total	900 000	Total	900 000

Example 8.4

Balance Sheet: End of Year 1

Liabilities	£	Assets		£
Long-term:		Fixed:		
Loan	300 000	Building and plant	500 000	
Shares	600 000	less Depreciation	50 000	450 000
		Investments		50 000
Current:		Current:		
Tax reserve	36 700	Stocks		16 000
Dividend	55 050	Cash		475 750
Total	991 750	Total		991 750

It seems clear at the end of the first year that Nufoods is excessively liquid, which means that too much of its total value is lying idle as cash. The company ought to consider the purchase of more buildings and plant, and the expansion of production. At the moment Nufoods is in danger of a takeover attempt, perhaps by one of the big agricultural chemical firms. By negotiating with the shareholders, nearly £½ million in ready cash is obtainable from Nufoods' bank account and that could seem attractive to a company experiencing difficulties in raising funds. Let us assume that Nufoods does buy new plant and buildings for the start of Year 2, so that the total becomes £750 000. All that has happened is a transfer of wealth from a current category to a fixed (capital) category and the balance sheet in Example 8.5 shows this. However, the new manufacturing capacity means that the output of foodstuffs in Year 2 can be increased significantly.

The value of the Nufoods company at the end of Year 1 is £991 750, i.e. £991 750 represents the cash evaluation of all the assets. However, at the start of Year 2 Nufoods is liable for tax and must declare a dividend to the shareholders. For simplicity's sake, let us assume that all the dividend reserve is paid out and, of course, all the tax. The balance sheet for the start of Year 2 is as given in Example 8.5.

Example 8.5

Balance Sheet: Start of Year 2
(after plant expansion, payment of taxes and dividend distribution)

Liabilities	£	Assets	£
Long-term:		Fixed:	
Loans	300 000	Building and plant	750 000
Shares	600 000	Investments	50 000
		Current:	
		Stocks	16 000
		Cash	84 000
Total	900 000	Total	900 000

We should notice how the company's bank balance has diminished. Largely it is a result of plant expansion but it has also been depleted by the payment of taxes and dividend. At this instant in time, Nufoods is again valued at £900 000.

8.3.5 The Second Year Experience

The change in productive capacity represents a 50 per cent increase over the previous year's. It is reasonable to assume that the same increase *could* occur in sales. Not all the costs need rise by the same proportion since labour, administration and electricity are not actively linked to output volume. Also, the plant may be expected to be more efficient at higher volume because of *economies of scale*. The following information arises from the second year's operation: sales 4220 tonnes, closing stock £34 000, wages and salaries £98 000, rates £3000, electricity £31 700, insurance premiums £2100, administration £15 600, packaging £32 325, purchases £212 000. The year's operating accounts are given in Example 8.6. Each tonne still sells at £140.

Example 8.6

Trading and Profit and Loss Accounts for Year 2
Trading Account

	£		£
Opening stock	16 000	Sales	590 800
Purchases	212 000		
	228 000		
Closing stock	34 000		
Cost of materials in sale	194 000		
Gross profit	396 800		
	590 800		590 800

Profit and Loss Account

	£		£
Wages and salaries	98 000	Gross profits	396 800
Rates	3 000	Investment income	3 000
Loan interest	24 000		
Electricity	31 700		
Administration	15 600		
Insurance	2 100		
Packaging	32 325		
Depreciation	75 000		
	281 725		
Pretax profit	118 075		
	399 800		399 800
Tax provision	47 230		
Available for distribution	70 845		
	118 075		

From these accounts we can assess the changing efficiency of Nufoods. The unit material cost for each tonne sold is about £46, hardly affected by the increase in scale. However, the other costs of £281 725 represent a unit non-material cost of about £66.76, which is a little more expensive than in Year 1. In the light of the fact that the depreciation charged against the business has increased by a half, this stability in unit cost shows a significant economy in other categories. Now consider the consequences of these changes upon the balance sheet in Example 8.7.

By the next day, the first day of Year 3, the company must discharge its tax liability and distribute a dividend to shareholders. The balance sheet for the start of Year 3 will show resultant reductions in both columns. Let us assume that a nine per cent dividend rate is regarded by Nufoods as acceptable for shareholders. Then £54 000 of the dividends' figure will be distributed to shareholders and the rest will be retained by the company as a reserve. Such a reserve is sometimes called 'undistributed profits' or 'retained profits' in a balance sheet and is accounted as a liability since it is due to shareholders but not actually passed on.

Example 8.7

Balance Sheet: End of Year 2

Liabilities	£	Assets		£
Long-term:		Fixed:		
Loans	300 000	Buildings and plant	750 000	
Shares	600 000	less Depreciation	75 000	675 000
		Investments		50 000
Current:		Current:		
Tax reserve	47 230	Stocks		34 000
Dividends	70 845	Cash		259 075
Total	1 018 075	Total		1 018 075

If, at the same moment, Nufoods spend £75 000 on maintaining buildings and plant, the balance sheet will appear as in Example 8.8.

Example 8.8

Balance Sheet: Start of Year 3

Liabilities	£	Assets	£
Long-term		Fixed:	
Loans	300 000	Buildings and plant	750 000
Shares	600 000	Investments	50 000
Current:		Current:	
Reserve	16 845	Stocks	34 000
		Cash	82 845
Total	916 845	Total	916 845

It is apparent now that Nufoods is managing to operate at a slight surplus, after fulfilling all its obligations to financiers and shareholders, and maintaining its productive capacity. In fact, its cash holdings still seem extravagant in relation to sales income (often referred to as turnover).

8.4 BUYING AND SELLING ON CREDIT

Not all the raw materials used by a company need to be paid for at the moment of their receipt from suppliers. Almost always there will be a delay in the clearing of cheques through the banking system and, in effect, the goods are delivered but not paid for. More important than this organizational delay, most firms have an arrangement with suppliers whereby they settle a purchasing account just once monthly or even quarterly. By this means the purchaser is obtaining credit from the supplier for which he may be required to pay a small additional charge on the account. Such a system of credit purchase will not appear in the current or operating accounts since they keep track only of funds actually going out of or coming into the firm. Credit purchases show up as a current liability on the balance sheet: the company must expect to pay it off sometime in the foreseeable future. Any other company taking over the liabilities must expect to pay off creditors immediately.

In the case of Nufoods, we may assume that about one-twelfth of their purchases are outstanding as credit, which is about £17 700 in Year 3. This means that the company will have materials of this value in stock and a corresponding liability to pay for them soon. The new balance sheet is shown in Example 8.9. Note how the totals are still equal since credit is the source of funds and stocks the application.

Nufoods will also be expected to supply on credit, because the distributor will not pay cash for each consignment. Nufoods will probably be paid once a month for goods received by the distributor (most agricultural suppliers receive a monthly cheque from their marketing board or other distributor). This means that the cash figure in Example 8.9 probably is unrealistic for a real company. More likely, a certain proportion of it is not cash but delivery notes outstanding to the customer, representing foodstuffs sent out but not yet paid for. These sums are debts owed to Nufoods and will be represented as a further subdivision of current assets. They are current because they are likely to change in the short term, and assets because they represent sums to the credit of Nufoods somewhere in the commercial system. Let us assume that about one-twelfth of the year's sales have been consigned on credit, then about £49 000 is owed to Nufoods and has not been received as cash. The new balance sheet in Example 8.10 shows the effect.

Example 8.9

Balance Sheet: Start of Year 3
(including credit purchases)

Liabilities	£	Assets	£
Long-term:		Fixed:	
Loans	300 000	Buildings and plant	750 000
Shares	600 000	Investments	50 000
Current:		Current:	
Reserves	16 845	Stocks	51 700
Creditors	17 700	Cash	82 845
Total	934 545	Total	934 545

Example 8.10

Balance Sheet: Start of Year 3
(including credit sales)

Liabilities	£	Assets	£
Long-term:		Fixed:	
Loans	300 000	Buildings and plant	750 000
Shares	600 000	Investments	50 000
Current:		Current:	
Reserves	16 845	Stocks	51 700
Creditors	17 700	Debtors	49 000
		Cash	33 845
Total	934 545	Total	934 545

This final balance sheet looks as if it could apply to a real business. The reader should now be able to scan down a balance sheet for a public or private company and recognize the various divisions in assets or liabilities. There are a few complications in published accounts, such as tax-reserve certificates in the assets column: these are certificates purchased by employers during a tax-year to help pay their various tax bills at the year's end. These certificates are accepted by the Inland Revenue in payment for tax and carry a useful rate of interest. They are merely a specialized form of very short-term investment and may be cashed at any time. The reader will see a variety of such entries in published accounts but each may be placed in one of the categories in Example 8.10.

8.5   GETTING MORE INFORMATION FROM ACCOUNTS

The construction of a set of annual accounts is not an end in itself, even though they do give a quick view of the company's operations; to the business analyst the *interpretation* of accounts is more important. Apart from simple profitability, the analyst is concerned with at least three important questions relating to (a) the company's ability to pay its way, (b) profitability of sales and (c) ability to make an acceptable return to the owners. This analysis is often referred to as *accounting ratio analysis*: most accounting textbooks introduce a long list of analytical ratios, some of which are too highly specialized to be of use here. We shall consider an essential set and so introduce the concept for the reader to extend as appropriate.

8.5.1   Liquidity: Paying the Way

By liquidity is meant the ease of obtaining purchasing power or alternatively staving off people who need paying. All companies must be liquid to some extent, because they need both cash and credit to be able to meet daily liabilities. For this reason, a simple ratio to consider is the *quick asset ratio* (sometimes called the acid test) since it measures the company's ability to meet short-term demands: it is defined as follows:

$$\text{Quick asset ratio} = \frac{\text{Cash} + \text{Debtors}}{\text{Current liabilities}} \times 100$$

This ratio is expressed as a percentage by convention and indicates whether a company is able or unable to cover short-term liabilities, or even if it is too liquid. Obviously, if a firm has sufficient cash and credit to cover current liabilities many times over, then it ought to seek ways of using its assets to a better purpose. For Nufoods, the quick asset ratio is 240 per cent which is unnecessarily high. For the sake of prudence the business analyst would prefer the ratio to be about 100 per cent to indicate that Nufoods could cover urgent calls for funds. Perhaps a figure of 105 per cent should be regarded as a target to give a margin of safety. In Nufoods' case, the problem seems to lie in the high ratio of debtors to creditors. Nufoods could attempt to buy more on credit: this would be a matter of policy for the directors.

As a matter of definition, the excess of current assets over current liabilities is called *working capital*: for Nufoods it amounts to £134 545 − £34 545, that is, £100 000. This is the 'excess liquidity' of the company at the start of Year 3 and it is probably too high a figure. An associated ratio of use to the analyst is the *working capital* (or *current*) *ratio*, which embodies this argument. It is defined as:

$$\text{Working capital ratio} = \frac{\text{Current assets}}{\text{Current liabilities}} \times 100$$

For Nufoods its value is 389 per cent, which shows, once again, how well endowed the company is. As a target, 200 per cent is often regarded as reasonable, which means that the company ought to reorganize its finances. It could, for example, convert its investments into productive plant or reduce its levels of stocks.

The question of excess stocks can be analysed by the rate of stock turnover. If a company has sufficient stock for six months' production, then we would say that too great a stock was being held. This may be calculated by the *time to sell stock*, which is defined as:

$$\text{Time to sell stock} = \frac{\text{Average value of stock}}{\text{Cost of goods sold}} \times 365 \text{ days}$$

For Nufoods, average stock value may be calculated from balance sheets at the start of Years 2 and 3. The cost of the goods sold in this case is the cost of materials in sales in Example 8.6, since the stocks in question are stocks of materials. This ratio is a comparison of the asset aspect of materials with the operating aspect.

From Examples 8.5 and 8.10 average stock value is £33 850 and the time to sell stock is:

$$\frac{£33\,850}{£194\,000} \times 365 \text{ days} = 63.7 \text{ days}$$

This is interpreted to mean that normally stocks may be converted into cash about once every two months. It also means that stock ties up money for about 64 days and does not yield any interest. In times of supply difficulties, time to sell stock could be allowed to rise to perhaps three or four months without seeming excessive.

Finally, there are other easy ratios which allow the analyst to decide on a company's ability to control its debtors or to gain credit from its suppliers. At least two final balance sheets are required since the ratios use averages. The first is *time taken to pay* which is defined as:

$$\frac{\text{Average debtors}}{\text{Turnover}} \times 365 \text{ days}$$

Over a number of years, most firms would prefer this value not to rise, since that would indicate a loss of control.

The other value is *time taken to pay creditors* which is defined as:

$$\frac{\text{Average creditors}}{\text{Turnover}} \times 365 \text{ days}$$

In a sense it is advantageous for a company to defer payment on materials simply because it puts off the day of reckoning! However, creditors is a category on the liability side of the balance sheet and most firms would prefer the amount not to rise beyond a reasonable value. One explanation for this lies in all firms' need to raise money at some time, whether it be a bank loan or a new share issue, and excessive creditors can make the company appear unattractive to prospective investors.

8.5.2   Profit: The Purpose of Selling

As we have seen, profit can be subdivided into a series of surpluses; on sales, before tax, after tax as distributed to shareholders. Each definition has its interest for a particular group of participants in a company because, for that group, it measures how effective the company is at selling. Ratios for this purpose are expressed in relation to sales income (turnover) and each is a measure of return on sales. First, consider a gross measure:

$$\frac{\text{Gross profit (on materials)}}{\text{Turnover}} \times 100\%$$

For Nufoods, over the two years of operation, the ratio is calculated as follows:

Year 1 $\dfrac{£307\,800}{£462\,000} \times 100 = 67\%$

Year 2
$$\frac{£396\,800}{£590\,800} \times 100 = 67\%$$

This indicates stability which would be regarded as desirable in times of economic recession. Also, it seems a sufficiently high value to be desirable at any time: over a number of years the owners of a company could feel well satisfied with a stable 67 per cent.

Another return-on-sales ratio is:

$$\frac{\text{Pretax profit}}{\text{Turnover}} \times 100\%$$

This ratio gives a similar impression to the gross measure except that it also takes into account all the company costs, not just purchase of materials. It is conceivable that a company's effectiveness varies over the years purely because of changing administrative costs, interest and depreciation.

For Nufoods this net measure is calculated as follows:

Year 1
$$\frac{£91\,750}{£462\,000} \times 100 = 19.9\%$$

Year 2
$$\frac{£118\,075}{£590\,800} \times 100 = 20.0\%$$

We can see that Nufoods' performance is improving slightly in this respect: non-materials' costs are rising at a lower rate than material purchases. This is one of the benefits arising from increased scale of operation, but management must keep track of the ratio. As companies grow into massive trading corporations, administrative costs and interest charges tend to rise. This ratio, compared with the gross measure, indicates that such a change is occurring and the business analyst would detect the signs.

8.5.3   Profit: Good Use of Someone Else's Money

The people and organizations who lend money to a company expect a return and the analyst usually considers *profitability*; that is, profit in relation to money being used. An immediate useful ratio is that between 'profit available to pay anyone with a claim' and 'money tied up in the business'. The first is usually referred to as *available profit* and can be taken to be defined as follows:

Available profit = Pretax profit + loan interest from profit and loss account.

The second is referred to as *capital employed* and may be defined as:

Capital employed = Total assets − current liabilities from balance sheet.

The ratio between these two is called *return on capital employed* and is expressed as a percentage. It is a measure of the profitability with which a company is operating.

$$\text{Return on capital employed} = \frac{\text{Available profit}}{\text{Capital employed}} \times 100$$

For Nufoods this return is calculated as follows:

Year 1 (end) $\dfrac{£(91\,750 + 24\,000)}{£(991\,750 - 91\,750)} \times 100 = 12.9\%$

Year 2 (end) $\dfrac{£(118\,075 + 24\,000)}{£(1\,018\,075 - 118\,075)} \times 100 = 15.8\%$

These figures indicate an increase in profitability in Nufoods. Interpreted in everyday language, this ratio tells the analyst that every £1 tied up in the business as fixed or net current assets yields about 16 pence in Year 2 for all those people and organizations who need to be paid. These are the European Regional Fund, the Inland Revenue and members of the public who hold ordinary shares.

An additional ratio to return on capital employed is *return on equity*. By *equity* is meant those sources of funds which are at risk in the business in the sense that they may never be repaid. Ordinary shares are such a source and, in Nufoods' case, so is the reserve since it represents a fund of indebtedness from undistributed profits. Reserves are not cash; they may exist as stock or plant, in fact anything on the assets side of the balance sheet. They are simply a measure of profits once earned but not distributed. Shareholders may never see them in cash form. Return on equity, therefore, is a measure of profitability on the use of money which is at risk:

$$\text{Return on equity} = \frac{\text{Net profit}}{\text{Equity}} \times 100\%$$

For Nufoods this ratio has the value calculated below. The everyday meaning is that each £1 placed at the company's disposal without security makes a return of about nine pence during Year 1 and about 11 pence in Year 2.

Year 2 (start) $\dfrac{£55\,050}{£600\,000} \times 100 = 9.2\%$

Year 3 (start) $\dfrac{£70\,845}{£616\,845} \times 100 = 11.5\%$

Whether this calculation is made at the end of one year or at the beginning of the next depends on what figures are available: it is valid in comparison so long as the analyst stays with a particular time reference. In this case, Nufoods seems to be improving from the point of view of equity-holders although, as we saw in section 8.3.5, not all the net profit is distributed. Even so, it shows that the firm is strong and seems able to continue returning a reasonable dividend on each £1 share.

8.6   CONCLUSION

This long chapter has introduced various elements of financial analysis and the reader should be in a position now to apply them to real published accounts. There are categories of assets and liabilities not included here but they are easily defined in a business dictionary or accounting textbook. In addition, accountants use a variety of ratios for analysis beyond those mentioned here, but the reader will find them easy to use now that the concept has been introduced. To give a single example, the ratio of wages and salaries to electricity costs is often a useful figure in that it measures the labour-intensity of a production process. There is almost no end to such ratios but their usefulness is often debatable.

ASSIGNMENTS

A8.1 Using the Nufoods accounts in Examples 8.6 and 8.10, derive a trading and profit and loss account for Year 3 and a balance sheet for the start of Year 4. You are given the following information: quantity sold 4600 tonnes; purchases £225 000; closing stock £32 000; wages and salaries £111 200; rates £3000; electricity £34 500; insurance premiums £2300; administration £16 000; packaging £36 250. The company will maintain its buildings and plant at £750 000 and will declare a nine per cent dividend to shareholders, if possible. Debtors and creditors remain the same as in Year 2.

(a) Prepare the accounts.
(b) Is Nufoods maintaining its performance as a profitable concern?
(c) Using appropriate ratios, discuss whether or not Nufoods is progressing in terms of liquidity and profitability.

A8.2 In the United States of America, the apparent success of Nufoods attracts the attention of a large pharmaceutical corporation. A subsidiary with the name Petronosh is set up to convert American oil waste into a variety of products including foodstuffs, fertilizers and plastic bedding materials for livestock pens. Petronosh is set up with the following assets and liabilities.

Petronosh Balance Sheet: Start of Year 1

Liabilities	$	Assets	$
Long-term:		Fixed:	
Loans	1 000 000	Buildings:	2 700 000
Shares	2 550 000	Plant	670 000
		Current:	
		Stocks	105 000
		Cash	75 000
	3 550 000		3 550 000

During the first year's operation, the following financial flows occur: sales $1 418 000; purchases $342 100; wages and salaries $290 000; administration $30 420; heating and lighting $140 000; local land tax $60 000; packing and transport $106 000. Loans bear interest at 15 per cent per year. Buildings depreciate at five per cent per year and plant at 10 per cent per year. Company taxation is at a rate of 20 per cent. Closing stocks are valued at $191 000. At the year's end, creditors total $80 000 and debtors $95 000.

(a) Construct a trading and profit and loss account as if it were governed by the accounting conventions of the United Kingdom.
(b) Construct the balance sheet for the start of Year 2 assuming that half the company taxes are paid at that time and half the net profit is distributed to the shareholders and fixed costs are maintained at their original value.
(c) Since Petronosh and Nufoods use different currencies, comparison between any two flows is difficult since it depends upon the rate of exchange. The use of ratios is helpful since their calculation removes any currency units. For Petronosh calculate a set of ratios to assess liquidity, return on sales and return to funds. Compare these values with those calculated for Nufoods.

(d) On a balance of arguments, which company do you believe is performing more effectively from the point of view of:
  (i)   Management;
  (ii) A bank considering a loan;
  (iii) Potential shareholders?

A8.3   The Widgett family agree to set up a company to manufacture and sell some of Uncle George's inventions. Twenty thousand ordinary shares of £2 each are issued to members of the family in return for cash. (The expenses of the issue are negligible and are born by Aunt Alice as a present to the family.) Two policies are available for immediate implementation with a view to getting the business off the ground. In a year or two, other developments will be considered.

Policy A: Make and sell 80 flumjets at £1000 each. Materials cost £250 per unit and labour costs £200 per unit; fixed costs are estimated at £8600 for a rented factory; delivery and packing for each flumjet is estimated at £100. Machinery for this product will cost £30 000 and will have a working life of ten years: depreciation will be accounted on a straight-line basis.

   Because of their newness, it is thought likely that flumjets must be offered for sale on three months' credit. However, the Widgett family are not well known in the trade and have been refused credit on purchases. Each unit will be built to order, so that there will be no stock.

Policy B: Make and sell 10 000 wijkins at £7 each. Combined materials and labour cost £4 per unit; packaging costs £20 per hundred units; an estimated £7000 worth of tools and equipment will be used each year but no heavy capital equipment; fixed costs are estimated at £6000 per year. Trading will be on a cash basis both in buying and selling. It is intended that a stock valued at £5000 of finished wijkins be held at all times to cover emergency orders.

For both policies administration is estimated at £10 000 per year for secretarial and management expenses. The company will be assessed for tax at 40 per cent of the profits, payable at the end of the year.

(a) Construct profit and loss accounts, and balance sheets for both policies after their first year's operations.
(b) Write a brief report on the prospective performance of each policy.
(c) Advise the Widgett family upon the choice of policy.

9—Deciding Between Investments

9.1 INTRODUCTION AND OBJECTIVES

9.1.1 The Subject of the Chapter

By 'investment' economists and business analysts usually mean expenditure upon buildings and plant for the purpose of creating a productive unit, such as a factory. For the fortunate business, there will be more than one worthwhile plan (or project) available at any moment, but having a number of good options can present the analyst with the problem of deciding which to recommend. Making the decision requires that each project be measured against a set of criteria and against the other projects. The purpose of this chapter is to investigate and answer the question, 'Into which project, if any, should the company put its money?' We shall review basic ideas of profit and return from Chapter 8 and present value from Chapter 1, and shall construct a series of tests which may be applied to any project or group of projects.

The intention is to provide the reader with an armoury of criteria whereby potentially expensive projects can be evaluated. If there was to be a simple name to describe this armoury it would be *investment appraisal* and some texts do use such terms. It should be noted that numerical methods of selecting projects are insufficient by themselves because all business people have predispositions towards and against certain activities, no matter how profitable. Thus a family construction firm may specialize in housing even though it is able to attempt industrial buildings: it sees itself as a housing company. Similarly, a firm of accountants may decide not to employ a specialist in tax avoidance because 'that is not the way we operate'. These are matters of *ethos* and cannot be quantified: frequently a project preferred by the analyst will be rejected by the decision-maker precisely on such grounds. Despite this, the analyst needs to be able to present evidence for and against each of a set of competing projects, and this chapter is written with that in mind.

9.1.2 Objectives

1. To review basic concepts of measurement in the context of investment plans.
2. To use profit and profitability as measures of a project's worth.
3. To extend the concept of present value and understand its importance when applied to multiple cash-flow situations.

4. To calculate and understand the payback period as a crude measure of performance.
5. To understand the internal rate of return for a project and to use it in conjunction with net present value.
6. To weigh all the available numerical evidence in investment appraisals, combine it with subjective criteria and advise upon the selection of one project.

9.2   BASIC PROBLEM DATA

Agrifund Ltd is a finance organization which lends money for the development of agricultural technology. It borrows from banks, insurance companies and various government agencies and pays interest at a rate of 16 per cent per year. Administrative costs are estimated as an additional two per cent on all business but otherwise Agrifund makes no profit.

Recently, Agrifund has received an application from a firm of engineers who wish to develop equipment for cultivating steep mountain sides. It is believed that such machinery would have a major impact on farming in developing countries. Also, the applicants believe that it would be some years before their technology was copied and any competition developed. Two proposals have been made, codenamed Project A and Project B. The first is thought likely to take three years to develop fully, after which time almost certainly competition will cause the project to be reviewed. The second is thought to be more promising in its early years but more easily copied, so that by the third year sales would decline significantly unless design changes could be introduced. In addition, Project B is thought likely to run into raw materials shortages after its first year. The estimated cash flows for the two projects are given below, for the three-year decision period.

	Project A Initial outlay £900 000			*Project B* Initial outlay £1 000 000		
	Costs	*Sales*	*Profits*	*Costs*	*Sales*	*Profits*
Year 1	£600 000	£600 000	Nil	£200 000	£1 000 000	£800 000
Year 2	£600 000	£1 150 000	£550 000	£850 000	£1 300 000	£450 000
Year 3	£600 000	£1 400 000	£800 000	£900 000	£1 000 000	£100 000
Totals	£1 800 000	£3 150 000	£1 350 000	£1 950 000	£3 300 000	£1 350 000

Agrifund must answer three questions before agreeing to finance one of the projects:

1. Are both projects worthy of consideration?
2. Is one project better than the other?
3. Is the better project sufficiently profitable to cover Agrifund's interest charges and administration?

9.3   COLLECTING EVIDENCE FOR THE JUDGEMENT

9.3.1   A Good Profit?

Both projects yield a net surplus of accumulated profits over initial outlay, in terms of a three-year operation. Both yield £1.35 millions gross, and therefore are worth while in purely financial terms. The importance to be attached to such a surplus will depend upon how much the projects cost and the timing of the profits from sales. As we saw in Chapter 1, waiting for money robs it of purchasing power in a manner we may analyse by discounting future sums. Since these two projects are so very different, such considerations could be crucial as we shall see later. As a first approach, however, Agrifund would consider simple profitability.

Project A costs £900 000 in initial outlay, a further £1 800 000 over three years and sells machinery worth £3 150 000. Therefore the *net return* is £450 000 as follows:

$$
\begin{array}{l}
\text{Project} \\
\text{net} \\
\text{return}
\end{array}
=
\begin{array}{l}
\text{Value} \\
\text{of} \\
\text{sales}
\end{array}
-
\begin{array}{l}
\text{Annual} \\
\text{operating} \\
\text{costs}
\end{array}
-
\begin{array}{l}
\text{Initial} \\
\text{outlay}
\end{array}
$$

$$= £3\,150\,000 - £1\,800\,000 - £900\,000$$

$$= £450\,000 \text{ over three years}$$

By the same procedure, Project B yields a net return of £350 000 over three years, which gives it the appearance of a poorer project. In fact, things look even worse for Project B since it costs £1 000 000 in initial costs and £1 950 000 in operating costs over the period. It is altogether a more expensive project and yields a lower net return.

Another aspect of profitability is *return on sales*. In Project A, the net return of £450 000 arises from sales of £3 150 000 which gives a crude measure with value 0.143 or 14.3 per cent over the three years. In Project B, this return on sales is 0.106 or 10.6 per cent (£350 000 on sales of £3.3 million) and Project A again is selected as the more worth while. Another way of interpreting these values is 'pence in the pound profit from sales': for Project A, it is 14.3 pence, and for Project B, it is 10.6 pence.

A third aspect relates profit to cost in one of two ways. Operating costs of £1.8 millions in Project A yield total profit of £1.35 millions over three years: therefore every £1 of expenditure upon production and associated activities yields 75 pence profit from sales in three years. For Project B this *return on costs* is given by £1.35 millions profit divided by £1.95 millions operating costs, and is equal to 0.69 or 69 pence in every £1. Project A again is supported as the better of the two.

The other way to analyse returns in relation to costs is to compare total profits to total initial and operating costs. It is obvious without calculation that Project A is preferred to Project B because it has a lower initial cost and a higher return to operating cost. For Project A, total costs are £2.7 millions and total profits £1.35 millions so the following calculation can be made:

$$
\begin{array}{l}
\text{Return on} \\
\text{total cost}
\end{array}
=
\frac{\text{Total profit}}{\text{Total costs}}
$$

$$= \frac{£1.35 \text{ million}}{£2.7 \text{ million}}$$

$$= 0.50 \text{ or } 50 \text{ per cent in three years}$$

Note that this refers to profit, over and above paying operating costs and repaying initial outlay. The same calculation for Project B gives the value 0.458 or 45.8 per cent, which is less than for Project A.

We may summarize the evidence so far, relating to profitability, as in Table 9.1. It appears that Project A is preferable to Project B in these important respects. Nonetheless, both projects are worthwhile in that both yield a net surplus and acceptable returns in their three years of operation.

Table 9.1   *Commercial comparisons*

Measurement	Value for Project A	Value for Project B	Preferred project
Initial outlay	£900 000	£1 000 000	A
Operating costs	£1 800 000	£1 950 000	A
Net return	£450 000	£350 000	A
Return on sales	14.3%	10.6%	A
Return on operating costs	75%	69%	A
Return on total costs	50%	45.8%	A

9.3.2   Debts Must Be Repaid

Any money lent by Agrifund Ltd must be repaid and both projects carry the promise of being able to do so. Project A is a 'slow starter' in the sense that the technological problems cost as much to solve in the first year as the value of sales so that there is expected to be no contribution to repaying initial outlay. By contrast, Project B experiences little technical

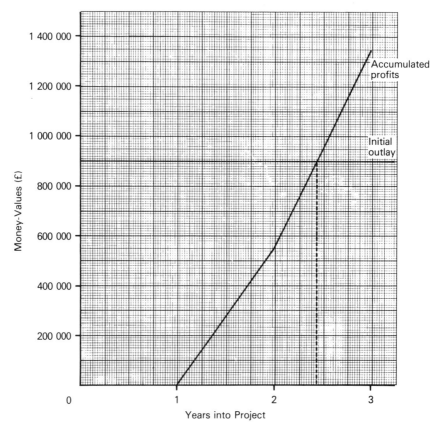

Figure 9.1   *Payback period for Project A*

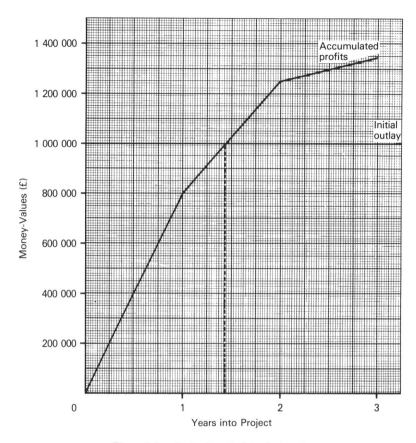

Figure 9.2 *Payback period for Project B*

expense in Year 1 but costs rise dramatically in Year 2 and again in Year 3. As a result, Project B makes a significant contribution in its first year towards repaying the initial loan (£800 000 out of £1 million) but relatively little thereafter. By the end of Year 2, Project B is expected to be able to repay its outlay: Project A is only just over halfway towards its £900 000. We may make a precise comparison between the two by calculating their *payback periods*. A payback period is defined as the minimum length of time over which accumulated financial surplus equals initial outlay. It is of particular interest to the lender since it measures a project's ability to pay for itself. In Figure 9.1 the payback period for Project A is seen to be 2.44 years. Note the assumptions that profits accumulate uniformly over each year, so that the graph consists of annual straight lines. Notice also, for Project A, that accumulated profits are zero until Year 2.

By comparison, Project B has a payback period of 1.44 years as Figure 9.2 shows. For the first time Project B is preferable to Project A: as a general rule, the shorter the payback period, the more attractive the project from the point of view of the financier since it carries the firmer promise of repayment.

The advantage of Project B's cash-flow pattern derives from the immediate sales performance in Year 1. As most business people will testify, a healthy cash flow during the early stages of any project gives confidence, to the extent that many commercial ventures have been shut down before they could prove their worth. Project B will not have such a problem and Agrifund Ltd will approve of its ability to make early returns.

9.3.3   Present Value Again

In Chapter 1 the idea was introduced that a sum of money received today is in some way worth more than the same amount in the future. We saw that future sums of money could be discounted to obtain their present value. For example, £100 to be received in two years' time, when interest is 12 per cent per year, can be discounted as follows:

$$\frac{\text{Present}}{\text{value}} = \frac{\text{Future value}}{\text{Compound interest factor}}$$

$$= \frac{£100}{(1.12)^2}$$

$$= \frac{£100}{1.254}$$

$$= \underline{£79.74}$$

The compound interest factor may be calculated or obtained from Table 1.2 in Chapter 1. The interpretation to be placed upon this present value is clear once we realize that £79.74 lent for two years at interest of 12 per cent per year becomes worth £100 eventually. In the context of the Agrifund decision, the timings of the various cash flows suggest a similar analysis over the three-year period in question. To simplify the calculation of present value, Table 9.2 gives the discounting factor for various times and rates of interest. Instead of dividing a future value by the compound interest factor, we need now only *multiply* it by this discounting factor. Each value in Table 9.2 is the reciprocal of the corresponding value in Table 1.2. The calculation now becomes:

$$\frac{\text{Present}}{\text{value}} = \frac{\text{Future}}{\text{value}} \times \frac{\text{Discounting}}{\text{factor}}$$

Discounting may now be applied to the two Agrifund projects. For example, the £800 000 received in profit after one year in Project B is not actually worth £800 000 at the moment the project commences because it must be waited for. The same applies to each of the net inflows enjoyed before discounting can be applied: we know the timings but not the rate of interest (*rate of discount*) to be applied. In section 9.2 we learned that Agrifund must pay 16 per cent upon its borrowing and must make a further two per cent to cover its own administration. Consequently, Agrifund must charge 18 per cent per year to stay in business. Another way of thinking about this is that every project Agrifund approves must be capable of making an 18 per cent return at least. This is the *minimum* rate of discount we may apply to the cash flows under the two projects. As we shall see later, it is also worth considering discounting at a higher rate to analyse the effects of a rise in interest rates, just in case that should occur.

Present values will be used to evaluate each project as follows:

1. Calculate the present value of each annual profit (net cash flow).
2. Sum the annual present values to obtain the total present value.
3. Compare total present value with initial outlay: the former should exceed the latter if a project is to be considered worth while.

Table 9.2 *Discount factors*

Years	6%	8%	10%	12%	14%	16%	18%	20%
				Rate of interest per year				
0	1.000	1.000	1.000	1.000	1.000	1.000	1.000	1.000
1	0.943	0.926	0.909	0.893	0.877	0.862	0.847	0.833
2	0.890	0.857	0.826	0.797	0.769	0.743	0.718	0.694
3	0.839	0.794	0.751	0.712	0.675	0.641	0.609	0.579
4	0.792	0.735	0.683	0.636	0.592	0.552	0.516	0.482
5	0.747	0.681	0.621	0.567	0.519	0.476	0.437	0.402
6	0.705	0.630	0.564	0.507	0.456	0.410	0.370	0.335
7	0.665	0.583	0.513	0.452	0.400	0.354	0.314	0.279
8	0.627	0.540	0.467	0.404	0.351	0.305	0.266	0.233
9	0.592	0.500	0.424	0.361	0.308	0.263	0.225	0.194
10	0.558	0.463	0.386	0.322	0.270	0.227	0.191	0.162
15	0.417	0.315	0.239	0.183	0.140	0.108	0.084	0.065
20	0.312	0.215	0.149	0.104	0.072	0.051	0.037	0.026
25	0.233	0.146	0.092	0.059	0.038	0.024	0.016	0.010

4. Subtract the initial outlay from total present value to obtain the *net present value* (NPV) for the project: this is the measure we require since it indicates the extent to which the project can pay its interest charges and still yield a return in excess.

The calculation is carried out in small tables such as Table 9.3 and Table 9.4, one for each project.

Table 9.3 *Net present value for Project A*

Time	Cash flow	18% discount factor	Present value
0	−£900 000	1.000	−£900 000
1	nil	0.847	0
2	+£550 000	0.718	£394 900
3	+£800 000	0.609	£487 200
	Net present value		−£17 900

Table 9.4 *Net present value for Project B*

Time	Cash flow	18% discount factor	Present value
0	−£1 000 000	1.000	−£1 000 000
1	+£800 000	0.847	£677 600
2	+£450 000	0.718	£323 100
3	+£100 000	0.609	£60 900
	Net present value		+£61 600

In both tables the cash-flow column gives the amount of money flowing and indicates whether it is an outflow (negative) or an inflow (positive). The present-value column is the product of cash flow and discount factors; note that initial outlay is not discounted at all since it occurs at the beginning, before any time has elapsed. The net present value is the arithmetic sum of the present-value column and is a measure of the overall effectiveness of the project in its ability to make an acceptable return. There is something obviously wrong with Project A: it bears a negative NPV which indicates that it is unable to cover the initial loan borrowed at 18 per cent. The sum total of all its profits when discounted to the beginning of the project's life is less than the cost of starting up. Stated bluntly, Project A is a loser at this rate of interest. The reason is clear: the £900 000 initial loan accumulates interest until the end of Year 2 without any repayment contribution being available from sales.

In Project B, the benefits of an early cash flow are clear in Table 9.4. After three years of operation it would be able to pay off the loan and also yield a return to its operators. Project B is preferred under this crucial criterion: Project A simply cannot pay its way.

The NPV's in Tables 9.3 and 9.4 should not be interpreted as profits or losses. They are precisely what the name implies: net profits or losses discounted to the project's commencement. Table 9.5 indicates the relationship between profit and NPV for Project A by analysing the reduction of the initial £900 000 loan. Repayments are shown as negative on the assumption that all annual profits are used for that purpose and that no further debt is incurred. The closing debt of about £30 000 shows that repayments have been unable to keep pace with interest. The present value of this residual debt may be found by the usual procedure:

$$\frac{\text{Present}}{\text{value}} = £29\,729 \times \frac{\text{Discount}}{\text{factor}}$$

$$= £29\,729 \times 0.609$$

$$= \underline{£18\,000} \text{ approximately (an owed amount)}$$

This is the NPV for Project A as found in Table 9.3. There is a discrepancy between the two because the discount factors in Table 9.2 are rounded to three places of decimals. As a consequence the £17 900 is a slight underestimate. This debt analysis makes clear again Project A's inability to pay for itself.

Table 9.5   *Management of debt in Project A*

Years into project	Opening debt (£)	18% interest (£)	Total debt (£)	Repaid from profits (£)	Closing debt (£)
1	900 000	162 000	1 062 000	nil	1 062 000
2	1 062 000	191 160	1 253 160	−550 000	703 160
3	703 160	126 569	829 729	−800 000	29 729

In conclusion here we can say that Project B is the one which would be worth considering for a loan at 18 per cent interest. The evidence for its superiority is beginning to gain weight.

9.3.4   What If Interest Rates Change?

Project B is viable at 18 per cent initial on capital loans, but Project A is not. Presumably, at some lower interest rate, Project A would become worth while and conversely, at some higher interest rate, Project B would cease to be. All realistic projects should be able to cover 10 per cent but hardly any would be expected to cover 50 per cent. Project A, for example, possesses a positive NPV of £155 597 at a discount rate of 10 per cent and of £41 892 at 15 per cent. If money could be borrowed at these rates, Project A would be worth while. Table 9.6 shows the effect upon Project A's net present value for a variety of discount rates and it is clear that between 16 per cent and 20 per cent the cutoff value exists at which NPV is zero. That rate is the maximum under which Project A could operate and we know that it is less than 18 per cent.

At a 16 per cent discount rate both projects would be economical, although Project B would be preferred, possessing an NPV of £88 144 against £21 266 for Project A. At a discount rate of only six per cent, Project A has NPV of £261 193 and Project B has NPV of £239 177 so that the former would be preferred if capital could be obtained so cheaply. The changeover at such low rates results from the £100 000 difference in the initial outlays: interest is relatively unimportant in comparison with the initial saving. For a wide range of discount rates, Figure 9.3 shows the NPV for both projects and it is clear that Project A is preferred only at very low rates.

Note that both curves intersect the vertical axis at their basic accounting net surpluses of £450 000 and £350 000 respectively. This is because at zero discount rate there is no interest to be paid and all profits are accumulated without suffering the reduction due to waiting. It is a general principle in managerial economics that the lower the interest rate, the more projects can be regarded as commercial propositions and Figure 9.3 is an explanation. It must be admitted that the calculation of points in Figure 9.3 is tedious and prone to error. However, many readers will have knowledge of elementary computing and a BASIC program can be specified simply as follows:

Table 9.6   *Sensitivity of Project A to interest rate*

Time	Cash flow (£)	Discount factors			Present values (£)		
		12%	*16%*	*20%*	*12%*	*16%*	*20%*
0	−900 000	1.000	1.000	1.000	−900 000	−900 000	−900 000
1	nil	0.893	0.862	0.833	0	0	0
2	+550 000	0.797	0.743	0.694	438 350	408 650	381 700
3	+800 000	0.712	0.641	0.579	569 600	512 800	463 200
			Net present values		+ 107 950	+ 21 450	−55 100

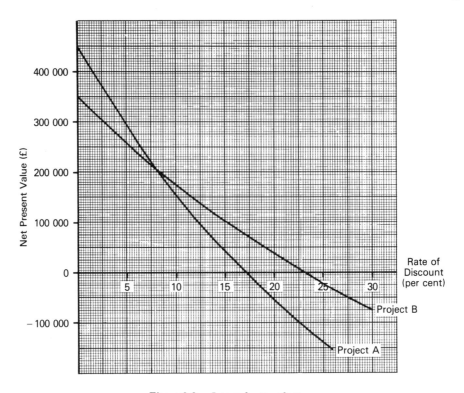

Figure 9.3   *Internal rates of return*

```
10 DIM P(10), V(10)
20 PRINT 'ENTER INITIAL OUTLAY ';
30 INPUT C1
40 PRINT 'NUMBER OF PERIODS ';
50 INPUT N1
60 FOR N2=1 TO N1 STEP 1
70 PRINT 'PERIOD ';N2;' PROFIT ';
80 INPUT P(N2)
90 NEXT N2
100 FOR R1=.0 TO .3 STEP .02
110 V1=−C1
120 FOR N2=1 TO N1 STEP 1
130 V(N2)=P(N2) * (1+R1)↑(−N2)
140 V1=V1+V(N2)
150 NEXT N2
160 PRINT 'FOR ';100 * R1;' PER CENT        NPV= ';V1
170 NEXT R1
180 END
```

This short program is appropriate for the Agrifund data and will produce a table of NPV's for interest rates up to 30 per cent. It is not especially efficient in computing terms but the reader may wish to run it, vary the cash-flow values and experiment with better lay-outs and output procedures. The printout for Project A is given below:

```
ENTER INITIAL OUTLAY !900000
NUMBER OF PERIODS !3
PERIOD 1    PROFIT !0
PERIOD 2    PROFIT !550000
PERIOD 3    PROFIT !800000
FOR  0 PER CENT              NPV= 450000
FOR  2 PER CENT              NPV= 382500.69
FOR  4 PER CENT              NPV= 319703.00
FOR  6 PER CENT              NPV= 261193.46
FOR  8 PER CENT              NPV= 206602.14
FOR 10 PER CENT                NPV= 155597.29
FOR 12 PER CENT                NPV= 107880.83
FOR 14 PER CENT                NPV= 63184.35
FOR 16 PER CENT                NPV= 21265.73
FOR 18 PER CENT                NPV= -18093.86*
FOR 20 PER CENT                NPV= -55092.59
FOR 22 PER CENT                NPV= -89910.16
FOR 24 PER CENT                NPV= -122709.87
FOR 26 PER CENT                NPV= -153640.31
FOR 28 PER CENT                NPV= -182836.91
FOR 30 PER CENT                NPV= -210423.30
```

*This is the correct value without the rounding errors of Table 9.3.
Note: Underlining indicates entry by the reader.

From Figure 9.3 and the computer printout we see that Project A would cease to be worth while at any discount rate greater than 17 per cent. Since the discount rate includes a two per cent administration charge by Agrifund Ltd, Project A could be considered only if finance were available at 15 per cent interest. It is usual to state this result by saying that Project A has an *internal rate of return* of 17 per cent. This figure measures the project's ability to cover the costs of borrowing. By the same process we see that NPV for Project B is zero at a discount rate of about 23 per cent so that is its internal rate of return.

Project B, therefore, could cover a rate of interest of about 21 per cent in addition to Agrifund's administration charge. This means that Project B is not only preferable to Project A at 18 per cent, as we have seen, but also is able to accommodate substantial increases in interest rates before its viability is jeopardized. Project B is said to be *robust to interest rate changes* and the decision to adopt it would be called a robust decision because slight alterations in the business environment should not cause it to be cancelled.

9.4   WEIGHING THE EVIDENCE

9.4.1   Taking a Numerical View

On commercial grounds, having regard to sales and costs, we saw in Table 9.1 that Project A was to be preferred. However, trading considerations are insufficient grounds for judgement because no business is involved only with selling. It also must be financed and these aspects are of greater importance since often they will be under the control of an external source of funds. All businesses must pay their way regardless of their market performance. Project A has superior market performance over three years but in terms of its debts it cannot discharge its liability. Table 9.7 summarizes all the analysis carried out in previous sections of this chapter and there can be little doubt that Project B is the one to recommend.

Table 9.7   *Full comparison between projects*

Type of comparison	Measurement	Value for Project A	Value for Project B	Preferred project
	Initial outlay	£900 000	£1 000 000	A
	Operating costs	£1 800 000	£1 950 000	A
	Net return	£450 000	£350 000	A
Commercial	Return on sales	14.3%	10.6%	A
	Return on operating costs	75%	69%	A
	Return on total costs	50%	45.8%	A
	Payback period	2.44 yrs	1.44 yrs	B
	NPV at 18%	−£18 000	+£61 600	B
Financial	Internal rate of return	17%	23%	B
	Maximum interest rate covered	15%	21%	B

9.4.2   The Unknown Quantities

Taking a three-year analysis of Agrifund's decision may be reasonable as regards the available estimates. But three years is not a long time in business and the analyst normally attempts to gain a longer perspective on problems. Project A has been rejected on a three-year comparison but consider again its performance at the end of the decision period: it has an increasing profit, steady costs and rising sales. Compare these with Project B which has diminishing profits, rising costs and falling sales. Reviewing both projects at the end of Year 3, there can be no doubt that Project A looks to be a better proposition than Project B, even though the former is still in debt to Agrifund Ltd. Project A has a promise of long-term viability but Project B has all the appearance of fading away very soon. What the analyst would like is a forecast of future sales, even if only for a further two or three years. If both projects continue for two years to make profits at their Year 3 rate, Project A is preferred under all the criteria in Table 9.7, both commercial and financial.

There may be other subjective aspects of decision-making which would be meaningless in terms of any numerical criterion. For example, expected loss, even in just one year, can be unattractive to shareholders, bank managers or a government agency. This is true even if a profit is expected in every other year and is due to the uneducated belief that only bad projects make losses.

9.4.3   Conclusion

Agrifund Ltd should decide that Project B be financed so long as interest rates remain at the 16 per cent level. If they do fall below 15 per cent, or if there is a likelihood of that happening in a year or so, then Project A would be preferred since it seems to display better long-term prospects. If a rise in interest rates seems probable, then there can be no doubt that Project B is the only one to choose. If they rise above 21 per cent, or if such a level is anticipated, then neither project should be accepted for financing by Agrifund Ltd.

ASSIGNMENTS

(The reader could use the computer program in these assignments.)

A9.1 A company has two alternative investment projects but only sufficient capital to embark on one of them.

> *Project 1* costs £1000 initially and £100 per year for the next *three* years thereafter. The sales incomes in years 1, 2, 3 and 4 are respectively: £300, £500, £500 and £400. There is no cost in the fourth year.
>
> *Project 2* costs £600 initially and £150 per year for the next four years thereafter. The sales incomes in years 1, 2, 3 and 4 are respectively: £200, £300, £550 and £400.

Both projects have a lifespan of only four years and the company normally expects a 12 per cent return on invested capital. You are asked to decide which project is the more attractive. Use commercial criteria to select one of the projects.

A9.2 For both projects in A9.1 calculate the net present value and derive the internal rate of return. Then comment upon the economic value of both of them and advise the adoption of one. (Note: in this case the discount rate is not related to rate of interest but instead to the company's expected rate of return. If the internal rate of return is not equal to the expected rate of return, the reader should ponder the meaning of the latter.)

A9.3 A small company has £150 000 at its disposal for modernization of plant. Two alternative plans have been put forward: one will take some years to put fully into practice and the other is expected to run into technical problems after an easy start. Evaluation of the projects is to be based on a four-year decision period. Interest rates are about 12 per cent.

> *Plan 1* Initial outlay £150 000; annual running cost £75 000; income in first year £55 000 rising each year thereafter by £50 000.
>
> *Plan 2* Initial outlay £150 000; annual running cost £50 000 in first year rising each year thereafter by £20 000; income constant at £130 000 per year.

(a) Which plan would you advise the company to adopt?
(b) How would your advice differ if a fifth year were to be considered?

A9.4 An inventor has £10 000 which he invests in the development of a new type of plant propagation cabinet. During the first year he makes a profit of £23 000 but during the second year he runs into a legal problem over patent rights. During the second year he makes a loss of £13 200 paying creditors and legal expenses. He decides to close down the business before his losses increase.

(a) Calculate his overall profit or loss in the two years of operation.
(b) Calculate the net present value of the business over the two years of its life, using a discount rate of 14 per cent.
(c) Calculate the net present value again at 20 per cent discount rate.
(d) Plot upon an NPV graph the three values found above and calculate as many other points as necessary to display the form of the function.
(e) Discuss the form of the NPV function. In particular, comment upon the internal rate of return for the business. (Note: this exercise points out a weakness in the earlier analysis since it suggests that borrowing money at 14 per cent is better than borrowing it free. All that can be said at this stage is that discounting methods are not always applicable when mixture of losses and profits occur.)

10–Decisions Under Risk and Uncertainty

10.1 INTRODUCTION AND OBJECTIVES

10.1.1 The Subject of the Chapter

Any view of the individual, the household, the firm or the government as a decision-making unit presupposes the existence of *choice*. While certain conditions ('states of nature') are given and hence beyond our control, we can choose a number of strategies—even choosing to do nothing is a strategy.

Given, let us say, three possible states of nature (E_1, E_2 and E_3) and two possible strategies (S_1 and S_2), there are *six* possible results (r). These results can be shown in one of two ways, either by:

1. A pay-off table; or
2. A decision tree.

Let us consider each in turn. Table 10.1 is an example of a pay-off table. If we adopt strategy S_1 and event E_2 occurs, then the result (pay-off) will be r_{12}. The same information may be displayed by means of a decision tree as in Figure 10.1.

If we knew with *certainty* which event (reflation or recession, say) would occur, the decision would be obvious. Unfortunately, however, events are seldom certain. There remain two situations; on the one hand, *uncertainty* and, on the other, *risk*. The distinction between the two involves probabilities. Risk is used to denote events to which probabilities of occurrence can be assigned and uncertainty where probabilities are unknown.

We shall deal first with decision-making under uncertainty and then under conditions of risk. Although at first the pay-off table will be employed, in the later sections decision trees will be used.

Table 10.1 *A pay-off table*

		Events		
		E_1	E_2	E_3
Strategies	S_1	r_{11}	r_{12}	r_{13}
	S_2	r_{21}	r_{22}	r_{23}

Pay-off

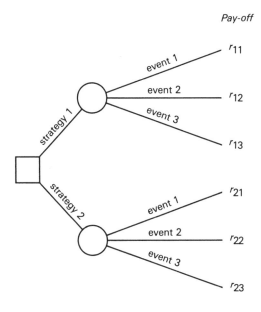

Figure 10.1 *A decision tree*

10.1.2 Objectives

1. To be familiar with the use of pay-off tables and decision trees.
2. To be able to apply a number of decision criteria under conditions of uncertainty and of risk.
3. To be able to calculate the EMV, EVPI and EOL for different strategies.
4. To be aware of the role played in decision-making by non-monetary factors.

10.2 BASIC PROBLEM DATA

A manufacturer must decide now his strategy for next year. There are four feasible strategies: expand, maintain present output level, cut back, and most drastic of all, liquidate. He has researched the monetary results of each of the strategies, given that one of two events, continued recession or reflation, will occur. This is best shown in the form of a pay-off matrix:

	Event	
Strategy	*reflation*	*recession*
Expand	+ £750 000	− £420 000
Maintain	+ £390 000	+ £150 000
Cut back	+ £210 000	+ £180 000
Liquidate	+ £125 000	+ £125 000

Table 10.2   *A pay-off table for the problem data*

			Event	
			reflation	*recession*
Strategy	1.	*expand*	+ £750 000	− £420 000
	2.	*maintain*	+ £390 000	+ £150 000
	3.	*cut back*	+ £210 000	+ £180 000
	4.	*liquidate*[a]	+ £125 000	+ £125 000

[a] Non-admissible strategy

10.3   NO CHANCE!

10.3.1   Dominance and Admissibility

After setting out the data in a suitable form, the next step is to identify any obvious 'non-starters' and remove them from further consideration.

Although at this stage there is no obvious best strategy, it is possible to exclude one from further consideration. It can be seen from Table 10.2 that strategy 4 (liquidate) is inferior to both strategies 2 and 3 for both possible events. If the firm's aim is to maximize pay-off, it would be irrational to select strategy 4 in preference to 2 or 3. We say that strategies 2 and 3 *dominate* strategy 4, rendering it *non-admissible*. We therefore remove it from further consideration. Notice, however, that strategy 1 does not dominate strategy 4; which one is preferred depends on which event occurs. However, for a strategy to be rendered non-admissible, it is only necessary for it to be dominated by any one alternative strategy. It is not possible to eliminate any other strategy, and so we are left with the three strategies shown in Table 10.3.

Table 10.3   *A pay-off table of admissible strategies*

		Event	
		reflation	*recession*
Strategy	*expand*	+ £750 000	− £420 000
	maintain	+ £390 000	+ £150 000
	cut back	+ £210 000	+ £180 000

Without additional information we are unable to select the 'best' strategy. What is required is a decision rule. There are four major rules available:

1. The pessimistic (maximin).
2. The optimistic (maximax).
3. Opportunity loss or regret (minimax).
4. Equal likelihood.

These will be considered in turn.

Table 10.4 *A pay-off table showing the worse outcome for each strategy*

		Event	
		reflation	*recession*
Strategy	*expand*	+ £750 000	− £420 000
	maintain	+ £390 000	+ £150 000
	cut back	+ £210 000	+ £180 000

10.3.2 Prepared for the Worst

A pessimist always expects the worst to happen. Adopting this outlook we must consider each strategy in turn and note the worst outcome possible. In the problem, there are only two possible outcomes for each strategy: one if reflation occurs and one if recession occurs. In Table 10.4 the worse outcome for each strategy is underlined.

These underlined figures represent the minimum pay-off possible for each strategy. Of these which is preferred? Clearly a profit of £180 000 is better than a profit of £150 000 or a loss of £420 000, and thus we should opt for strategy 3 (cut back). This is termed the *maximin criterion* because it aims to maximize the minimum pay-offs, that is, to make the best of a bad situation.

If, instead of attempting to maximize something such as profit or revenue, the nature of the exercise is to *minimize* some quantity such as losses or costs, the appropriate criterion for the pessimist is termed the *minimax criterion*. In this case we choose the action which minimizes the maximum pay-off.

10.3.3 Looking Through Rose-Tinted Glasses

Where optimism reigns, the manufacturer will expect, for each strategy, the best possible outcome. The corresponding pay-offs are underlined in Table 10.5.

The firm will then select the strategy associated with the best of the three under-lined pay-offs. This is to expand, giving a profit of £750 000. This is termed the *maximax criterion*. To apply this in general we identify the best event that can happen, i.e. the largest value of each row of the pay-off table, and then select the strategy which will bring about the largest of these. If the object is to minimize something (losses, costs, etc.), the criterion is termed *minimin*.

Table 10.5 *A pay-off table showing the better outcome for each strategy*

		Event	
		reflation	*recession*
Strategy	*expand*	+ £750 000	− £420 000
	maintain	+ £390 000	+ £150 000
	cut back	+ £210 000	+ £180 000

10.3.4 Lost Opportunities

The opportunity loss, or regret approach, focuses on the opportunity cost of not choosing what eventually turns out to have been the best strategy; hence the term 'regret'.

Consider our manufacturer. If he decides to expand and the recession continues, his *opportunity loss* (OL) is not just the £420 000 loss he actually makes but also the £180 000 he would have made had he made the right decision (to cut back). The opportunity loss is therefore £600 000. The complete picture is given in Table 10.6. A zero occurs where the best strategy has been selected, since no opportunity loss is involved.

Table 10.6   *An opportunity loss table for the problem data*

		Event	
		reflation	*recession*
	expand	0	£600 000
Strategy	*maintain*	£360 000	£30 000
	cut back	£540 000	0

In general, if the pay-offs represent quantities we wish to make large (such as profit or revenue), we calculate opportunity losses by subtracting each pay-off in an event column from the largest value in that column. Conversely, for losses or costs, we subtract the smallest column value from each value in that column. Thus, the OL for the 'maintain' strategy if reflation occurs is £750 000 − £390 000 = £360 000 as in Table 10.6.

Having calculated the opportunity losses what decision rule should we apply? The *minimax* criterion is applied because this will lead us to choose the strategy which will ensure that the greatest possible opportunity loss (if the less favourable event should occur) is kept to a minimum. These maximum opportunity losses are underlined in Table 10.7.

Table 10.7   *An opportunity loss table with the maxima marked*

		Event	
		reflation	*recession*
	expand	0	£600 000
Strategy	*maintain*	£360 000	£30 000
	cut back	£540 000	0

On this basis, the manufacturer should choose to maintain current levels of output since that strategy is consistent with the minimum (£360 000) of the three maximum opportunity losses.

10.3.5 Equal Likelihood

In our example, we have considered two possible events, reflation and recession. We made no attempt to say which is more likely because this would involve assigning probabilities and this section deals with uncertainty (no known probabilities).

In the absence of information on probabilities we could assume that all events are *equally likely*. The probability for each of n events is then given by $p(E) = 1/n$. In our example, since there are two possible events (reflation or recession), each is assigned a probability of 1/2, i.e. 0.5. If we adopt this approach we are implicitly assigning probabilities to events, albeit in a rather negative manner. Each strategy would then be evaluated by the mean of its pay-offs, resulting in £165 000 for expansion, £270 000 for maintaining output and £195 000 for a cutback. The second strategy would then be selected. We shall now consider decision criteria where probabilities are more positively and explicitly employed.

10.4 DEGREES OF RISK

10.4.1 Mathematical Expectations

Clearly, decision-making under conditions of uncertainty is less than satisfactory and some knowledge of the likelihood or probability of events is desirable. While informal, subjective views of probabilities (such as 'hunches') may be used, many firms employ specialists for this task and often surveys are conducted in advance.

Given that we can now assign probabilities, it is possible to calculate mathematical expectations which enable us to base decisions on EMVs (expected monetary values) of the alternative strategies. This involves us in the use of *Bayes' decision rule*, named after a pioneer analyst. Consider the manufacturer's pay-off table again (Table 10.3).

Suppose there is reason to believe that the odds are 2 to 1 in favour of reflation. The probability of reflation is therefore $2/(2 + 1) = 2/3$. The probability of recession must then be 1/3. In general, the expected monetary value (which in this case is profit) is obtained for each strategy by summing the product of each pay-off and its probability of occurrence. For the problem data we obtain the following expected monetary values:

1. Expand: expected profit $= (£750\,000 \times 2/3) + (-£420\,000 \times 1/3) = +£360\,000$.
2. Maintain: expected profit $= (£390\,000 \times 2/3) + (£150\,000 \times 1/3) = +£310\,000$.
3. Cut back: expected profit $= (£210\,000 \times 2/3) + (£180\,000 \times 1/3) = +£200\,000$.

Since an expected profit of £360 000 is preferable to an expected profit of £310 000 or £200 000 the Bayesian decision rule would lead the manufacturer to decide in favour of expansion.

10.4.2 A Sensitive Issue

It is important to note that the assigned probabilities could turn out to be wrong. As a result, depending on the probabilities assigned, different decisions may be made. To illustrate this last point let us assign different probabilities to the manufacturer's problem.

Let the probability of reflation be 3/5 and of recession be 2/5. Then the EMVs (expected profit) are as follows.

1. Expand: (£750 000 × 3/5) + (− £420 000 × 2/5) = + £282 000.
2. Maintain: (£390 000 × 3/5) + (£150 000 × 2/5) = + £294 000.
3. Cut back: (£210 000 × 3/5) + (£180 000 × 2/5) = + £198 000.

A slight change in assigned probabilities has led to a different decision; this time maintenance of present output levels will be the preferred decision. Measuring how sensitive decisions are to changes in assigned probabilities is a problem of *sensitivity analysis* and will not be considered further in this volume.

Since Bayesian expectation is calculated as the product of the pay-off and the appropriate probability, decisions may also be sensitive to change in the pay-off values themselves. A prudent firm will keep assigned probabilities and estimated pay-offs under constant review.

10.4.3   Expected Opportunity Loss

When prior probabilities are available, the Bayesian decision rule may be applied to calculate not only EMVs but also *expected opportunity losses* (EOLs). The EOLs, using the original probabilities of 2/3 and 1/3, are shown in Table 10.8.

Table 10.8   *Expected opportunity losses.*

		Expected Opportunity Loss
	expand	£200 000
Strategy	*maintain*	£250 000
	cut back	£360 000

The EOL of £200 000 for the expansion strategy is obtained by multiplying the opportunity loss for each event by the probability that the event will occur. Thus the EOLs for all the strategies are as follows.

1. Expand: (£0 × 2/3) + (£600 000 × 1/3) = £200 000.
2. Maintain: (£360 000 × 2/3) + (£30 000 × 1/3) = £250 000.
3. Cut back: (£540 000 × 2/3) + (£0 × 1/3) = £360 000.

Therefore, in order to minimize the expected opportunity loss, the expansion strategy should be chosen.

10.4.4   How Much Is Advice Worth?

Bearing in mind that the worst possible outcomes result from selecting precisely the wrong strategy for a particular event, think how useful perfect information would be. How much then should a firm be willing to pay for such information? The answer is the *expected value of perfect information* (EVPI). Note that the pay-off with perfect information is that which results from making the best decision for each particular event. In the manufacturer's problem, if reflation occurs, the optimum decision would have been to expand, and conversely if recession occurs, it would have been to cut back. Thus the expected profit with perfect information is:

$$(£750\,000 \times 2/3) + (£180\,000 \times 1/3) \ = \ £560\,000$$

We can now calculate how much of an improvement would result from having perfect knowledge. Remember that using these prior probabilities led us to estimate the maximum expected profit (by selecting the expansion strategy) to be £360 000. The difference, £560 000 − £360 000 = £200 000, indicates the maximum the manufacturer should be willing to pay for perfect information. The result, EVPI = minimum EOL, is not a coincidence. In fact, EVPI always equals the minimum expected opportunity loss.

10.4.5   Choose One Strategy

It is the purpose of risk analysis to identify one strategy which satisfies a broad range of criteria and so may be judged best overall. From the lists below, we can see that this does not happen.

Criterion	*Optimal strategy*
Maximin pay-off	Cut back
Maximax pay-off	Expand
Minimax regret	Maintain
Equal likelihood	Maintain
EMV (with probabilities of 2/3 and 1/3)	Expand
EMV (with probabilities of 3/5 and 2/5)	Maintain
EOL	Expand

Clearly, the uncertainties of the situation have swamped the analysis; this is a frequent experience in business. On a purely personal, subjective level, many analysts in such a case would opt for the maximin selection, to allow for the worst that could happen.

10.5   TREE DIAGRAMS AGAIN

10.5.1   Trees as an Alternative to Tables

The analysis so far has relied on pay-off tables, but decision trees could have been employed. In fact, decision trees are often preferred, especially for complex problems.

In short, decision trees can be employed where:

1. Sequential decision-making is required which involves a large number of possible results.
2. Events are not the same for each possible strategy.
3. The decision-maker may wish to experiment or conduct a survey at particular stages.

In this section we shall apply decision-tree analysis to the manufacturer's problem under conditions of risk and then develop a more complex example to illustrate the true worth of decision trees.

10.5.2   Components of a Decision Tree

All decision trees have the same overall structure, in the way that living trees all have roots, branches, bark, leaves and so on. The analogy can be applied to decision trees since they all consist of:

1. Branches representing a single strategy or event.
2. Decision nodes represented by □. Branches from these represent possible strategies.

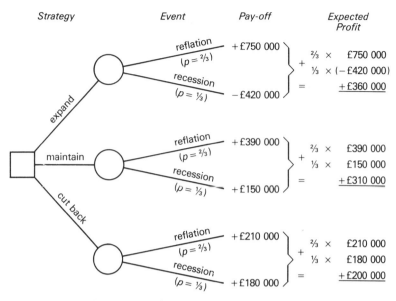

Figure 10.2   *The problem in decision-tree form*

3. Event nodes represented by ○.
4. Outcomes (pay-offs) which are the results of a sequence of strategies and events that define a unique path in the tree from the initial node to the final node.

The *optimal decision* is to choose the set of strategies that yields the *best expected value* for the initial node.

10.5.3   The Manufacturer Problem Again

Using the probabilities assigned in section 10.4.1, i.e. the probability of reflation = 2/3 and the probability of recession = 1/3, the manufacturer's problem is illustrated in Figure 10.2.
       Thus, in order to maximize expected profit we should opt for the expansion path. The situation if we had perfect information is shown in Figure 10.3 .
       Notice how, in Figure 10.3, certain paths are discarded because, with perfect information, the best path for a given event will always be followed. To show how they were arrived at, the expected profits have been shown at the far right of each diagram. However, it is conventional to work from *right to left* and show the expected value associated with each decision branch at each decision node, selecting the best and discarding the rest until we eventually arrive back at the original choice of strategies armed with an EMV for each. This is shown in Figure 10.4.
       Clearly the best strategy is to expand and this should be chosen. Discarded strategies are indicated by lines across the branch at the decision node. Let us now consider a more complex problem in which the decision tree will really come into its own.

10.6   A MORE COMPLEX PROBLEM

10.6.1   The Problem Stated

A country, anxious to stimulate the industrial development of its economy, will grant a licence to the firm tendering the best scheme for the manufacture of sheet metal. In order

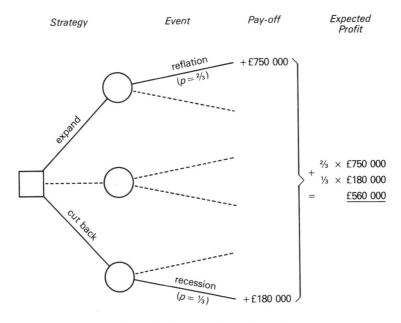

Figure 10.3   *Decision tree with perfect information*

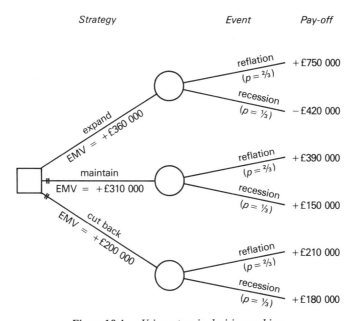

Figure 10.4   *Using a tree in decision-making*

to compete, Tinpot Metals Ltd will have to spend £800 000 on modifications to its production process to suit local conditions. If this is done, the firm is reasonably confident ($p = 0.8$) of obtaining the licence. If it is unsuccessful, the project will be terminated, but if successful, a decision must be made on the scale of operation. Much depends on whether the firm can subsequently capture the market of the neighbouring country ($p = 0.3$). If

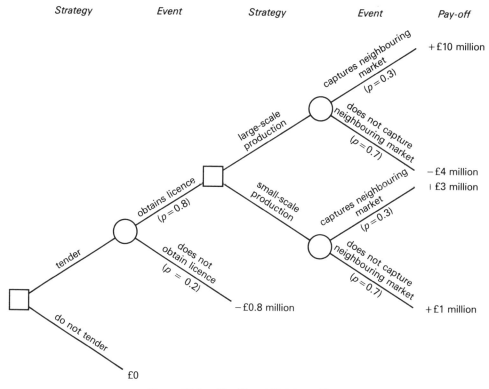

Figure 10.5   *The Tinpot Metals problem*

large-scale production is undertaken and the neighbouring market is captured, the net profit is estimated at £10 million but a loss of £4 million will be incurred if the second market is not secured. For small-scale manufacture if the neighbouring market is captured, a profit of £3 million is anticipated while, if it is not, a profit of £1 million will be made.

Advise Tinpot Metals.

The information showing the correct sequence of events is set out in Figure 10.5.

10.6.2   To Tender or Not to Tender?

Figure 10.6 illustrates the calculations necessary to enable a decision to be made on the basis of EMVs.

Working from *right to left* we commence at the topmost decision branch (large-scale manufacturing). The EMV for this option is calculated as follows:

$$\text{EMV (high)} = (+£10 \text{ million} \times 0.3) + (-£4 \text{ million} \times 0.7) = +£0.2 \text{ million}$$

and the figure, £0.2 million is entered at the appropriate decision node. The low-level manufacturing option gives the following EMV:

$$\text{EMV (low)} = (+£3 \text{ million} \times 0.3) + (+£1 \text{ million} \times 0.7) = +£1.6 \text{ million}$$

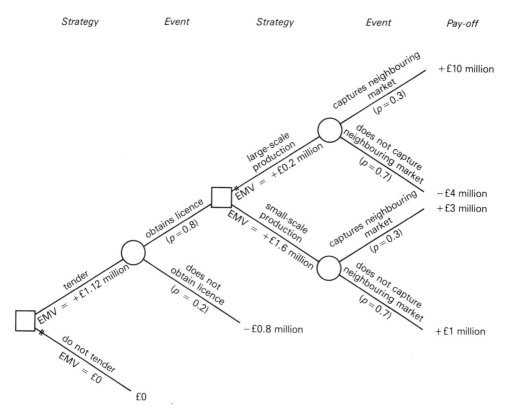

Figure 10.6 *Decision-making for the Tinpot Metals problem*

and this value is entered at the appropriate decision node. At this point we are in a position to eliminate one of the decision branches (large- or small-scale manufacturing) in favour of the other.

Clearly the branch with the higher EMV is to be preferred. We choose small-scale manufacturing (EMV = +£1.6 million) and discard (note the parallel lines through it) the large-scale manufacturing decision branch.

We now continue our right to left search for the optimal decision. In this example the next decision point is in fact the initial decision point. The EMVs for the two decision branches are calculated as follows:

$$\text{EMV (carry out modifications and make tender)} = (£1.6 \text{ million} \times 0.8)$$

$$+ (- £0.8 \text{ million} \times 0.2)$$

$$= £1.12 \text{ million}$$

$$\text{EMV (don't)} = £0$$

When these are inserted at the appropriate (initial) decision node, the choice of decision is obvious, *the firm will choose to modify with a view to tendering.* Note again how we show that the 'do not tender' strategy is discarded by means of parallel lines.

10.7   FURTHER DEVELOPMENTS

10.7.1   Events Need Not Be Accidents

So far it has been assumed that events (the Es) just occur. However, in business the relevant events may well be the actions of competitors. In other words, whether E_1, E_2 or E_3 etc., occurs is within the control of a *competing firm*. In the manufacturer's case, the two events E_1 and E_2 could, instead of reflation or recession, be: E_1 = competitor chooses not to expand; E_2 = competitor chooses to expand.

In this case the strategies of one firm become the events of the other. A pay-off table can be constructed and the decision criteria previously discussed applied. However, the *theory of games*, as this is often termed, is beyond the scope of this text.

10.7.2   Odd Behaviour!

So far the analysis has assumed, like much of economic theory, that firms attempt to maximize easily measurable (tangible) quantities such as profit or revenue, or alternatively seek to minimize losses or costs. Behavioural theories of the firm suggest that intangibles conferring *utility* can play an important part in decision-making. Where this is so, the monetary value of a pay-off may under- or overstate the utility gained. If this occurs, the firm may make what appears to be the 'wrong' decision on the basis of purely monetary values. For example, if the manufacturer in the original problem knows that an essential bank loan would be called in if he failed to make a profit in the forthcoming year, this would make the possibility of a £420 000 loss (see Table 10.3) even more to be feared. In this case he might opt *not* to expand even where prior probabilities would otherwise lead him to do so.

Clearly, to include utility considerations in our decision analysis requires that we can in some way measure them. This is not an easy task and will not be considered here. Let it suffice to say that monetary pay-offs do not always show the complete picture and therefore some apparently 'irrational' decisions are in fact rational when all such factors are considered.

10.8   CONCLUSION

A number of decision criteria of varying degrees of complexity have been considered in this chapter. It is important to bear in mind throughout that the selected decision criterion is only as good as the data (including, where appropriate, probabilities) on which it is based.

ASSIGNMENTS

A10.1   A businessman has to travel to Birmingham to negotiate a contract, which may take one or two days to complete. He has to decide on a purely monetary basis whether to travel by car, or by train. If he chooses the latter he must also decide whether to buy a cheap day return or an ordinary return. He estimates the cost by car to be

£50 regardless of whether the business is concluded in one or two days. The cost of a day-return rail ticket is £40, of an ordinary return £60, and of a single £30.

(a) Which of the strategies is non-admissible and why?

Using the following decision criteria advise the businessman.

(b) Pessimistic (minimax).
(c) Optimistic (minimin).
(d) Opportunity loss/regret (minimax).
(e) Equally likely.

Now, if the businessman estimates the probability of completion in one day to be 0.7, advise him by means of:

(f) Expected monetary values.
(g) Expected opportunity losses.

Also:

(h) What is the expected value of perfect information?
(i) What factors, other than the purely monetary cost, might be taken into account, and how?

A10.2 An individual who has won £10 000 on the football pools intends using it to buy a house in a year's time. In the meantime she is undecided between two options. First, she could deposit it in a building society and obtain 10 per cent interest per annum. Second, she could become a sleeping partner in a friend's business venture. If the venture is successful she will be able to sell her interest in the venture for £30 000 in 12 months' time. If it is unsuccessful she will lose her £10 000.

Advise the individual on the better alternative by means of the following criteria:

(a) Pessimistic (maximin).
(b) Optimistic (maximax).
(c) Opportunity loss (minimax).
(d) Equally likely.

Having researched her friend's proposed venture, the individual estimates its probability of success to be 0.3. Advise her using the following criteria:

(e) Expected monetary value.
(f) Expected opportunity loss.

Finally:

(g) What is the maximum she should be willing to pay for perfect information on the venture's future?

A10.3 A newly formed taxi firm must decide on the size and nature of its fleet. It must decide whether to purchase one or two vehicles, and if it chooses the former, whether to supplement it with an option on a lease of an extra vehicle, as and when required. The problem is summarized in the following pay-off table, which shows estimated profits.

Strategy	Event (level of demand)	
	moderate	*large*
purchase 1	£20 000	£20 000
purchase 1 + lease 1	£18 000	£24 000
purchase 2	£2000	£30 000

Advise the firm on the best strategy using the following decision criteria:

(a)   Pessimistic.
(b)   Optimistic.
(c)   Opportunity loss.
(d)   Equally likely.

Now, assuming the relevant probabilities to be moderate demand (0.6) and large demand (0.4), advise the firm using the following decision criteria:

(e)   Expected monetary value (net profit).
(f)   Expected opportunity loss.

Finally:

(g)   What is the maximum amount it would be worth the firm paying for perfect information on future demands?

A10.4   A well-known publisher is contemplating making a £5000 contribution to an expedition to the Amazon basin. It is hoped to publish a book as a result, although there is a probability of 0.2 that one will not materialize. If a book is forthcoming, a decision will have to be made on the scale of the first print-run being moderate or small. If the former is chosen and the book is popular ($p = 0.6$), a net profit of £200 000 is anticipated, but if it is not popular ($p = 0.4$), a loss of £40 000 may be incurred. On the other hand, the anticipated pay-offs for a small print-run are +£50 000 and −£10 000 respectively.

(a)   Draw a decision tree for the problem.
(b)   By calculating the expected monetary values, advise the publisher whether or not, from the purely financial aspect, to make the £5000 contribution.
(c)   What considerations, other than the pure and immediate financial aspects, might the publisher take into account?
(d)   As a result of recent reviews, the likelihood of the book being popular is reduced to 0.1. Advise the firm on the basis of this new information.

A10.5   A firm wishing to send a consignment of spares to Greece has to decide between three modes of transportation, air, overland and sea. The transport costs are £8000, £5000 and £3000 respectively. In addition, there is a penalty clause in the contract involving an additional £5000 if the consignment arrives late. The probabilities of arriving on time are estimated to be 0.9, 0.7 and 0.5 respectively.

(a)   Draw a decision tree for the problem.
(b)   Advise the firm on the best mode of transport to minimize expected cost.
(c)   If a seamen's dispute increases the probability of late delivery by sea to 0.7, will this lead you to alter your advice?

11–Business Forecasting: Part 2

11.1 INTRODUCTION AND OBJECTIVES

11.1.1 The Subject of the Chapter

Forecasting from time-series, as in Chapter 6, is not always appropriate since the data are not always available in a form which lends itself to that analysis. Sometimes information comes to hand at unequal discrete intervals so that seasonal influences cannot be deduced. In addition, data may be available at one moment in time from a variety of sources and thus is not time based at all. For example, a hundred companies may reply to a survey about interest rates and the number of employees made redundant during a certain period. Such information is said to be *cross-section data* since it derives from an instantaneous observation across a complex situation. Forecasts made from such information need methods of analysis other than those used for time-series and attempt to answer the question, 'What if . . . ?' For example, 'What if interest rates rise by two per cent?'

The hundred companies in the survey will be affected, probably all differently, and the analyst wishes to forecast the effect upon the 'average' company. In this chapter, we are concerned with forecasting one variable, such as redundancy, on the basis of changes in another, such as the level of interest rates. In a sense, we are moving towards *prediction* because 'What if . . . ?' implies the answer, 'I predict that . . . ' The word 'prediction' will be used from time to time instead of 'forecast' for this reason and also because it carries the connotation of a formula which states 'If this, then that'. Such an approach has been used in Chapter 1 for the conversion of temperature from Fahrenheit to Celsius and vice versa: the simple formula predicts the reading on one thermometer scale from that on another. It would be useful to be able to forecast redundancies from interest rates by means of a simple prediction formula and the derivation of such a formula is the subject of the chapter.

The reader must beware that in using words such as 'forecast' and 'prediction' he does not accord them greater respectability than they deserve. The authors do not believe that the future can be foretold in any human activity and certainly not in business analysis. Consequently, predictions are statements which are likely or probable or credible, in the sense that they attempt to remove the 'don't know' from business and substitute the 'I think'. Thus there are philosophical links between the forecasts of this chapter, the probability of Chapter 3 and the risk analysis of Chapter 10. All human behaviour systems are uncertain: it is the purpose of analysis to understand uncertainty, convert it to measurable risk and to advise on the basis of the best available information.

11.1.2   Objectives

1. To understand the concept of functional association between two variables.
2. To construct two-variable scattergraphs and discuss patterns in data points.
3. To understand the form of a linear equation applied to visual analysis of data points.
4. To calculate the coefficients of a regression line by the split-plot method and by least squares.
5. To use regression lines for prediction, being aware of their limitations and employing subjective methods as appropriate.
6. To calculate the coefficient of correlation and interpret it in the context of linear regression.
7. If possible, to use a specific computer program for the least-squares method.

11.2   BASIC PROBLEM DATA

Mega-Sell Incorporated is a marketing organization which employs freelance selling agents, each of whom acts as a local representative for a wide range of products advertised on television. Each agent receives £2000 per year as a retaining fee plus three per cent of the value of sales, up to a maximum income per agent of £6500 per year.

Mega-Sell experiences the problem faced by many such employers which is that the retaining fee is sometimes paid to agents who make little effort to sell. In an attempt to predict the selling performance of agents, in addition to the interview, applicants will be asked to complete an aptitude test. The first year's sales figures for those who joined the company immediately after the introduction of the test are shown below, together with their scores in the test. Note that the sales performance is given in thousands of £s.

Recruit	A	B	C	D	E	F	G	H	I	J
Aptitude score	13	8	31	40	26	5	47	42	17	21
Sales (£000s)	132	118	141	144	139	121	142	142	126	135

Recently, three applicants (X, Y and Z) were interviewed and obtained respective aptitude scores of 45, 30 and 10. It is decided to appoint in future only those agents who seem able to sell at least £138 000 of goods in their first year, using the available information to make predictions.

11.3   CAUSE AND EFFECT

11.3.1   Predicting Sales

Mega-Sell Inc. obviously believe that there is a link between their aptitude rating for a recruit and that recruit's sales performance. In effect, they are saying, 'Tell us an aptitude score and we'll tell you a credible sales figure'. In statistical jargon, this is usually phrased as, 'aptitude score is the *independent* variable and sales performance is *dependent* upon it'. The clear implication is that aptitude causes sales and not vice versa, which is reasonable. To

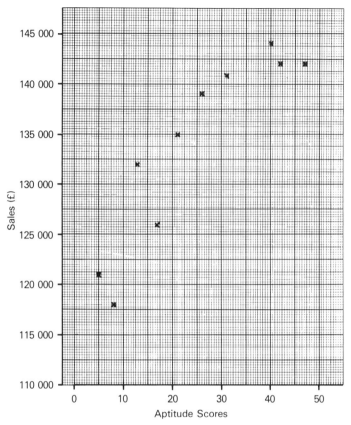

Figure 11.1   *Scattergraph for Mega-Sell data*

assess the strength of any relationship between these two, consider first Figure 11.1 which is the *scattergraph* for the data.

As a general rule, Mega-Sell's belief seems to be borne out by the data. We see that low aptitude scores produce lower sales than do higher aptitude scores, which supports the validity of the test given to recruits. If the cause–effect relationship is sufficiently strong, then predictions from aptitude score to sales should be possible. In statistical terminology it would be said that there exists a *regression of sales upon aptitude score*: this use of the word 'regression' is specific to the techniques of prediction analysed in this chapter. We shall identify the *regression equation*, which will be a formula for converting scores into sales. It could take the form of a straight line, as introduced in Chapter 1, with the following structure:

$$\text{Sales} = a + (b \times \text{Score})$$

As in section 1.3.1, *a* and *b* in this equation are the constants that define the straight line. If both of them could be found for the Mega-Sell data, we should have a prediction formula.

11.3.2   Find the Formula: Part 1

If we adopt the model that there is a straight-line relationship between aptitude score and sales, then we must identify the slope and the intercept for the data in Figure 11.1. Visually, the linear model seems reasonable and we could lay a ruler on the graph to pass through the scatter. Such a free-hand method would be acceptable if the points lay very close to a straight line but the Mega-Sell data are quite widely spread and no-one could be sure that the ruler made the 'best line' for forecasting purposes. What is required is an analytical method to identify *a* and *b* in the regression line.

The agents employed by Mega-Sell, for whom data are available, sell between them £1 340 000 of products in the first year. The reader should check that this is the total for the sales data. Since there are ten agents, the mean sales are £134 000 per agent. Similarly, the total score from the aptitude test is 250, so that the mean score is 25. If the regression equation is to mean anything as a prediction formula, it must predict that a score of 25 in the test would lead to sales of £134 000: if it does not, it cannot be said to represent all the data. Therefore we have a point on the scattergraph which *must* lie on the regression line. Let this point be called *P* and let its position be denoted by (25, 134 000) to represent its horizontal and vertical values in Figure 11.2. To identify a straight line, at least one other point is required and we shall use the *split-plot* method to find two of them.

Since Mega-Sell assumes the aptitude score to be the independent variable, it is reasonable to consider agents in two categories: those with below-average scores and those with above-average scores. By this means, we can analyse low values of the 'cause' and relate it to 'effect', and the same for high values of the 'cause'. In Figure 11.2 the graph is split by a line perpendicular to the 'cause' axis (the scores) and passing through *P*(25, 134 000).

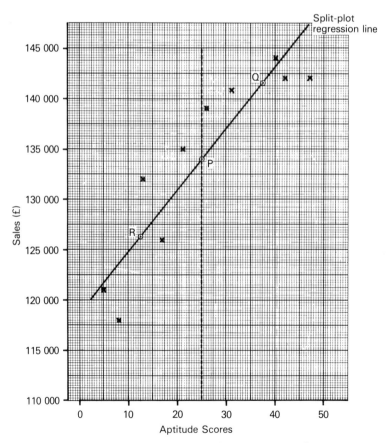

Figure 11.2   *Split-plot regression of sales upon aptitude score*

As an aid to memory, the regression of sales *upon* score requires a split line to drop *upon* the score axis.

For above-average aptitude scores, the mean is 37.2 with mean sales of £141 600, and for below-average aptitude scores the values are 12.8 and £126 400 respectively. These results are calculated as follows:

Below-average scores

Recruit	A	B	F	I	J		
Score	13	8	5	17	21	Total 64;	Mean 12.8
Sales (£000s)	132	118	121	126	135	Total 632;	Mean 126.4

Above-average scores

Recruit	C	D	E	G	H		
Score	31	40	26	47	42	Total 186;	Mean 37.2
Sales (£000s)	141	144	139	142	142	Total 708;	Mean 141.6

We can now add these points as in Figure 11.2. Since they represent the upper and lower ends of the aptitude range among recruits, we will use them to indicate the slope of the regression line. Let the high-score point be $Q(37.2, 141\,600)$ and the low-score point be $R(12.8, 126\,400)$. The regression line must pass through the overall mean at P and be parallel with points Q and R. In Figure 11.2 the result is the straight line which passes so close to all three points that they appear to lie on it: in fact Q and R do not, but no graph of this size could show the error. Now we have a method of predicting sales performance from aptitude scores and its reliability can be judged visually by the way the regression line passes through the data points. It represents the 'average relationship' between score and sales for the ten recruits in question. Curiously, it fails to predict the position of any single data point but that is a common occurrence with all types of average.

The three latest recruits X, Y and Z had aptitude scores of 45, 30 and 10 respectively. From Figure 11.2 the expected sales obtained by each may be read off from the regression line to yield the following predictions:

Recruit	X	Y	Z
Aptitude score	45	30	10
Predicted sales (£000s)	146.5	137.1	124.7

Since it is Mega-Sell's intention to appoint only agents who appear able to sell at least £138 000 of products, only recruit X will be appointed. Recruit Y is a marginal case and the company may exercise discretion because no forecast can be perfect, even if it is called a prediction. Recruit Z certainly will be rejected.

11.3.3   Find the Formula: Part 2

Carrying a graph around is not a convenient way to remember a formula. As we saw in Chapter 1, an alternative would be to derive an expression in the form of an equation which, in this case, will be the equation of the straight line in Figure 11.2. The slope of the line is given by the points Q and R and it must pass through the point P. Therefore, we have sufficient information to identify a and b in the equation: Sales $= a + (b \times \text{Score})$.

To find b, consider the vertical and horizontal distances between points Q and R in Figure 11.3. A 24.4 increase in aptitude score leads to a £15 200 increase in sales and therefore the slope of the line is given as follows:

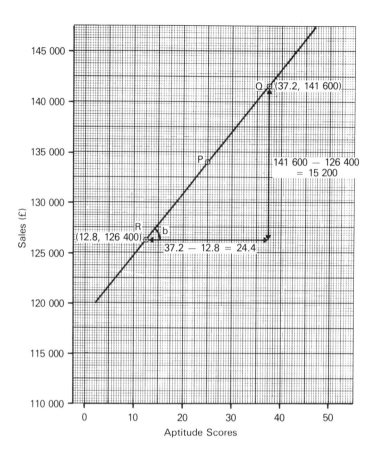

Figure 11.3   *Gradient of the split-plot regression*

$$b = \frac{\text{Change in sales}}{\text{Change in score}}$$

$$= \frac{£15\,200}{24.4}$$

$$= £623 \text{ per point of score}$$

Note that a downward-sloping line would have a negative gradient since an increase in the horizontal direction would cause a reduction in the vertical, so that the numerator would be less than zero. There is an assignment at the end of the chapter in which this happens.

To find *a*, substitute the £623 and the values for point *P* in the regression equation, since we know that *P* must lie on the line. Thus:

$$£134\,000 = a + (£623 \times 25)$$

$$a = £134\,000 - £15\,575$$

$$= £118\,425$$

The prediction formula for sales from any value of aptitude score is obtained by substituting the *a* and *b* values to yield:

$$\text{Sales} = £118\,425 + (£623 \times \text{Score})$$

Applying the formula to recent recruits X, Y and Z, predicted sales are £146 460, £137 115 and £124 655 respectively. The reader should compare these values with those obtained from the graph in section 11.3.2. They are more precise in the sense that a formula can be calculated exactly, whereas reading a graph always involves errors and loss of accuracy. Even so, graphical estimates are usually adequate in practical management.

11.3.4   Predicting Aptitude

If there is a strong connection between aptitude score and sales, then there is no reason why Mega-Sell could not assess all its agents in the sales force to establish their aptitudes. There is probably no reason to carry out this particular analysis but there are circumstances when such an approach would be useful, as will be seen in the assignments at the end of the chapter. If it was desired to predict aptitude from sales, then sales would be the independent variable and aptitude would be dependent upon it. The equation would then be for the *regression of aptitude score upon sales* and would be different from that for the inverse relationship. This may be a new concept for some readers, especially since it goes against the simple example of temperature conversion in section 1.3.1. There we saw that temperature in degrees Fahrenheit (f) could be calculated from degrees Celsius (c) by the formula $f = 32 + 1.8c$. To find c from f we simply manipulated the equation to give $c = (f - 32)/1.8$. However, this easy transposition works only for a *deterministic* relationship, in which all the values lie on a single line on a graph, which is the case for temperature conversion. Quite clearly, the Mega-Sell data do not lie on a single line or even on a curve, although there does seem to be a fairly strong visual connection in Figure 11.1. The points display a *stochastic* relationship, which means that we are in the realm of probability and the best we can hope for is an estimate of one variable, score or sales, attaching to it a description such as 'estimated value'. There are influences on sales other than just the aptitude score and these have been omitted, perhaps because they are unknown or immeasurable. As a consequence the regression of sales upon aptitude will be an entirely different line on a graph from that for the regression of aptitude upon sales. The reader is left to carry through this calculation in the first assignment at the end of the chapter, in which it should be shown that the prediction formula should be:

$$\text{Aptitude score} = (0.00146 \times \text{Sales}) - 170.64 \text{ for sales in £s}$$

Note that the a value in this equation is negative and is subtracted at the end, which is a common convention in writing formulae or equations.

11.4   A MORE TECHNICAL APPROACH TO REGRESSION

11.4.1   The Nature of Errors in Forecasts

By the nature of forecasting-type data, no single line or smooth curve would be expected to pass through all the data points. Therefore, every prediction will probably contain an error because they are all made to lie on a regression line. As an alternative to the split-plot

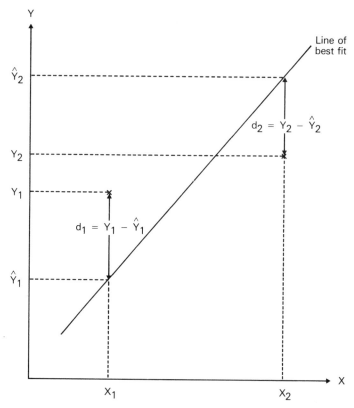

Figure 11.4   *Deviations from the line of best fit (Note: the points X_1, Y_1 and X_2, Y_2 are actual data values)*

method, we could actually analyse these errors and obtain a regression line which minimizes them in some way. In fact, this alternative is referred to as the *least-squares* method because it yields the regression line which minimizes the sum of the squared deviations between the actual data points and their predicted values. Figure 11.4 shows a general scattergraph with the horizontal axis labelled X and the vertical labelled Y. Only two data points are shown but the technique may be applied to any number.

11.4.2   Find the Least-squares Formula

From Figure 11.4, the unknown regression line is the line of best fit defined by the following analysis:

let Y be the data on the vertical axis,
               X be the data on the horizontal axis,
               $\hat{Y}$ be the predicted vertical value from the (unknown) line of best fit;

then the line of best fit will be of the form:

$$\hat{Y} = a + bX$$

There will generally be a discrepancy between the data and the prediction; let this discrepancy be called d for each point on the scatter, then:

$$d = (Y - \hat{Y}) = Y - (a + bX) \text{ for any value of } X \text{ corresponding to } Y$$
$$d = Y - a - bX$$

Let us define the line of best fit as that for which the sum of such squared discrepancies is a minimum, that is $\min(\Sigma d^2)$. Then $d^2 = (Y - a - bX)^2 = Y^2 - 2aY - 2bXY + 2abX + b^2X^2 + a^2$ for any single point. Sum over all points to give Σd^2. Let this be called U for simplicity, then $U = \Sigma d^2 = \Sigma Y^2 - 2a\Sigma Y - 2b\Sigma XY + 2ab\Sigma X + b^2\Sigma X^2 + na^2$ for n points in the scatter.

We require U to be a minimum for the line of best fit and it can be shown that U is minimized when the following equations are satisfied. Since the only unknowns are a and b, solution of these equations will yield the constants of the line of best fit. They are called *normal equations*.

1. $\Sigma Y = na + b\Sigma X$.
2. $\Sigma XY = a\Sigma X + b\Sigma X^2$.

The reader should not be too concerned about this derivation but the application is easily understood once the two equations can be solved. For the Mega-Sell data, the various summations are obtained as follows. The aptitude scores are labelled X and the sales values (in £000s) are labelled Y.

Score X	13	8	31	40	26	5	47	42	17	21	$\Sigma X =$	250
Sales Y	132	118	141	144	139	121	142	142	126	135	$\Sigma Y =$	1 340
X^2	169	64	961	1600	676	25	2209	1764	289	441	$\Sigma X^2 =$	8 198
XY	1716	944	4371	5760	3614	605	6674	5964	2142	2835	$\Sigma XY =$	34 625

Substitution of these values into the normal equations gives the following, both of which must be solved simultaneously.

1. $1340 = 10a + 250b$.
2. $34\,625 = 250a + 8198b$.

The reader may already be able to obtain a and b from equations by the process known as linear elimination; but if not, the procedure is simple and centres on the elimination of one unknown as shown below. Here, we shall eliminate a and solve for b; then obtain a using the b already found.

Step 1 Compare the numbers of a in the two equations and decide what number must be multiplied into one equation to make the two a equal: here, we should multiply Equation 1 by 25 to yield $250a$ in both.

$$(\text{Equation 1}) \times 25: \ 33\,500 = 250a + 6250b$$

Step 2 Subtract (or add as appropriate) the new equation from (or to) Equation 2 to eliminate the a component.

$$34\,625 = 250a + 8198b \text{ Equation 2}$$

subtract $\qquad 33\,500 = 250a + 6250b$ from Step 1

whence $\qquad\qquad 1125 = 1948b$

$$\underline{b = 0.578} \text{ rounded to 3 places of decimals}$$

Step 3   Substitute $b = 0.578$ into one of the original equations, say, Equation 1, since
it is the simplest.

$$1340 = 10a + (250 \times 0.578)$$

whence $a = 119.55$

Step 4   Write down the resulting regression equation as found, remembering that certain
units are reduced by a factor for convenience (in this case, sales are measured in
thousands of pounds). Thus:

$$\hat{Y} = 119.55 + 0.578X$$

Step 5   Convert the symbols X and Y to their variable names and multiply through by the
reduction factor.

$$\text{Sales (£000s)} = 119.55 + (0.578 \times \text{Score})$$

$$\text{Sales (£)} = 119550 + (578 \times \text{Score})$$

The reader should compare this prediction equation with that obtained from the split-
plot method in section 11.3.2. Both the gradient and intercept are different but not greatly
so and the predictions for recruits X, Y and Z are as follows:

Recruit	X	Y	Z
Aptitude score	45	30	10
Least-squares predicted sales	£145 570	£136 900	£125 340

The two regression lines are shown plotted together on Figure 11.5 and the reader
should check that both pass through the joint mean point at (25, 134 000). Both regression
lines possess the essential feature that they pass through the scatter of points in a manner
which seems to describe the general pattern whereby a high score indicates high sales.

The least-squares regression method is widely used because it is derived from the
desire to minimize errors. Its calculation can be quite complicated and the reader perhaps
will be dismayed at the prospect of carrying it out without tuition: to some extent this
difficulty is overcome by the use of a calculator or a computer. A simple computer program
is given in section 11.6 of this chapter, which yields the a and b values for any set of data.

11.4.3   How Good is the Best Fit?

The Mega-Sell data scatter around a straight regression line without very great errors being
apparent. Therefore, we could conclude that the 'line of best fit' fits very well. Of course,
if all the data points lay much closer to the line, or even on the line, then the fit would be
better still. There is a variety of circumstances in which the fit of the least-squares regression
line will be poor and each is worth considering in some detail since it will cast light upon this
section's question.

Data points may be so widely scattered that no straight line adequately describes the
underlying relationship. In Figure 11.6, the horizontal variable is not a good predictor of the
vertical variable. In Figure 11.7 the fit is poor for a different reason: the data are not linear.
There is a predictive relationship of a curved form but no straight line affords the confidence
that the analyst would require. In Figure 11.8, there is a good fit to a straight line but the
line has no purpose for prediction since the vertical variable is practically constant regardless
of the values on the horizontal axis.

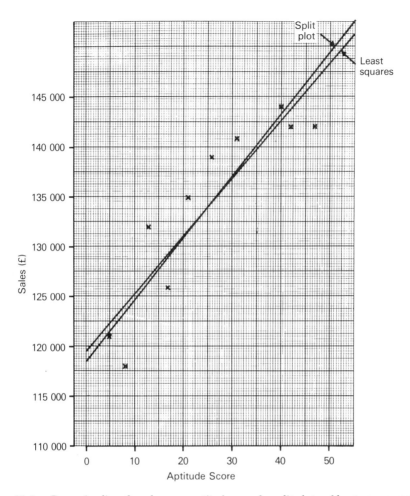

Figure 11.5   *Regression lines for sales upon aptitude score by split-plot and least-squares methods*

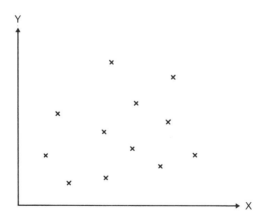

Figure 11.6   *Zero linear association: case 1*

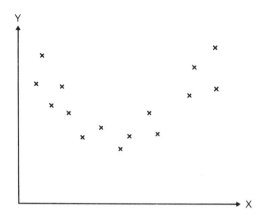

Figure 11.7   *Zero linear association: case 2*

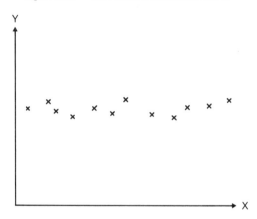

Figure 11.8   *Zero linear association: case 3*

In each of these cases, it may be said that there is no *linear association* between the horizontal and vertical variables, which is not to say that there is no relationship whatsoever: only that a straight line is an inadequate explanation of the positions of data points. If either the split-plot or least-squares method was applied to data like these, the result would be a straight line which passed through the points, but it would tell the analyst nothing. There are assignments in which this problem may be explored further.

From the analyst's point of view, the fact that a straight line can be constructed for a set of data is of interest only if it can be established that a straight line is appropriate. What is required is a measure of the goodness of fit and the next section considers this problem.

11.5   CONFIDENCE IN PREDICTIONS

11.5.1   Measuring Goodness of Fit

The least-squares regression line is the most widely used method of obtaining prediction formulae. One reason is that it leads to a useful theory about goodness of fit, which is

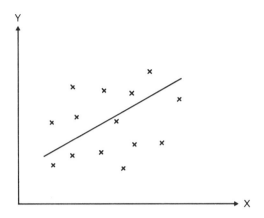

Figure 11.9 *Low degree of linear correlation*

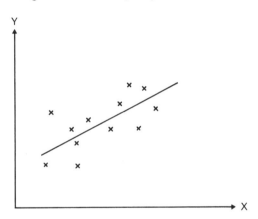

Figure 11.10 *Moderate degree of linear correlation*

usually referred to as *correlation analysis*. As this term implies, we are concerned with the co-relation between two sets of variables. One approach to its measurement is to answer the question, 'How much of the scatter is explained by the regression line?' Obviously, the greater the degree of explanation, the better must be the line for prediction purposes. In Figure 11.9, the scatter is very great and the line explains almost nothing. In Figure 11.10, the scatter is less and the line begins to explain the positions of some of the points. In Figure 11.11, the scatter is small and the line tells us quite a lot about the positions of the points. In the first case, there is little evidence of correlation; in the second, there is some evidence; in the third, there can be no doubt that correlation exists.

Measuring the scatter is quite a simple problem since we already have a measure of dispersion from Chapter 3; the standard deviation. Therefore, we can calculate the dispersion of the points in both their horizontal and vertical directions by the product of the two standard deviations. Consider a simple numerical example:

$$X \quad 1 \quad 2 \quad 3 \quad 4 \quad 5 \qquad \text{Standard deviation } S_X = 1.41$$
$$Y \quad 4 \quad 8 \quad 5 \quad 10 \quad 8 \qquad \text{Standard deviation } S_Y = 2.19$$

The reader may wish to sketch these points on a scattergraph and confirm that they do not lie upon a straight line although there is some degree of association apparent between them.

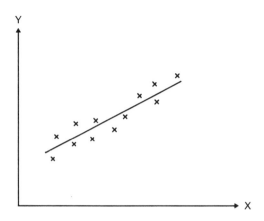

Figure 11.11   *High degree of linear correlation*

The total scatter can be measured by the product $S_X \times S_Y$ which gives 3.09 approximately. The closeness of the points to a least-squares regression line can be measured by the *covariance*, which is a hybrid calculation involving both X and Y and has the formula:

$$\text{Cov}(XY) = \frac{\Sigma(XY)}{n} - \frac{(\Sigma X)(\Sigma Y)}{n^2} \text{ for } n \text{ points}$$

For data points lying perfectly upon a straight line $\text{Cov}(XY) = S_X \times S_Y$ which implies that the line explains all the scatter. For our simple example, $\text{Cov}(XY)$ is calculated as follows

X	1	2	3	4	5	$\Sigma X = 15$
Y	4	8	5	10	8	$\Sigma Y = 35$
XY	4	16	15	40	40	$\Sigma(XY) = 115$

$$\text{Cov}(XY) = \frac{115}{5} - \frac{(15)(35)}{25} = 2.00$$

The degree of association may now be measured by the *correlation coefficient* which is the quotient of $\text{Cov}(XY)$ and $S_X \times S_Y$ as follows:

$$\text{Correlation coefficient} = \frac{2.00}{3.09} = 0.65$$

It is conventional to give the correlation coefficient the symbol r, so in our example we could state $r = 0.65$ and analysts the world over would be able to interpret it.

In a simple numerical example, calculation of r is quick and easy. In the Mega-Sell data, there are complications arising from the larger volume of arithmetic. In may be summarized as follows, where X is the aptitude score and Y is sales.

Aptitude score	*Sales*
$\Sigma X = 250$	$\Sigma Y = 1340$ (in £000s)
$\Sigma X^2 = 8198$	$\Sigma Y^2 = 180\,356$
$S_X = 13.96$	$S_Y = 8.92$

$$\Sigma(XY) = 34\,625$$

$$\text{Cov}(XY) = 112.50$$

Combining these results we obtain that r is 0.903 as follows:

$$r = \frac{\text{Cov}(XY)}{S_X \times S_Y} = \frac{112.50}{13.96 \times 8.92}$$

$$r = \frac{112.50}{124.52}$$

$$\underline{r = 0.903}$$

The authors are convinced that this is the way to understand correlation coefficients but some textbooks and tutors explain in terms of a formula like the one below. If the reader is content to substitute values in such a formula, then calculation of r can be simplified. However, it is not easily remembered and in an examination, the reader could expect it to be made available.

$$\text{Correlation coefficient for } n \text{ points} \quad r = \frac{n\Sigma(XY) - (\Sigma X)(\Sigma Y)}{\sqrt{n\Sigma X^2 - (\Sigma X)^2} \times \sqrt{n\Sigma Y^2 - (\Sigma Y)^2}}$$

More important than the evaluation of this formula is the ability to interpret results. To ease calculation, the computer program in section 11.6 is included.

11.5.2   How Good Is a Good Line?

If all the points in a scattergraph lie on a straight line, then the correlation coefficient will take the value 1.0, indicating *perfect correlation*. If the points are very widely scattered as in Figure 11.6 or Figure 11.9, it will take a value close to zero, indicating an absence of correlation. If all the points lie on a downward-sloping line, r will take the value -1.0, indicating a perfect inverse association. These extreme cases are portrayed in Figures 11.12, 11.13 and 11.14. The value of r must lie at or between -1.0 and $+1.0$.

The nearer to 1.0 or -1.0 the calculated value for r is, the better the fit of a straight regression line and the greater the confidence of the analyst in making predictions. For the Mega-Sell data, $r = 0.903$ which is positive and close to 1.0, indicating that confident

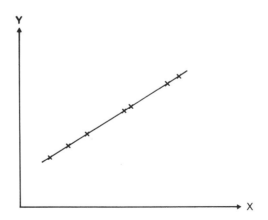

Figure 11.12   *Perfect positive linear correlation*

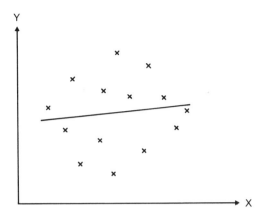

Figure 11.13   *Zero correlation*

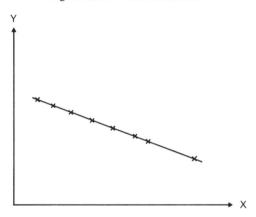

Figure 11.14   *Perfect negative linear correlation*

estimates of sales may be made from aptitude scores. There are assignments at the end of the chapter in which r has values very different from 1.0 and the reader should aim to understand their implications for business forecasting.

The reader may find in other texts that some authors refer to a second measure of goodness of fit, the *coefficient of determination*. This is defined as the square of the coefficient of correlation, r^2, and is said to measure the proportion of variation in a set of data points which is explained by a least-squares line. At this stage, the reader should only note the existence of this coefficient; it will not be referred to further in the assignments.

11.6   A USEFUL COMPUTER PROGRAM

The following program asks for a variety of information, calculates the two least-squares regression lines (Y upon X, and X upon Y) and the correlation coefficient. It is not especially efficient in computing terms but it is intended to be of use and interest to the reader with an elementary knowledge of the BASIC language. The DIM statement which normally would start the program is omitted here since most BASIC systems now operate a default procedure for simple arrays such as the X and Y variables.

```
10 PRINT 'HOW MANY DATA POINTS';
20 INPUT N1
30 PRINT 'ENTER DATA VALUES IN THE FORM X, Y'
40 S1=0
50 S2=0
60 S3=0
70 S4=0
80 S5=0
90 FOR N2=1 TO N1 STEP 1
100 INPUT X[N2],Y[N2]
110 S1=S1+X[N2]
120 S2=S2+Y[N2]
130 S3=S3+X[N2]↑2
140 S4=S4+Y[N2]↑2
150 S5=S5+X[N2]*Y[N2]
160 NEXT N2
170 B1=(S5-(S1*S2)/N1)/(S3-(S1↑2)/N1)
180 A1=(S2-B1*S1)/N1
190 PRINT
200 PRINT 'FOR REGRESSION OF Y UPON X'
210 PRINT ' Y = ';A1;' + (';B1;')X'
220 PRINT
230 B2=(S5-(S1*S2)/N1)/(S4-(S2↑2)/N1)
240 A2=(S1-B2*S2)/N1
250 PRINT 'FOR REGRESSION OF X UPON Y'
260 PRINT ' X = ';A2;' + (';B2;')Y'
270 R1=SQR((N1*S3-S1↑2)*(N1*S4-S2↑2))
280 R2=(N1*S5-S1*S2)/R1
290 PRINT
330 PRINT 'CORRELATION COEFFICIENT R = ';R2
310 END
```

The printout for Mega-Sell Incorporated is given below. Note that the regression line for sales upon aptitude score is as found in section 11.4.2 and that $r = 0.903$ approximately. The least-squares regression line for aptitude score upon sales will be new to the reader but is comparable with that mentioned for the split-plot method in section 11.3.2. In this printout, values entered on the keyboard by the reader/programmer are underlined.

```
HOW MANY DATA POINTS? 10
ENTER DATA VALUES IN THE FORM X, Y
? 13,132
? 8,118
? 31,141
? 40,144
? 26,139
? 5,121
? 47,142
? 42,142
? 17,126
? 21,135
```

FOR REGRESSION OF Y UPON X
Y = 119.562 + (0.577515)X

FOR REGRESSION OF X UPON Y
X = −164.384 + (1.41332)Y

CORRELATION COEFFICIENT R = 0.903445

ASSIGNMENTS

Where possible, the reader should use the program in section 11.6

A11.1 (a) For the data in section 11.2 find the split-plot regression line of aptitude score upon sales. The reader should note that the data values should be split this time by the mean sales dividing line.

(b) Use the regression line from part (a) to forecast the aptitude score of a recruit who sold £126 000 worth of products in her first year.

A11.2 In a fruit-growing area, the quantity of strawberries produced and the previous winter's mean daily temperature have been as follows:

Year	1979/80	1980/81	1981/82
Mean temperature	4.5°C	6.5°C	7.0°C
Quantity (million kilo)	2.2	2.7	3.4

(a) Plot these data upon a scattergraph.
(b) Obtain the split-plot regression line and plot it upon the scattergraph.
(c) If 1983 showed a mean winter daytime temperature of 8.5°C, estimate the subsequent strawberry crop.
(d) By consideration of the scattergraph and any other factors you believe to be important, comment upon your confidence in the estimate of crop weight.

A11.3 Over a six-month period, the weekly output from a small workshop has varied and so has the total cost as estimated by the accountant. The following data are available.

Week ending	16 Jan	13 Feb	13 Mar	10 Apr	16 May	13 June
Weekly output (Q)	30	36	40	42	38	34
Production cost (C) in £000s	£75	£91	£96	£101	£87	£76

(a) Plot these data on a scattergraph in which Q is the independent variable.
(b) Find the least-squares regression line of C upon Q.
(c) Forecast production costs for a week in which output was 20 units.
(d) Calculate the coefficient of correlation and comment upon its value in relation to the forecast in part (c).
(e) From the regression line estimate:
(i)   The fixed costs of the workshop.
(ii) The average unit cost of the items produced.

A11.4 A motoring magazine believes that the petrol consumption of a car is related to its engine capacity. It arranges for a family of five with a small caravan to cover the same route at the same time on a certain day of the week in a variety of motor cars. The results are as follows:

Engine capacity (litres)	1.0	1.5	1.8	2.0	2.2	2.8	3.0	3.5
Miles per gallon	26	32	40	38	33	28	20	19

(a) The least-squares regression line for these data is:
MPG = 41.3 − (5.32 × Capacity).
Plot the data on a scattergraph and also the regression line.
(b) Calculate the coefficient of correlation.
(c) Discuss the problem of using this regression line for forecasting purposes.
(d) Using the least-squares line above, or by any other means, forecast the petrol consumption for a 2.3 litre car.

A11.5 The business analyst for a large charity has investigated the effects of inflation upon annual receipts from street collections. He obtains the following data:

Year	Annual Inflation (A) rate (% p.a.)	Collection (C) (£000 p.a.)
1973	5.7	93
1974	8.3	104
1975	9.4	121
1976	18.6	126
1977	22.4	102
1978	21.0	96
1979	17.9	133
1980	16.1	131
1981	11.5	127
1982	14.2	129

(a) Plot these points upon a graph to show the effect of inflation upon charitable collection.
(b) A least-squares regression line through these data is: $C = 111.3 + 0.34A$; C in £000s, A in per cent.

   (i) State and explain which variable is *independent* in this equation.
   (ii) Plot the regression line upon your graph.
   (iii) Predict from the line the charitable collection for 1983, when the inflation rate is thought likely to be about 12 per cent.

(c) Discuss the usefulness of the regression line, commenting upon the linear assumption and the fact that the correlation coefficient is $r = 0.122$ for the ten points.
(d) Without reference to the regression line, make a prediction for the 1983 collection, explaining how you arrived at it, and comparing it with your answer to (b) (iii) above.

A11.6 Plot the following points on a scattergraph. They relate to the output from a high-precision machine which is thought to be affected by the working temperature.

Mean daily temp. (°C)	18	19	19	19	20	20	21	22
Max. daily error (microns)	60	70	80	90	75	65	80	60

(a) Plot the data on a scattergraph, deciding which is the independent variable.
(b) Calculate the coefficient of correlation and comment upon its values.
(c) Would you feel confident predicting the maximum daily error for a mean daily temperature of 23°C? Explain your answer.

A11.7 A ticket tout has several hundred tickets for an important international soccer match. Each day he varies the price at which he sells them in an attempt to maximize takings. The following table gives his experience over a ten-day period.

Price (£)	49	48	47	46	45	44	43	42	41	40
Number sold	130	120	120	150	140	180	160	200	190	180

(a) Plot these data on a scattergraph with price as the independent variable.
(b) Obtain the split-plot regression line of tickets sold upon price.
(c) Forecast the number of tickets sold at a price of £39 and at a price of £50.
(d) At which price over the ten days did the tout take in the greatest sum of money?
(e) At which price, £39 or £50, do you forecast he will take the greater sum of money?
(f) If possible, input these data to a computer using the program in section 11.6 and answer parts (c), (d) and (e) again.
Comment upon the differences which emerge.

12 – Planning Production Schedules

12.1   INTRODUCTION AND OBJECTIVES

12.1.1   The Subject of the Chapter

There are some jobs that one person will start and finish by himself. For example, a crafts-man working in stone or precious metal will divide his time so that the processes he must carry out will be scheduled in an appropriate order to achieve the end result. For such a worker, the schedule is derived from his experience in the job.

However, most modern production processes involve many trades and numerous people, each specializing in a particular part of the overall job. Consequently, more than one activity may be pursued in any period of time and the total job time will thereby be reduced. Consider the building of a house: while it is not possible to work on the roof and the foundations at the same time, it may be possible to install the electrical wiring con-currently?'. 'What is the best order for the various jobs?', 'Which jobs are so important that questions arising in such a multi-job situation are, 'How many jobs may be carried out con-currently?' 'What is the best order for the various jobs?', 'Which jobs are so important that their delay will prolong final completion?' and 'Which jobs may be delayed without interfer-ing with the general flow of other activities?' These are questions of scheduling.

The methods introduced in this chapter are often referred to as *project network tech-niques* or *critical path methods* and these names suggest the very nature of the analysis. We shall be considering the timing and ordering of complex production processes, looking at which jobs are 'critical' in the sense that their timings are crucial to the duration of the overall process.

12.1.2   Objectives

1.   To understand the component nature of activities within a complex project.
2.   To construct the project network from stated durations and priorities between activities.
3.   To identify important events in the project's completion.
4.   To determine and analyse the sequence of critical activities, and their influences on overall duration.
5.   To appreciate and partially analyse the resource constraints operating within a complex project.

12.2   BASIC PROBLEM DATA

A company has decided to install its own computer data-processing facilities instead of renting time through a bureau. The activities involved in this project, and their estimated durations are listed below.

	Activity	Duration
A	Carry out pilot survey of needs	17 days
B	Carry out pilot survey of costs	26 days
C	Carry out pilot survey of accommodation	14 days
D	Arrange conference with manufacturer	7 days' notice
E	Hold manufacturer's conference	3 days
F	Advertise for and appoint Computer Manager	49 days
G	Train computer operators	120 days
H	Find contractor for building conversion	24 days
I	Obtain materials for building conversion	17 days
J	Find contractor for air conditioning	21 days
K	Convert buildings	77 days
L	Install air conditioning	29 days
M	Prepare new office stationery	90 days
N	Install computer and peripheral equipment	5 days
O	First test run	2 days
P	Correction of system errors	11 days
Q	Second test run	2 days
R	First commercial run	3 days

Priorities for activities

1.   The pilot surveys B and C may proceed together after A.
2.   The conference must await the outcomes of the pilot surveys but may be arranged during their time.
3.   Finding contractors, staff appointments and clerical activities must await outcome of conference.
4.   The Computer Manager must be appointed before any equipment is installed.
5.   The installation of the air conditioning must proceed during building conversion.
6.   All stationery must be prepared and errors corrected before the second test run.

12.3   DRAWING THE PROJECT PLAN

12.3.1   Getting the Right Order

We know from the list of priorities above that activity A (pilot survey of needs) must be the first activity in the project and clearly activity R must be the last. Between these two all the others must be scheduled to take place. We are told that B and C may occur together after A and that they must be complete before the conference (E) is held. After the conference, the number of activities that may be commenced becomes too high to keep a simple list but a crude schedule could be drawn up as follows:

First activity	A
Second set of activities	B, C, D
Third set of activities	E
Fourth set of activities	M, G, F, J, H
and so on until	
Next to last activity	Q
Final activity	R

The middle section of this list is too complicated to write down in words. For example, activity K (convert buildings) may take place during activities M, G, F, I and L but before N, O, P, etc. The reader should check that this is so by applying the priorities and common sense to the list of activities. To write down this time dependence is not worth while: a diagrammatic approach is employed instead. The first step in constructing such a diagram is to draw up a complete list of activities and prerequisites for the commencement of each of them. Such a list is given below: it is made by application of the priorities and a little common sense. Note that if B follows A and E follows B, then E also follows A but it is repetitive and a waste of effort to say so.

	Activity	*Duration*	*Prerequisite activity*
A	Pilot survey needs	17	none
B	Pilot survey costs	26	A
C	Pilot survey accommodation	14	A
D	Arrange conference	7	A
E	Hold conference	3	B, C, D
F	Appoint Computer Manager	49	E
G	Train operators	120	E
H	Find contractor (building)	24	E
I	Obtain building materials	17	H
J	Find contractor (ventilation)	21	E
K	Convert buildings	77	I
L	Install ventilation	29	I, J
M	Prepare stationery	90	E
N	Install computer	5	F, K, L
O	First test run	2	G, N
P	Error corrections	11	O
Q	Second test run	2	M, P
R	Commercial run	3	Q

The reader should consider each line of this list and be certain that the prerequisites are absolutely necessary and conform to the stated priorities or common sense. Having done this, we are now in a position to construct the special diagram which is called a 'project network'.

12.3.2 Doing and Being

Every moment in the duration of a project must be either:

1. A moment during an activity after its commencement but before its completion; or
2. That moment when an activity has ended and another may be commenced.

Thus, all moments correspond to *doing* an activity or *being* at the end of an activity. This second type of moment is called an 'event' since it is recognizable as a distinct instance during a period of time. Corresponding to this, we can define an activity as the *period of time between events*. Let each activity (A to R in our basic problem) be denoted by an arrow. The length of the arrow is not indicative of the duration of the activity: it merely joins a particular event at the commencement with another at the completion. These events we shall call 'activity start' and 'activity finish' respectively. These are indicated by circles, as in Figure 12.1.

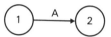

Figure 12.1 *An event is defined as the start or completion of an activity*

If activity A must be completed before activity B starts, then event 2 is the activity start for B, as in Figure 12.2.

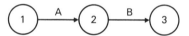

Figure 12.2 *Event 2 indicates the priority of activity A*

Figure 12.2 states that activities A and B cannot be carried out concurrently. However, if the completion of A triggers the commencement of two activities B and C which may occur together, then the network will be constructed as shown in Figure 12.3.

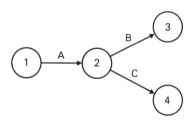

Figure 12.3 *Activities B and C may start together, proceed together but end at different times*

If event 4 is the starting event for activity E, but must await completion of activity B, then a timeless dummy activity must be drawn to show the connection (see Figure 12.4).

The dummy indicates activity E must await completion of both B and C *even though they complete at different times* (events 3 and 4). The dummy may be simply a wait after completion of B before commencement of E. If we now apply this method to our basic problem, we see that the early activities form Figure 12.5.

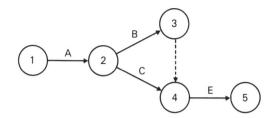

Figure 12.4   *Activity E must await completion of both B and C*

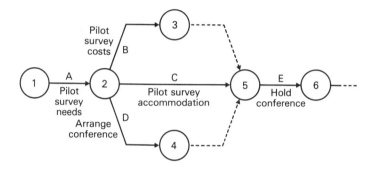

Figure 12.5   *The beginnings of the project network*

The conference must await the outcomes of the pilot surveys and its own arrangement but these three need not be completed at the same moment. Hence the dummies. Note the arrows for activities B, C and D may be labelled as shown or in any other combination provided E follows them all. In general, an event cannot be said to have occurred until all the activities leading to it have been completed.

As regards the rest of the network for our basic problem, the complexity of the project is simplified somewhat by considering each activity in turn. We have already decided in the previous section that after the conference (E) the activities F, G, H, J and M may commence. From event 6, therefore, these activities emerge as in Figure 12.6.

The procedure for drawing the rest of a network can be quite difficult but the secret is to follow through sequences of activities from the list of prerequisites. The simplest sequence is F, N, O, P, Q, R, in that order. The student should re-read the list of prerequisites to see that these activities do indeed form a sequence conforming to the priorities. Drawing these onto the network, we obtain Figure 12.7, which forms the backbone of the entire network.

After the basic formation of the network is obtained, all the branches from event 6 must be terminated. This will then indicate that those activities which started after the conference have been completed by the times appropriate for later ones to be started in correct sequence. For example, M (prepare new stationery) must be complete before the second test run (activity Q) can start. Therefore M must terminate by the start time of Q. Similarly, G (train operators) must be completed before the first test run (activity O) can start. Both of these are shown in Figure 12.8. However, the branches labelled H and J are a little more complicated and require further discussion below.

It is a matter of technique in the drawing of project networks to ensure that arrows flow towards the right-hand side whenever possible. Also, in general, crossings should be

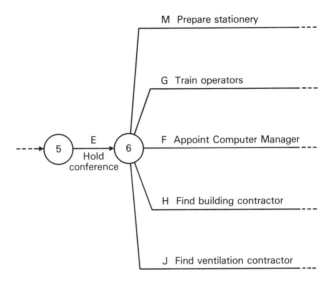

Figure 12.6   *Event 6 signals the start of various activities. (Note: these five activities may proceed concurrently but not until the conference is finished.)*

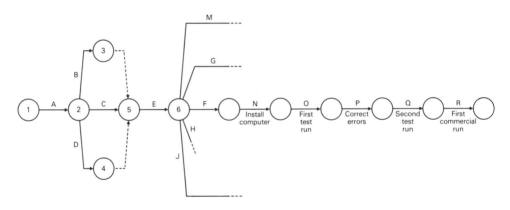

Figure 12.7   *The essential backbone of the project*

avoided, although this is not always possible. However, a redrawing of a network will usually permit both these niceties to be observed and the resulting diagram will be all the clearer for them.

Now we come to the remaining branches from event 6, that is, activities H and J. They may proceed together and both lead to other activities. For H, the sequence leading to the backbone at N is H then I then K then N, which is shown in Figure 12.9.

For activity J, we know from the list of prerequisites that it is followed by L. Also, we know that L must await completion of I as much as J. In other words, both K and L (the various building works) must await the conversion materials for the accommodation. The sequence from J must be J then L (after I also) then N, as shown in Figure 12.10.

Note how the network is altered in appearance to ensure that the forward flow of arrows is preserved. The sequence is more important that the positions of the circles or the lengths of arrows. The overall project network is shown in Figure 12.11.

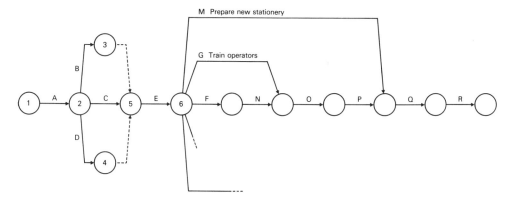

Figure 12.8 *Prerequisites for the test runs*

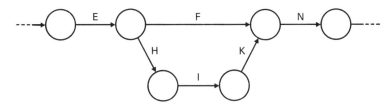

Figure 12.9 *The H–I–K link*

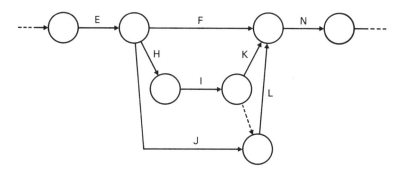

Figure 12.10 *The sequences after activities H and J*

Even though Figure 12.11 is merely a picturesque statement of the order in which activities must be carried out, it is already a useful way to identify the end times of activities. It shows that E (the conference) is critical in the sense that delay at that stage will inevitably prolong the overall project. The same must be true of A, Q and R. Each of these activities must be carried out alone, with no other concurrent. By contrast, activity M (prepare stationery) may not be critical since it may be carried out at the same time as G, F, H and J, and possibly as late as activity P. Provided it is complete by event 13, its operation is satisfactory. The numbering of events is unimportant, but by convention all arrows must lead from a lower event number to a higher one. This means searching through the network, at each event, and numbering accordingly.

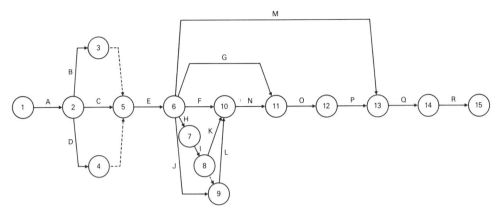

Figure 12.11   *The network for the entire project*

12.3.3   A Moment in Time

In addition to simply stating the order of activities (the production schedule), Figure 12.11 permits a close analysis of the actual times involved in each event. We know that activity A takes 17 days. Therefore, event 2 cannot occur at any other time than 17 days after event 1, unless A is delayed for some reason. Similarly, event 3 will be timed, at its earliest, at 43 days after the start because activity B lasts an estimated 26 days. Also, event 4 will be timed at 24 days after the start (17 plus 7 days). What then will be the earliest time for event 5? We know that it must await completion of activities B, C and D, and the dummies indicate the dependence. Activity C takes 14 days so its earliest completion could be at day 31 after the start. The earliest time for event 5 is that moment when B, C and D are all completed which is day 43 after the start. There is a paradoxical use of words here: the 'earliest event time' is the *latest time* for completion of activities leading to it. This arises from the definition of an event as that moment when an activity finishes. In this context, we can see that activity E cannot commence until event 5 has been reached and that will be at day 43. We may add this information to Figure 12.11 to give Figure 12.12.

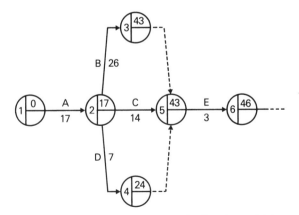

Figure 12.12   *Earliest event times for first few activities*

We can see that the earliest time for the completion of activity E (the conference) is day 46 after the start. Note the method of showing the earliest times: the circle representing an event is split into three parts as in Figure 12.12, the event number is given in the left part and the earliest time in the upper part. The lower part of the circle will be used for another item of information later.

Applying the same earliest time calculation to the rest of the network, we obtain Figure 12.13. The student should check particularly on the earliest time of events 9, 10, 11 and 13 since they denote situations where waiting may occur. For example, event 9 must await completion of J and I. Therefore, the event is timed at its earliest at the latest of these two:

1. Event 6 + activity H + activity I = 46 + 24 + 17 = 87.
2. Event 6 + activity J = 46 + 21 = 67.

The first route takes the longer, so event 9 must be timed at 87 days at the earliest. In this case, event 10 must be timed at 164 days since 87 + 77 exceeds 87 + 29. Figure 12.13 shows all the other earliest times.

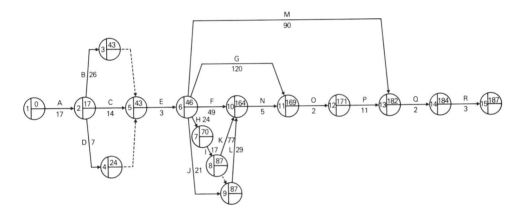

Figure 12.13   *Earliest event times for the entire project*

We can see now that the earliest time by which this computer can be installed and running satisfactorily is 187 days after commencement. Also, the timings show that certain activities, such as J, L and M, have more time available than they actually take to complete. As an example, activity M can start as early as day 46 and *must* finish by day 182; yet it has only 90 days duration. It has 46 days 'leeway'. The reader should check other activities with this property.

Let us now investigate further this property of leeway. Consider again activity M. Its latest start time is day 92, calculated by subtracting the activity duration (90 days) from the finishing time (day 182). Clearly, activity M possesses 46 days leeway between its earliest start time and its latest. The leeway is called *float* and numerous activities in the project will possess float of some magnitude. It is a useful property in an activity, since it tells the analyst that it may be postponed should circumstances warrant it. Staffing difficulties, postal delays, sickness and unforeseen problems can all cause delay in an activity and it is important to know those that can accommodate it, and those that cannot. A full analysis of float requires that we start at the end of the network and work back to the beginning deducting durations. As a general rule we must ensure that any event with two or more activities leading from it must be timed no later than is required to prevent delay in any of them. In some textbooks this is called the 'backward pass' over the network: it yields the latest event times. The 'forward pass', which we have already completed, yields the earliest event times.

From Figure 12.13 we can see that event 14 must occur not later than day 184 if the project is not to be prolonged. This is shown by deducting the three-day duration from the end time of 187 days. Similarly, event 13 must be timed no later than 182, event 12 no later than 171, event 11 no later than 169 and event 10 no later than 164. If these latest times are exceeded, then the entire project will be prolonged beyond day 187.

Event 6 is not so easy to time in the backward pass since numerous activities emanate from it. Figure 12.14 shows the timings that arise from activities M, G, F, J, H and so on. Event 9 must have the latest time of day 135 (164 minus 29 for activity L) and therefore J must start no later than day 114. Similarly, F must start no later than day 115 (164 minus 49), G no later than day 49 (169 minus 120) and M no later than day 92 (182 minus 90).

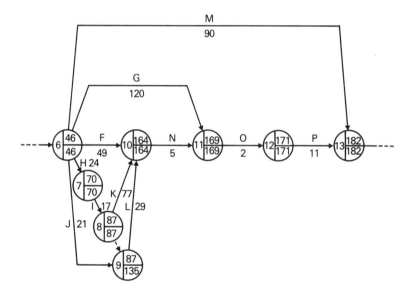

Figure 12.14   *Latest event times for the central group of activities*

The lower sequence of activities is more complicated. Activity L (install air conditioning) has a duration of 29 days and must be completed by day 164. Therefore, its latest permissible start time (event 9 latest time) must be day 135. Clearly, activity L possesses a float of 48 days between the day upon which it *may* start and that upon which it *must* start. Event 8, by contrast, must be timed no later than day 87, since activity K must be complete by day 164 and has a duration of 77 days.* Activity K possesses no float and we say that it is a *critical activity*: no delay is permissible. The same is true for event 7 and activity I. Therefore, the latest permissible time for event 6 is the earliest day required to prevent delay at event 10, or event 11 or event 13 since these are linked to it. We may list the times for the sequences leaving event 6 as follows:

---

* Note that dummies have zero duration in both forward and backward passes.

Latest start for M = day 92 (182 minus 90).
Latest start for G = day 49 (169 minus 120).
Latest start for F = day 115 (164 minus 49).
Latest start for H = day 46 (70 minus 24).
Latest start for J = day 114 (135 minus 21).

Clearly, activity H must start first and thus event 6 must not occur later than day 46. Activity H is *critical* but the others are not: they possess float.

Continuing the backward pass to event 1, we see that event 2 must be timed no later than day 17 and the entire project must start at day 0. The latest time for event 2 is the earliest of the three activities leading from it as follows:

Latest start for B = day 17 (43 minus 26).
Latest start for C = day 29 (43 minus 14).
Latest start for D = day 36 (43 minus 7).

We see that activity B is *critical* since it cannot be delayed beyond its earliest start time. Figure 12.15 gives the event timings for the whole project.

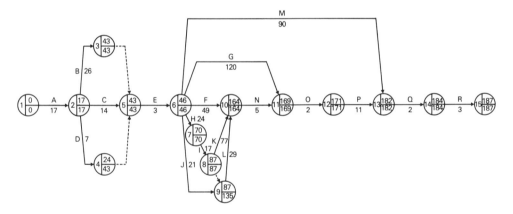

Figure 12.15 *Full event timings*

12.3.4 Some Actions Are More Important Than Others

The analyst is always concerned with shocks to the business system. That is why he must know where, in a plan, there exists flexibility to accommodate difficulties. In our vocabulary, he needs to know which activities are critical and which are not. If an activity is not critical (often said to be *sub-critical*) then it may be postponed to make life easier in the face of problems.

We shall now list all the activities in this computer installation project and calculate two important periods of time for each. First, the time *available* for completion and second the actual *duration*. If, for any activity, the two are equal then that activity must be critical. Otherwise, it is sub-critical.

Activity		Earliest start time	Latest finish time	Available time (days)	Duration (days)
A	Pilot survey: needs	0	17	17	17*
B	Pilot survey: costs	17	43	26	26*
C	Pilot survey: buildings	17	43	26	14
D	Arrange conference	17	43	26	7
E	Hold conference	43	46	3	3*
F	Appoint manager	46	164	118	49
G	Train operators	46	169	123	120
H	Find building contractor	46	70	24	24*
I	Obtain building materials	70	87	17	17*
J	Find ventilation contractor	46	135	89	21
K	Convert buildings	87	164	77	77*
L	Install ventilation	87	164	77	29
M	Prepare stationery	46	182	136	90
N	Install computer	164	169	5	5*
O	First test run	169	171	2	2*
P	Correction of errors	171	182	11	11*
Q	Second test run	182	184	2	2*
R	First commercial run	184	187	3	3*

The durations marked with an asterisk show critical activities since there is no float available to them. In all the others, there is float to a greater or lesser extent. For example, the preparation of stationery (M) possesses 46 days float: that is a measure of its non-criticality. By contrast, the training of operators (G) possesses only three days' float in an activity lasting nearly four months. It is only just sub-critical. Figure 12.16 shows all the critical activities as bold arrows to distinguish them from the sub-critical.

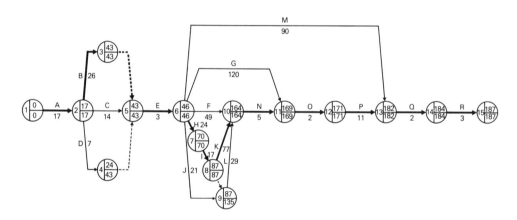

Figure 12.16   *The critical activities in the project. (Note that there is a critical dummy which means that there must be no wait between Event 3 and Event 5.)*

We are now in a position to ask important questions about the scheduling of this project and a few examples are considered here.

Question 1   Is it worth while to reduce the time taken on the pilot survey of buildings (activity C)?

Answer   No, because C already possesses 12 days' float. Reducing its duration will simply increase its float but not in any way affect the overall project time. What will reduce the total project time is a reduction in the time taken by the pilot survey of costs (activity B) since it is critical to the overall timing.

Question 2 If the estimated training period for operators turns out to be too short, will an extra fourteen days endanger the project's completion time?

Answer   Yes, because the training period (activity G) possesses float of only three days. Therefore a fourteen-day delay will prolong the entire project by 11 days.

Question 3 A building contractor is found (activity H) in a shorter time than expected. Will this permit a reduction in the total project time?

Answer   Yes, because H is on the critical path: any changes in its timing will affect every subsequent activity and therefore the total project time.

12.4   RESCHEDULING THE WORK

12.4.1   Some People Are Just Idle . . .

The network in Figure 12.16 gives a visual impression of the complexity of the computer installation as a capital project. Also, it permits further analysis of the management problems associated with the administration of such a project. For example, are there enough activities going on at any moment in time to employ fully the staff available? Conversely, at some times there may be too few members of staff to co-ordinate the numerous activities underway. To demonstrate this feature of the problem, let us now say that two principles have been established:

1.   Every activity must be supervised and participated in by a manager from the Accounts Department of the company.
2.   There are four Accounts Managers available for these supervisory responsibilities.

Clearly, by inspection of the network, we can see that not all four managers will be employed at all times. The most obvious situation exists with activity E, the administration of the conference, where only one manager need be in charge. Similarly, towards the end of the network only one needs to administrate activities Q and R. Presumably, the other managers will not actually be involved in the project at these times and, to that extent, will be 'idle' until their next supervisory activities require attention. Of course, since there is always at least one activity in progress, there will always be one manager employed directly on the project. At other times there will be more than one.

Let us now investigate the manager requirements of the project. The method we shall employ uses special charts, called Gantt charts, to obtain a graphical treatment of the problem. Let every activity be commenced at its *earliest time*, then how many managers will be required at any moment?

This question may be answered in parts. First, the critical path of the project requires one manager throughout the project time from day 0 to day 187. Figure 12.17 shows this as a block of time employing one person at every moment.

Similarly, we can chart the requirements of other activities, off the critical path, as shown in Figure 12.18. Remember that each activity is charted as *commencing at its earliest possible time*. For simplicity and ease of drawing, activities C and D are separated so that each block represent the requirements of one job.

From these two sets of charts, we may now compose the overall manager requirements

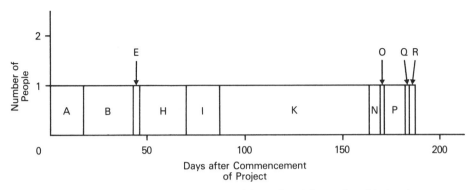

Figure 12.17 *One manager is required for each activity on the critical path*

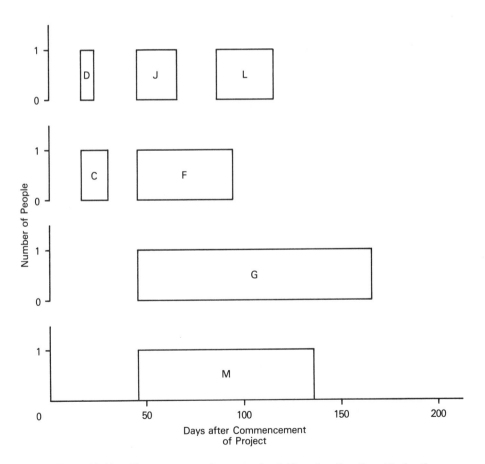

Figure 12.18 *The manager requirements of activities other than the critical path*

of the whole project. The technique is to scan along the time axis, inspecting the starts and finishes of activities, adding or subtracting their requirements as appropriate. For example, at the start time (day 0) there is only one activity commencing; that is activity A and this requires one manager. However, at day 17 activities B, C and D can each commence and this is seen from the charts to require a total of three managers. To obtain this number, simply add together the bars in the chart at the time in question, day 17. Such a process of vertical addition is continued throughout the analysis. Activities D and C are completed by day 24 and day 31 respectively, leaving the critical activity B to continue to day 43 when the conference will be the only activity in progress. We can see this from the Gantt charts, where only E has any manager requirement between day 43 and day 46. After E, activities J, F, G and M can all commence and they will each employ one manager. The total requirement at that moment will rise to five people. Such a search process is continued throughout the total project time and results in Figure 12.19.

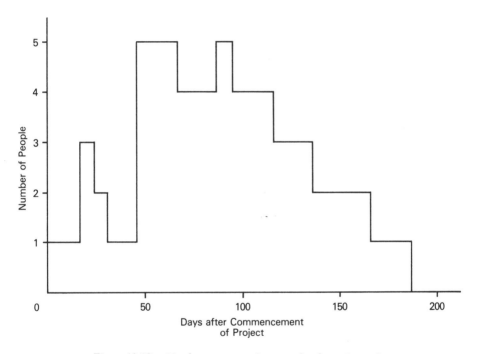

Figure 12.19   *Total manager requirements for the entire project*

One of the most noticeable features of Figure 12.19 is its uneven profile. We might suppose the ideal shape for a Gantt chart to be a block with a straight top, indicating a constant manager requirement throughout the project. To expect such a pattern is unrealistic since all complex projects will make variable demands upon resources and perfect uniformity must be regarded as exceptional. Even so, the unevenness in Figure 12.19 is particularly acute and raises numerous questions.

Whenever the height of the Gantt chart in Figure 12.19 is less than four people, one manager or more will have nothing to do in relation to the project. From the chart we can see that this occurs on 117 days out of the total project time of 187 days: for 63 per cent of the time there are managers waiting for their next activity to start. Of course, all the managers will have other duties but the computer's installation represents a drain upon their other responsibilities. The fact that the drain is not constant may be regarded as undesirable since it causes disjointedness in the work schedules of any particular manager. Stated simply, there is some degree of manager idleness for nearly two-thirds of the time the computer is being installed.

12.4.2   . . . Others Are in Short Supply

Another feature of Figure 12.19 is the fact that the total manager requirement exceeds four people for some of the time. That is, there will be times when activities are scheduled to be in progress without a manager available for their supervision. Especially this is the case for the periods between day 46 and day 67, and day 87 and day 95. During these times, the administration of the project will run short of appropriate staff. Such a situation must be avoided.

There are a number of ways in which the uneven profile of Figure 12.19 may be rectified. We shall consider the easiest method since it leads to a quick solution. In the real world the easiest method is not always available or desirable. For our purposes, consider the possibility of removing the two 'humps' in Figure 12.19 by deferring such activities as will lead to a generally smoother appearance. By so doing we are intervening in the general rule that all activities commence at their earliest times. The next section considers how this process may be applied.

12.4.3   Smoothing Out the Humps

Two activities in particular are sufficiently flexible in their timings to be considered for postponement. There are J (finding the air conditioning contractor) and L (installation of air conditioning); their manager requirements were shown in Figure 12.18. By contrast, activities C and D have not such flexibility since they must be completed by day 43. The full timing information for J and L are given in the table below. The various timings may be read from Figure 12.16 and the latest start times obtained by subtracting durations.

Activity	Latest finish time	Duration	Latest start time
J	135	21	114
L	164	29	135

To retime the start of J to day 114 will push both of these activities to the far right of their positions in Figure 12.18 to yield a new line of requirements as in Figure 12.20.

The result of such a rescheduling is shown in Figure 12.21 and we can see that the profile is generally more uniform. More of the four managers are employed for a greater proportion of the time and at no time is there a shortage of staff.

Certain problems may still remain which could further complicate our analysis. For example, the float available in activities J and L may have been insufficient to permit the scheduling we have accomplished. If that were so, then in this example we would be required to extend the total project time to fit in a schedule of activities which would not require more than four managers at any moment. Such methods of analysis are beyond the scope of this book.

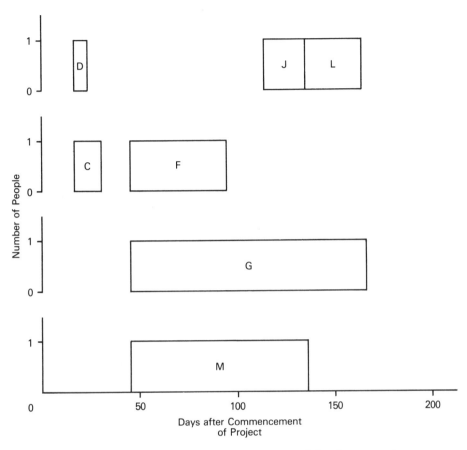

Figure 12.20 *Postponement of activities J and L until their latest start times*

Figure 12.21 *Total manager requirements for the project when activities J and L are postponed*

ASSIGNMENTS

A12.1   Compute the event timings throughout the illustrated network. The duration of each activity is shown in days against its arrow.

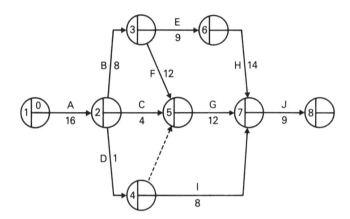

Show that the total project time will be 57 days and that the critical activities are A, B, F, G and J.

A12.2   (a) List the activities involved in two people getting up in the morning, making breakfast, getting ready for work, feeding the cat and so on until they walk through the door of the house. Do not be too precise but leave each activity at a fairly crude descriptive level.

(b) Construct the network for the two people, following the rules laid down in the chapter.

(c) Discuss problems which arise in the sequencing of activities and comment upon the allocation of time and facilities.

(d) Estimate the duration of each activity in (a) and calculate the overall duration of the exercise, marking out any critical activities.

A12.3   A major electronics company receives an order for the emergency replacement of a satellite-tracking telescope. The Planning Manager decides that there are ten activities which must be carried out in as short a time as possible. Labour or machine effort is to be no object. He lists the activities with their estimated durations and labour requirements, as below.

	Activity	Duration (days)	Labour
A	Obtain casing components	7	nil
B	Prepare casing components	14	3
C	Design internal chassis	5	2
D	Design electronic circuits	11	4
E	Assemble casing	4	4
F	Assemble electronics on chassis	4	3
G	Design carrying crate	2	2
H	Install chassis in casing	3	5
I	Make carrying crate	8	3
J	Crate and deliver	4	2

Discussion with technical staff leads to the establishment of priorities so that the illustrated network can be drawn up.

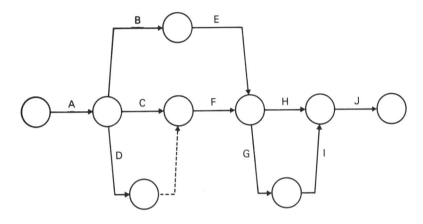

You are required to:

(a) Calculate event timings, state the total duration and deduce the critical activities.
(b) State the consequences for the total duration if activity F takes twice its normal time.
(c) Construct the Gantt chart for the project and state the maximum labour requirement, on the basis that every activity commences at its earliest time.
(d) Show that maximum labour requirement cannot be reduced by delaying activity C.

A12.4 A printer is planning to install a new press. The various activities are listed below with their duration and labour measurements. Before the new press (machine C) is installed, a site must be prepared for it. This is done by removing another press (machine B) to a site released by moving a packing machine (machine A) to a new site that also must be prepared. It is necessary, before moving machine B, to build up stocks of the stationery which it produces so that there will be stock in hand during the disruption. There are tools in store which can be used on the new machine C but only after they have been modified. New handling equipment will be required for C: some of it (basic equipment) is needed before the machine can be tried out, but other (final equipment) is not essential until the machine goes into production working.

Activity	Duration	Labour
Prepare site for machine A	2 weeks	3 men
Prepare site for machine C	8 weeks	3 men
Move machine A	4 weeks	3 men
Move machine B	1 week	3 men
Obtain machine C (waiting time)	8 weeks	–
Install and wire up machine C	2 weeks	4 men
Test, trouble-shoot, and prepare machine C prior to final handing over	13 weeks	4 men
Modify all tools for machine C	13 weeks	2 men
Obtain and install basic handling equipment	12 weeks	2 men

(cont'd)

Activity	Duration	Labour
Obtain and install final handling equipment	19 weeks	4 men
Build stocks to release machine B	2 weeks	1 man
Final handing over ceremony	–	–

(a) Determine the minimum time in which this project may be completed.

(b) State which activities are critical to the project's duration. In this context, discuss briefly the importance (or otherwise) of the longest activity, relating to final handling equipment.

(c) Graphically or otherwise, determine the maximum labour requirement if every activity commences at its earliest time.

(d) Suggest one change in the schedule which will result in a reduction of at least one man in maximum labour requirements.

A12.5 A local council is planning a major international arts festival and you are given the responsibility of arranging the various conferences and meetings which must be held. One of the constraints you will face arises from the fact that the council can accommodate only four important meetings at any one time. Apart from rooms, this limitation applies also to secretarial support, library facilities and administrative personnel. The table below lists the meetings which must be held and their duration. Also shown for each meeting is the activity (or activities) which must precede it: these are called the *prerequisites* for an activity. Similarly, for each meeting, the list shows the activity (or activities) which must follow it: these are called the *postrequisites* of an activity.

	Activity	Duration (weeks)	Pre-requisite(s)	Post-requisite(s)
A	Initial Planning Session	4	nil	B, C, D, E
B	Sculpture Conference	5	A	F
C	Pottery Conference	5	A	G, H
D	Picture Arts Conference	10	A	I, J
E	Folk Arts Conference	8	A	K
F	Sculpture Planning Committee	6	B	L
G	Pottery Planning Committee	7	C	L
H	Pottery Publicity Sub-committee	12	C	M
I	Picture Arts Planning Committee	5	D	M
J	Picture Arts Publicity Sub-committee	8	D	N
K	Folk Arts Planning Committee	5	E	N
L	Hard Arts Working Party	6	F, G	O
M	Publicity Working Party	8	H, I	O
N	Soft Arts Working Party	8	J, K	O
O	Final Action Group Session	2	L, M, N	nil

(a) Construct the project network for this festival and show that the total project time will be 32 weeks. Also, show that the critical meetings are A, D, J, N, O.

(b) Construct the Gantt chart to show the number of meetings in session at each moment during the 32-week period. Does it exceed four at any time when meetings commence at their earliest times?

(c) Show that the Gantt chart can be reduced to a maximum height of four meetings, and be generally more uniform, if activities L, G and I are deferred to their latest starting times.

(d) Draw up a timetable for the meetings, on the basis of the schedule in part (c). Assume that 'week' refers to a period of five consecutive working days, omitting public holidays, and that the first meeting can be held on 1 August.

Index